Collected writings of
Michael J. Ovey

The Goldilocks Zone

Edited by
Chris Green

INTER-VARSITY PRESS

36 Causton Street, London SW1P 4ST, England

Website: www.ivpbooks.com

Email: ivp@ivpbooks.com

First published 2018

British Library Cataloguing-in-Publication Data

A catalogue record for this book is available from the British Library.

ISBN: 978-1-78359-609-6 paperback
       978-1-78359-610-2 ebook

Set in Monotype Garamond 11/13pt
Typeset in Great Britain by CRB Associates, Potterhanworth, Lincolnshire
Printed and bound in Great Britain by Ashford Colour Press Ltd, Gosport, Hampshire

Inter-Varsity Press publishes Christian books that are true to the Bible and that communicate the gospel, develop discipleship and strengthen the church for its mission in the world.

IVP originated within the Inter-Varsity Fellowship, now the Universities and Colleges Christian Fellowship, a student movement connecting Christian Unions in universities and colleges throughout Great Britain, and a member movement of the International Fellowship of Evangelical Students. Website: www.uccf.org.uk. That historic association is maintained, and all senior IVP staff and committee members subscribe to the UCCF Basis of Faith.

In grateful memory of Michael J. Ovey,
and in loving fellowship with
Heather, Charlie, Harry and Anastasia

CONTENTS

Mike Ovey as a theologian   1
Mark D. Thompson

A steward of knowledge: Mike Ovey 1958–2017   23
Chris Green

Part 1: 'Off the Record' articles from *Themelios*   31

1. The Goldilocks zone   33
2. The right to ridicule?   37
3. Sorrow at another's good?   41
4. Colonial atheism: a very British vice   45
5. From moral majority to evil disbelievers: coming clean
   about Christian atheism   48
6. Liberty, what crimes are committed in thy name?   53
7. The covert thrill of violence? Reading the Bible in disbelief   57
8. Projection atheism: why reductionist accounts of humanity
   can lead to reductionist accounts of God   61
9. Is it a mistake to stay at the crossroads?   65
10. Courtier politicians and courtier preachers   70
11. Can *Antigone* work in a secularist society?   74

12. Is the wrath of God extremist?   78
13. The art of imperious ignorance   83
14. The echo chamber of idolatry   88
15. Choose your fears carefully   92

Part 2: The *Cambridge Papers*   97

16. Women, men and the nature of God: equality but not symmetry   99
17. Deconstruction: gagging the speaking God?   107
18. The human identity crisis: can we do without the Trinity?   117
19. Does Athens need Jerusalem? A Christian context for secular
    thought   127
20. Idolatry and spiritual parody: counterfeit faiths   137
21. Beyond scrutiny? Minorities, majorities and postmodern tyranny   148
22. Victim chic? The rhetoric of victimhood   159

Part 3: Gospel and atonement   171

23. Can we speak of 'the' gospel in a postmodern world?
    Pluralism, polytheism and the gospel of the one, true God   173
24. Appropriating Aulén? Employing *Christus Victor* models
    of the atonement   203

**Part 4: Global Anglican Futures Conference (GAFCON)
lectures**   235

25. The gospel 'how' of theological education (Jerusalem, 2008)   237
26. The gospel 'what' of theological education (Jerusalem, 2008)   249
27. The grace of God *or* the world of the West? (Nairobi, 2013)   261

Sermon at the thanksgiving service for Mike Ovey   278
Peter F. Jensen

Afterword: Mike Ovey – the best possible gift   285
Daniel Strange

MIKE OVEY AS A THEOLOGIAN

Mark D. Thompson, Principal, Moore College, Sydney

In August 2016 Mike Ovey gave a lecture on 'Justification in the Reformation' at the Protestant Reformation Society Conference in Oxford.[1] As the second of his introductory comments he said this:

> Secondly, I should say a word about where I am coming from theologically and
> not just geographically. I am in temperament, I suppose, a sixteenth century
> Anglican in a kind of Cranmerian mould in terms of faith and understanding, and,
> I hope, in terms of final confession too. But I would say sixteenth century, rather
> than seventeenth, eighteenth, nineteenth or even twentieth. I think, for me, Cranmer
> was a theological giant and we need to recover that. That is where I am coming from
> and I want to be completely upfront about that so that you know precisely how to
> hear what it is I have to say this evening.

Here is Mike's theological self-description. He located himself as an heir of the Reformation and particularly of the evangelical Anglicanism associated with Thomas Cranmer. Like Cranmer, his passion was to see God honoured as the gospel of the Lord Jesus Christ is proclaimed throughout the world in the glory with which it is presented to us in the Bible. Like Cranmer, he was determined to stand on the great Reformation truth of justification only by faith and to explore the consequences of this truth in all areas of life and ministry. Like Cranmer, he took seriously the writings of the church fathers and his contemporaries but placed all under the final authority of Holy Scripture. Mike Ovey was a Reformation man, a Cranmer man, but more importantly a Bible man, because he was always and above all else a Jesus man. He had been brought to God the Father through Jesus Christ and in the power of the Holy Spirit.

Yet while these convictions were clear and unwavering, they did not make Mike narrow-minded in any sense. He was an heir of the Reformation but he read and engaged theology from the entire course of Christian history. He turned repeatedly to the early church fathers, to Athanasius and Augustine, and especially to Hilary of Poitiers, as Christians in whose company he could read the Scriptures with profit. He read and appreciated both the strengths and the weaknesses of medieval theologians like Thomas Aquinas and Gabriel Biel. He read the Reformers and their immediate heirs, discovering and rejoicing in their contributions to our understanding of God and his purposes. Alongside Calvin, Luther and Cranmer, he would cite Chemnitz, Leigh, Junius, Turretin and Pictet, but others as well. He had read widely in modern theology too: Thielicke and Barth, Niebuhr and Tillich, Packer, Gunton, Torrance, Vanhoozer, and others. Mike knew he wasn't the first to read and seek to learn from Scripture and he was prepared to listen carefully to those who had read it before him or, in the loosest sense, alongside him. He was genuinely intellectually curious and was prepared to learn from those with whom he disagreed as well as those who thought like him. Yet when he chose to speak of where he could best be located theologically he chose the confessional Anglicanism of Thomas Cranmer.

Similarly, while his first theological instinct was always to turn to the Scriptures, he understood the theological, philosophical and cultural factors which influenced the way he, like everyone else, read the Scriptures. He was particularly well read in philosophy and was able to cite classical and modern writers accurately and insightfully. He read history and works of modern cultural analysis, to which he added his own astute observations of what was happening around him in popular culture as well as in the intellectual and academic life of the West. To read Mike deftly moving between classical and contemporary references, more often than not uncovering deep and insightful resonances to which could be addressed the teaching of Scripture and its magnificent themes of grace, forgiveness and hope, was to marvel at the breadth of his grasp but also the profundity of his analysis. Yet he could be deliberately playful in this as well, enjoying the apparent absurdity of comparing the Goldilocks story and the machinations of contemporary thought leaders, or the latest blood-and-gore vampire thriller and recent goings-on in the Church of England. I smiled reading his citation of 'Top Ten Christian Chat-up Lines' in a lecture on justification and Augustine's view of sin as misdirected love, especially when I realized how apt it was! Sometimes the very absurdity of the comparison made the point (as well as lightening the mood).

The chief themes in Mike Ovey's theology

Mike never saw himself as having a distinctive theology. In a section on 'Intellectual Vice' in one of his addresses at GAFCON in Jerusalem in 2008, he warned of the way 'the prime intellectual virtue, truth', could be undermined by the 'quest to find something new, something original, no matter how eccentric, a thought that one can call one's own and possess'. He asked, 'Is that not, to be honest, a snare for the academic, the yearning to have a school of thought or line of argument named after one? For one's doctoral thesis to be all too definitive?'[2] So Mike would no doubt squirm at the idea of having 'his theology' summarized in this way. He saw himself as a steward of an inheritance passed on to him, the inheritance of Christian doctrine disciplined by the actual words of Scripture read attentively and responsibly. That inheritance had been explored and expounded by the church fathers and in an important sense rediscovered at the time of the Reformation. It had been passed on to him by men like John Stott, Jim Packer and Peter Jensen. Though I never heard him actually say it, I am absolutely certain that he would have agreed with the promise made by Methodist theologian Thomas Oden: 'The only promise I intend to make, however inadequately carried out, is that of unoriginality.'[3] The theologian's responsibility is rightly to handle the word of truth (2 Tim. 2:15), faithfully to pass on what we have received (2 Tim. 2:2), to guard the deposit entrusted to us (1 Tim. 6:20), to contend for the faith once for all delivered to the saints (Jude 3). We do not fashion a theology, but cherish, guard and pass on, as clearly and faithfully as we are able, the theology of the Bible. Of course, there remains the question of how best to communicate that theology to men and women in a rapidly changing context. Mike certainly realized there is plenty of hard work to be done if we are to pass on the deposit both faithfully and effectively in the midst of the unique pressures of this moment. Nevertheless, he would insist that this work does not involve recrafting the deposit itself. We are stewards who must give an account of how we have treated what has been entrusted to us. So what follows is not original to Mike. Rather, here are at least some of the biblical and theological themes to which he returned again and again.

The Creator–creature distinction

Mike Ovey had a keen sense of the distinction between the one almighty and eternal God, and everything else. God is the Creator and we are his creatures.

The implications of this simple, inviolable truth are manifold. God remains sovereign over all he has made and we as his human creatures are accountable. God cannot be mastered or controlled, manipulated or put in service of our personal or cultural agendas. All attempts to do so are human delusions. The distinction cannot be crossed from our side. It can only be crossed from God's side as it was when the Word became incarnate. Yet even in the new era ushered in by the life, death and resurrection of Jesus Christ, and even though Christian men and women are united to Christ through faith and by the Spirit, we remain creatures and it is incumbent upon us to remember our place in walking before our creator in his world and especially when speaking of him. We need to be reminded of the question the Lord posed through the prophet Isaiah:

> To whom then will you compare me,
>   that I should be like him?
> (Isa. 40:25, ESV)

The uniqueness of God is associated there and elsewhere in Scripture with God's creative activity. Everything owes its existence to him. He owes his existence to nothing and no one. Everyone is dependent upon him for life, light and love. He is dependent on no one. He alone is the Creator and we are all his creatures – finite, constrained by time and space and the myriad of influences that shape us, while he is infinite, uncontainable and unconditioned.

Mike knew that this has highly critical implications for our knowledge and talk of God. This was evident from even his earliest published work. However, it was the particular focus of his contribution to a collection of essays in honour of New Testament scholar and evangelical statesman Don Carson:

> To some extent, looking back, I think evangelical Christians had been closer to the rationalists than we should have been and we found it hard to articulate a way of talking about truth without falling over into something like a claim of exhaustive knowledge. Theologically I think our proximity to rationalism was (and perhaps still sometimes is) more toxic than we realized: rationalism is close to the sins of intellectual pride, and pride, argues Augustine, is fundamental to human sin. Claims to exhaustive knowledge have an ugly way of blurring the distinction between creature and creator in the realm of knowledge.[4]

Mike found a way of countering the claim – or the appearance of a claim – to exhaustive knowledge through reading the work of Franciscus Junius, Professor of Theology at Leiden from 1592 to 1601 (where he was controversially succeeded by Jacobus Arminius), and especially his distinction between archetypal and ectypal theology. Archetypal theology is the 'unbounded wisdom, which God possesses concerning His own person and all other things'.[5] Ectypal theology is 'wisdom which the creatures have concerning God according to their own manner, and concerning those things that are oriented toward God through His communication of Himself'.[6] Mike saw that this distinction allowed for human beings to know the truth about God and everything else considered in relation to him, but only in 'a creaturely way'.[7] Ectypal theology is 'God's created gift of knowledge of divine matters to his human creatures in terms conformed by him to their creatureliness'.[8] That includes finitude and dependence. Only God knows himself and all things in relation to him exhaustively or comprehensively, and unconditioned by anything outside himself. In Mike's book on Hilary of Poitiers, he made the point by distinguishing between the *apprehension* of truth about God in distinction from the *comprehension* of truth about God.[9] In knowing God and speaking about him we must remember we are creatures who can never 'master' our creator. Our knowledge of God arises from God's knowledge of himself and all things, but is always different from it. This carries with it one more important corollary: 'only the one with archetypal theological knowledge could validate a theology that derives from archetypal theology. The connection lies on the Godward side of the Creator–creature divide, not on the creature's side.'[10]

The end product of such reflection is humility. Humility in this area expresses itself as a recognition and acceptance of our limitations and God's surpassing greatness:

> For my thoughts are not your thoughts,
>   neither are your ways my ways, declares the LORD.
> For as the heavens are higher than the earth,
>   so are my ways higher than your ways
>   and my thoughts than your thoughts.
> (Isa. 55:8–9, ESV)

> Now I know in part; then I shall know fully, even as I have been fully known.
> (1 Cor. 13:12, ESV)

As Mike put it to a group of theological educators at GAFCON:

> Humility discourages the attitude that seeks to possess and master God's Word,
> or tell others what God should have said on particular topics. Humility opens the
> door to a trust that God does speak and speaks truthfully, but does not insist that one
> has grasped him and his word exhaustively. In that sense learning humbly really does

reflect the relationships the Gospel establishes, and there would be something
odd about expecting a minister who has been taught in ways that make him proud,
to be able to live the gospel life of humility.[11]

There is the sting in the tail for any approach to theology which ignores the
Creator–creature distinction: claiming we know either too much or too little.

The genuine sonship of the Son

Mike Ovey was most clearly a trinitarian theologian. The very first of the
Cambridge Papers he wrote, from 1992, included reflection upon the Trinity and
especially the nature of the relation between the Father and the Son:

> Looking at the relationship of the Father and the Son within the trinity shows that
> having different roles in a relationship does not imply necessarily an inferiority of
> being, even where that difference relates to authority and submission. To say that
> it necessarily does would logically falsify the eternal trinitarian relationship of the
> Father and Son. That in turn would suggest that Jesus cannot give us accurate
> information about God and therefore casts doubt on him as the incarnate God.[12]

The nature of the relationship between the Father and the Son, and an
insistence that they genuinely are Father and Son and not two Fathers or two
Sons – since this would put in jeopardy our salvation – was a lifelong feature
of Mike's theology. His third contribution to the *Cambridge Papers*, from 1995,
returned to the theme:

> It has been suggested that there is a symmetrical, mutual submission between the
> persons of the Trinity. This makes the Father completely interchangeable with the Son
> and the Spirit in their relationships. That in turn starts to eliminate the individuality
> of the persons of the Trinity since they are a common coin. Obviously that is not
> the way the persons appear in salvation history. (Biblically, the Father does not submit
> to the Son: in fact, 1 Corinthians 15:24 makes it clear that the Father is the final
> monarch after the general resurrection and the conquest of evil.) This suggestion
> is disastrous, both for our doctrine of God, because it tends to make the persons
> of God contingent and not essential, and also for our doctrine of humanity, because
> we would be persons in the image of a clone-type God who could not guarantee our
> unique value as human individuals.[13]

Mike's point was not a mere esoteric one. Nor was it merely a device created to
serve the interests of another debate. He understood that our knowledge of
God, our relationship with him, and our very constitution as human beings

created in his image, is at stake. Jesus' revelation of the Father immediately begins to unravel since Jesus crucially claimed, 'no one knows the Son except the Father, and no one knows the Father except the Son and anyone to whom the Son chooses to reveal him' (Matt. 11:27, ESV).

Mike's doctoral thesis under Colin Gunton, and then Judith Lieu, at King's College London, was entitled 'The Eternal Relation Between the Father and the Son and Its Handling by Selected Patristic Theologians, with Particular Reference to John's Gospel'. His conclusions from John's Gospel reflect the same convictions:

> The Trinitarian picture this creates is of distinct Persons who mutually indwell each other and act both distinguishably and as a unity. Their relations are characterised by mutual glorification and love, yet the love is asymmetrically expressed, by the Father's giving and the Son's obedient receiving – for he receives and exercises his cosmic monarchy as the Father wills. In this the Father conforms to the ideal of fatherhood, and the Son to true Sonship.[14]

Mike understood that the true sonship of the Son is vital to a proper understanding of God's triune nature. He challenged Barth's predilection for 'glossing the revelation of a son by his Father as essentially a self-revelation' with a reflection upon Jesus' exchange with the Pharisees in John 8. When Jesus was charged with testifying about himself (v. 13), he answered that his self-testimony, while true (v. 14), does not stand alone but is corroborated by the testimony of another, namely his Father (v. 18). At this point as at others, 'the plurality of subjects and the non-reflexive nature of revelation by the Persons is vital'.[15]

This theme was explored again by Mike in a book chapter published in 2015,[16] and in more detail in his book *Your Will Be Done: Exploring Eternal Subordination, Divine Monarchy and Divine Humility*.[17] This book is, without doubt, the most stretching of Mike's published works. Once again he returned to the writings of Tertullian, Athanasius and Hilary, with sprinklings of Augustine. More importantly, once again the discussion was anchored in John's Gospel. He argued that to suggest a symmetric relation of Father and Son, a complete reciprocity between them, is to fail to do justice to what Jesus himself revealed about this eternal relationship:

> in relational terms, as distinct from questions of substance, the Father and the Son are different persons, with unique attributes within their relationship ... Each is who he is by virtue of the relationship, but each is individuated and not simply a mirror image of the other. They are asymmetrical in the relationship.[18]

At the heart of the book is a careful treatment of the themes of giving and sending in John's Gospel and Jesus' own defence of the charge that he has set himself up as a second God by claiming to be the Father's Son (John 5:18–30). Jesus refers to himself repeatedly as the one who was sent (John 3:34; 5:38; 6:29; 20:21), who comes to do the will of the one who sent him (4:34; 5:30; 6:38–39) and speaks the words given to him by the one who sent him (7:18; 8:26; 12:49; 14:24; 17:8). The Father has sent the Son and this sending is not just something that happens during his incarnate life. 'He is sent from "outside"' – something that is not true of the prophets.[19] This dynamic of sending and being sent reflects the eternal relations between the persons. It is entirely appropriate that the Father should send the Son. It would be utterly inappropriate for the Son to send the Father. Furthermore, not once is there any suggestion in the Gospels or anywhere else in the New Testament that the Son sends the Father. Likewise, the Father gives the Son 'all judgment' with a view to all honouring the Son as they honour the Father (5:22–23). Critically, he gives him 'to have life in himself' (5:26) – the same life the Father has in himself. The Father gives the Son work to do (5:36) and words to say (12:49; 17:8, 14). He gives him 'all things' (3:35; 13:3).[20] It is in every case the Father who does the giving and the Son who receives the gift he has given. Here again is an unambiguous indication that their relationship is asymmetrical. The Son is a true Son, acting in a filial way. The Father is truly the Father of the Son, acting in a paternal way.

To speak of the Son as a true Son, and to explain this in terms of the Son's filial submission to the will of his Father, not just while incarnate but eternally, raises other questions. How is the will of the Son related to the will of the Father? Are there two wills in God? Wouldn't this be tantamount to saying there are two Gods? Furthermore, since Jesus Christ is both fully man and fully God, are there two wills in Christ? Would this not jeopardize the unity of his person? Mike took questions like these seriously and responded to them in the light of Jesus' prayer in the Garden of Gethsemane on the night of his arrest, and the Christological debate centuries later, finally resolved through the contribution of Maximus the Confessor. The distinction of wills between Father and Son is 'at the level of personal relation' not 'at the level of nature'.[21] There is only one divine will at the level of essence or nature, but we may speak properly of the will of the Father and the will of the Son at the level of persons. We must not forget that the Gethsemane prayer is from beginning to end an expression of a personal relationship. 'Jesus the Son in his unified coherent Person is praying for, and in the light of, the priority of his Father's will in their relationship.'[22]

Mike realized that understanding the truth about the Son's eternal sonship has monumental implications. It keeps our doctrine of God from lurching towards a form of modalism, where the persons of the Trinity are interchange-able and ultimately indistinguishable. It anchors more deeply our creedal confession of the Son as 'eternally begotten of the Father'. It acknowledges the humility of Philippians 2, properly understood, as an eternal divine attribute which stands in harmonious relation to our confession of God's glory and sovereign authority: 'because he was in the form of God, he did not count equality with God something to be grasped' (Phil. 2:6).[23] As Karl Barth famously wrote:

> Therefore we have to state firmly that, far from preventing this possibility, His divine unity consists in the fact that in himself He is both One who is obeyed and Another who obeys ... That is the true deity of Jesus Christ, obedient in humility, in its unity and equality, its *homoousia*, with the deity of the One who sent Him and to whom He is obedient.[24]

Penal substitutionary atonement

Mike Ovey was a champion of penal substitution as the critical centre of the New Testament's teaching about the cross. In October 2004 he was involved in a public debate on the subject, following denials of penal substitution by a number of high profile evangelical leaders. That he knew there was more to the cross than penal substitution is evident from an earlier piece produced for the Fourth Annual School of Theology at Oak Hill College.[25] However, he defended the centrality of penal substitution: 'restoration of this cosmos, the one God actually created, demands a penal substitution'.[26] He was the driving force behind one of the most extensive defences of this doctrine ever to appear in print: *Pierced for Our Transgressions: Rediscovering the Glory of Penal Substitution*.[27] More than half of the book examines key biblical texts, assembles the theo-logical framework, explores the implications and recounts the contributions made by leading figures in Christian history. The second half addresses no fewer than twenty-six objections to the doctrine and demonstrates that none of them is able to overthrow the doctrine or dislodge it from its central place.

The chapter on the theological framework for penal substitution (ch. 3) bears the hallmarks of Mike's approach to Christian doctrine more generally. Once again the teaching of the Bible directed the discussion. Once again he addressed the possibility of a true knowledge of God and his ways that is not exhaustive and is the gift of God by means of his written word:

> Now, certainly it is true that our finite minds cannot fully comprehend the infinite mind of God: we can never give a complete and exhaustive account of him, nor reach the point where there is nothing more about God to know. But does this mean we

cannot understand Christian theology at all? In particular, does it mean we cannot
understand even enough to see whether penal substitution fits in? . . . to attempt to
draw the 'big picture' of Christian theology is simply to pay due attention to what God
says about himself. We must not ignore our speaking God; instead we must recognize
that his wisdom is infinitely greater than ours, and root out any thinking that conflicts
with his word.[28]

Characteristically, Mike wrote of sin and the fall as 'decreation', or 'the
undoing of creation'. In the Garden, the first man and woman denied God's
truthfulness and goodness and 'inverted the proper ordering of relationships
between God, humanity and the rest of creation'.[29] Counter to the prevailing
tendency towards an anaemic view of sin and confidence in our capacity to
secure our future, Mike insisted:

The problem of our sin runs so deep that we cannot and will not save ourselves.
Sin is decreational, and only the Creator can recreate his world. Yet he must do this
in a manner that upholds the goodness and truth of his word.[30]

In this chapter, Mike again returns to trinitarian theology as vital to a presentation of penal substitution that seeks to guard against distorting the biblical
teaching on the atonement. In this context, he knew it was necessary to speak
of the relation of the Father and Son in some detail (rehearsing much of what
we have seen above) because it is precisely at this point that an important
criticism of the doctrine has been raised. In particular, he reflected on the fact
that

although the persons of the Trinity act inseparably, their actions remain
distinguishable, just as the persons themselves are distinguishable. Although each
is involved in the work of the others, it does not mean they all perform exactly the
same function.[31]

'This is important in the present debate about penal substitution', he wrote,

because some have suggested that for the Son (subject) to propitiate the Father
(object) would be to divide the Trinity. But this simply is not true. The principle of
inseparable operation underlines that the Father and the Son shared a unity of will
and purpose. Penal substitution does not imply that the Father is unwillingly coerced
into an attitude of forgiveness, or that the Son is unwillingly coerced into offering
himself. When we say that the Son propitiates the Father, this is not to be understood
as if the Son and the Father are acting against each other. They are fulfilling different

roles in a plan to which both are equally committed, in pursuit of outcomes they both desire.[32]

It is just as important to affirm the simplicity of God, the recognition that God is not composed of parts and that his attributes are in harmony with one another and in fact cohere. Any construction of a doctrine which privileges God's love over his truthfulness, or his justice over his mercy, fails at precisely this point. No single attribute is more essential than another. The atonement is effected by the God who is love, justice and mercy, and each of these things 'all the way down'. 'Penal substitution', Mike wrote, 'emerges as a central aspect of God's redeeming work in Christ, integrating fully with God's justice and truthfulness, and safeguarding God's simplicity by preserving the harmony of his attributes of justice and mercy, holiness and love'.[33]

As mentioned above, Mike did not see penal substitution as the only biblical motif expressed in the cross of Christ. Nevertheless, he did not simply subscribe to a smorgasbord approach to atonement imagery, where each is free to choose the image that seems most appropriate. Penal substitution is critical to many of the images, enabling us to see how they function. Mike ended this critical chapter on the theological framework for penal substitution in this way:

> Penal substitution coheres perfectly with other biblical understandings of the atonement. It sheds light on Christ's victory over evil powers, explaining in particular how the devil is stripped of his power to accuse. It is the basis of our reconciliation with God, for there was a moral enmity between us and God, and our guilt had to be overcome. In its emphasis that God gave his Son for his *enemies* (Rom. 5:10), penal substitution deepens our appreciation of God's love. Finally, it places the theme of ransom in the correct biblical perspective, underlining the fact that we are indebted not to the devil but to God, and it is to him that a ransom must be paid.[34]

Justification only by faith

Mike Ovey was passionate about the doctrine of justification only by faith. He regularly lectured on the subject at Oak Hill College and elsewhere.[35] He was disturbed by the way modern movements, like 'The New Perspective on Paul' (in its various guises) and 'Federal Vision', distorted the teaching of the Bible on this critical subject. In particular, he insisted on a more serious approach to human sin, both before and after conversion. The problem with the Roman Catholic view of justification, Mike did not tire of saying, is that it allows for cooperation with God, justifying grace by joining faith with acts of love at this vital point. We must affirm 'faith alone' precisely because our guilt is located not just when we are at our worst but even when we are at our best. 'The critical issue is our good deeds', he wrote. Mike cited Luther at this point: 'The righteous man also sins while doing good.'[36]

> In spiritual matters, however (that is, in our understanding, our righteousness, our chastity, our piety), it is most difficult to see whether we are seeking only ourselves in them. For the love of these things, since it is honorable and good, often becomes an end in itself for us and does not permit us to regulate them in accord with God and refer them to Him, so that as a result we do them not because they are pleasing to God but because they delight us and quiet the fears of our heart, because we are praised by men, and thus we do them not for the sake of God but for ourselves.[37]

We simply are not able to cooperate with God in establishing our righteousness. Mike pointed to the inadequacy of Gabriel Biel's famous illustration of the impact of sin in his sermon on the circumcision of the Lord: 'We are like birds who have stones attached to our feet that are too heavy to let us fly.'[38] That still concedes too much to us, Mike argued. The bird in that illustration is still intact. 'Poor old bird, all that's wrong is the stones . . . it doesn't capture what our hearts are actually like . . . It's saying that there are parts of me that are untouched by the Fall.'[39] Our inability to save ourselves is absolute and so our right standing with God must come entirely from outside and as a gift. It is, as Luther used to say, 'an alien righteousness'. Far too many accounts of justification, Mike concluded, even ostensively evangelical accounts, sail dangerously close to semi-Pelagianism (and isn't semi-Pelagianism in the end merely a variant of Pelagianism?).

Mike's expositions of this doctrine followed a familiar pattern: deep anchoring in the teaching of Scripture, a broad knowledge of the history of the doctrine, an acute analysis of contemporary trends, and a rich, pastoral application. Once more special attention was given to the doctrine of God. Mike asked, 'What kind of God lies behind our justification debates?' His answer was 'a God of infinite perfection', with a tip of the hat to Anselm's *Monologion*. God's perfect grace is entirely sufficient and entirely unmerited. God's perfect love is unswervingly other-centred, uncontaminated by self-interest, constant and unrestrained. God's perfect justice has not the slightest defect, unclouded by ignorance or incompetence or corruption: the Judge of all the earth always does what is right (Gen. 18:25). God's perfect holiness means he is totally opposed to all sin and evil. At this point Mike would often quote from the Anglican 'Homily on Salvation':

> So that in our justification is not only God's mercy and grace, but also his justice; which the Apostle calleth the justice of God; and it consisteth in paying our ransom

and fulfilling of the law. And so the grace of God doth not shut out the justice of God in our justification, but only shutteth out the justice of man, that is to say, the justice of our works, as to be merits of deserving our justification.[40]

If too many accounts of justification pay insufficient attention to the seriousness of our sin and the doctrine of the God who is and acts with all his attributes, Mike saw that they also often play down the importance of imputation as the mechanism of justification. In justification, righteousness is not 'given to me so as to become my very own and part of my nature' but rather 'I am counted as righteous for the sake of another's righteousness'. The mechanism of imputation and the instrument of faith – faith is not the ground or basis of our status as those who are righteous in God's eyes but the empty hand by which this status is received by us – uphold the truth that our salvation is entirely by grace alone.

What is it that is in fact imputed to us in justification? Mike followed Calvin and others in arguing that our justification went beyond forgiveness but rather 'consists in the remission of sins *and* the imputation of Christ's righteousness'.[41] 'Penal substitution sees us as having our punishment met', Mike insisted, 'but it does not meet God's requirement that his human creatures be positively righteous. Hence the significance of justification as more than pardon . . .' At this point of the argument Mike would sometimes quote W. H. Griffith Thomas, an English theologian of the early twentieth century:

> Justification is, therefore, much more than pardon, and the two are clearly distinguished by St Paul (Acts 13:38, 39). A criminal is pardoned, but is not regarded as righteous. But Justification is that act of God whereby He accepts and accounts us righteous, though in ourselves unrighteous. The Christian is not merely a pardoned criminal, but a righteous man. Forgiveness is an act and a succession of acts; Justification is an act issuing in an attitude. Forgiveness is repeated throughout the life; Justification is complete and never repeated.[42]

Mike's deep acquaintance with the theology of the church fathers led him to add a distinctive note to the discussion of this central Christian doctrine from the writings of Irenaeus and Athanasius. He proposed a metanarrative for the doctrine which was set at the level of creation. Justification properly fits 'within God's one plan of creation renewed and fulfilled'. God created human beings 'to be in right (righteous) relation with our creator'. The fall amounts to an assault upon 'God's creation purpose of righteousness', which God will not abandon. Critical in this plan is Christ the last Adam who recapitulates God's purpose *by his obedience*. Here he cited Irenaeus with delight:

For as by the disobedience of the one man who was originally moulded from virgin soil, the many were made sinners, and forfeited life; so it was necessary that, by the obedience of one man, who was originally born from a virgin, many should be justified and receive salvation. Thus, then, was the Word of God made man, as also Moses says: 'God, true are His works'. But if, not having been made flesh, He did appear as if flesh, His work was not a true one. But what He did appear, that He also was: God recapitulated in Himself the ancient formation of man, that He might kill sin, deprive death of its power, and vivify man; and therefore His works are true.[43]

'[S]o that what we had lost in Adam – namely, to be according to the image and likeness of God – that we might recover in Christ Jesus', wrote Irenaeus.[44] No doubt Mike smiled as he concluded that 'salvation is in that sense not so much about divinization as humanization: justification by Christ's righteousness *humanises* us' (his emphasis).

Mike outlined with clarity and simplicity the metanarrative of justification he learnt from Irenaeus:

- God is perfectly righteous.
- We were created to be righteous (therefore righteousness is a creation concept).
- We have fallen from this originally intended righteousness.
- Creation by its very constitution 'needs' a righteous man.
- Christ is the righteous 'Last Adam' (not just innocent like Adam but righteous in obedience throughout his life *and* in his death and resurrection).
- The obedience of one is a source of righteousness for many.

And this righteousness, Mike insisted again and again, is received only by faith.

The public nature of truth and of theology

Mike Ovey's commitment to God as the creator of all carried with it the conviction that the truth about God and how all things relate to him was not a private matter but had relevance for all of God's creatures. His earliest published theological writing was in the *Cambridge Papers*. He was part of a group of writers from various denominations and academic disciplines who 'shared the conviction that if Jesus is Lord, he is Lord of all creation. Every sphere of knowledge and every human activity should be considered in the light of God's communication to us in the Scriptures.'[45] His contributions to *Themelios* were, likewise, reflections on current trends and events from a biblical and theological perspective. One of the things which marked out Mike's contributions in this area was the breadth of perspective that was shaped by the Bible but informed by wide reading in classical and contemporary thought. Mike's analysis was profound but it was directed towards understanding and responding appropriately to what is happening in the world around us.

Two pieces in particular demonstrate Mike's convictions in this area. The first is his justly acclaimed address to GAFCON II in Nairobi in 2013 entitled 'The Grace of God *or* the World of the West?'[46] His opening challenge set the tone:

> The modern west, in both culture and church, is, overall, graceless, and has become so because of its worldliness. That is why I have called this plenary talk the grace of God *or* the world of the west. Ultimately you cannot have both. It is either/or. My prayer is that as global Anglicans we choose grace, not the world of the west. For those of us who have tried to have grace and the world, I pray for our repentance. My fear is as global Anglicans we will try to have grace AND the world, and that God justly hands us over to the consequences of our sin in rejecting his grace as it truly is and builds his kingdom through others.[47]

What is clear from the start is that Mike brought theological categories to bear on the situation in which the faithful Anglican leaders gathered there in Nairobi found themselves. What is also clear is that he did not pretend to pursue this analysis from a position of privilege but as one who was faced with these same choices. He spoke of '*our* repentance' and 'my fear . . . *we* will try to have grace AND the world'. He knew the problem lies in all our hearts.

Mike assessed the grace about which the West spoke so much as, in fact, 'cheap grace', using Bonhoeffer's expression, that downplays the gospel call to repentance and ultimately is, in fact, graceless. A superficial appeal to the language of mission, witness and gospel is uninformed by the Bible's emphasis on repentance alongside faith. In stark contrast, 'the content of Jesus' gospel is "repent and believe" [Mark 1:15]', Mike reminded us. Matthew 28 has to be read alongside Luke 24, where, in verse 45, 'Jesus opened their minds to understand the Scriptures, and he said to them, "thus it is written, that the Messiah is to suffer and to rise from the dead on the third day, and that repentance and forgiveness of sins is to be proclaimed in his name to all nations, beginning from Jerusalem"'.[48] To these should be added the call to repent in response to Peter's sermon at Pentecost (Acts 2:38) and Paul's words about repentance at the end of his sermon at the Areopagus (Acts 17:30). Mike's conviction that God's word has the critical thing to say to the contemporary malaise is consistent with what we've seen of Mike's work in other areas. His public theology is biblically shaped theology as much as anything else.

Mike's analysis was deeper than that of many commentators. He recognized that talk of repentance is not entirely absent from contemporary discourse. It is too easy to say that repentance is absent from the churches of the West. Yet Mike argued that our repentance is very largely reserved for those things which the world itself finds offensive. The West is largely comfortable in condemning racism, for instance, and to call on people to stop using racist language or acting in ways that marginalize people on the basis of race. There is popular support in the West for the condemnation of colonialism with its attendant murder of indigenous peoples. Yet 'the acid test of whether our repentance is really towards God is when God and the world disagree'. What about the sexual sins which the West celebrates and the Bible condemns? Is our repentance, where it occurs, 'really turning *to God*, or acknowledging the *world*'?[49] He drew on Kant, on Nietzsche, on the essayists in *Lux Mundi* and the contemporary analysts of the age of entitlement, to show how we got to this point. Then he returned to Bonhoeffer and his alternative to cheap grace: 'a costly grace which costs us everything in that it is grace that we receive repentantly and with humility not presumption'.[50]

The second 'piece' is three talks Mike delivered at the Freedom for Faith Conference in Sydney in August 2016. Memorable for Mike's self-description as 'a hag ridden hoary old operator in the rough tough world of English theological education', where it is 'not all thin-sliced cucumber sandwiches', these talks enabled him to bring together his classical education, his understanding of the law and the workings of the English political system, his analysis of contemporary trends and challenges, with his deep engagement with the Bible in order to speak truthfully and, indeed, prophetically to the world in which he lived. The two keynote addresses were entitled 'But Who Is Antigone? Sophists, Pharisees, Sexuality and the Gospel'.[51] His conference dinner address had no title but its central subject was 'juridification' – the 'paradox of a law-bloated society that is covertly law-less'.[52]

Mike's two keynote addresses sought to make sense of three theses: (1) 'We work in a world that thinks it is good and we aren't'; (2) 'We work in a world that thinks it is pro-love and we aren't'; and (3) 'We work in a world where sophists have become Pharisees'. The first two of these observe that the world hears evangelical Christians 'calling them away from conduct which is right and doing so wrongly' and the conduct from which we are calling them is 'the righteous conduct of love'. It is a simple but penetrating analysis that helps to explain why the opposition to Christian teaching in many areas is so vehement and so unyielding. Christian teaching has been recast as a denial of human freedom, an entrenchment of inequality, and a source of violent intolerance. Against these things stands the Western liberal agenda with its catastrophic rate of marriage breakdown, the almost unimaginable scale of murdered children through abortion, a rapidly widening gap between the rich and the poor, and such things as the 'Nordic Paradox'.[53] Yet Mike did not simply take the easy route of exposing the contradictions and inconsistencies in the liberal agenda. His third thesis went further to examine how an ancient philosophical distinction between human convention on the one hand and divine or natural law on the other has been misused to justify liberal revisionism in a way that is deeply reminiscent of the strategy of the Pharisees in Mark 7 and Luke 11. The mark of the Pharisees was 'substituting human words for God's words' in a way that allowed them to judge themselves exemplars of righteousness. Yet character-istically Mike refused to speak simplistically of 'them' and 'us': he reminded his hearers that 'Luke's Gospel presents Pharisaism as the archetype of all our hearts'.

Both of these examples show how Mike was not content with the kind of armchair theology in which theologians simply speak among themselves. This is God's world. In Abraham Kuyper's terms, 'There is not a square inch in the whole domain of our human existence over which Christ, who is Sovereign over all, does not cry: "Mine!"'[54] The Christian theologian has something vital to say to the world, but that something vital must clearly arise from God's revelation of himself and his purposes in Scripture, if it is not just to be human speculation and opinion. In the last few years of his life, Mike had increasing opportunities to speak into the issues of the moment in both the churches and the world, unmasking what was really happening and how we got to this point (his Sydney addresses cited Alexis de Tocqueville, J. S. Mill, John Henry Newman, Charles Gore and Zygmunt Bauman, among others), but always from the per-spective of the good word which God has given us and a marvellous confidence in the living God who has given that word to us. God has something positive to say, a good that surpasses the longings of the world that refuses to acknow-ledge him.

The shape of Mike Ovey's theology

There is no gift more envied by teachers than the ability to excite their students about their subject. Mike had that gift in spades. He joked about wanting to make theology sexy, but the truth is his enthusiasm for God and his gospel, his love of the Scriptures and the delight he gained from taking the details of theology with the utmost seriousness regularly mesmerized his students. It is amazing how many times he could use the word 'intriguing' in a single lecture. His quirkiness at times just added to the alluring mix of personality and truth.

Mike's great achievement was not some new school of thought or some unheard-of yet genuinely profound insight. It was rather that he opened his students' eyes to see the glory of God revealed in the gospel of the Lord Jesus Christ.

Mike Ovey was confident, not in his own ability but rather in the goodness of God. He was confident too in the Bible as the written word of God. It was a confidence he wanted those around him to share. When a prominent evangelical in England raised questions about the authority of Scripture, Mike sat down with his colleague and friend Dan Strange and wrote *Confident: Why We Can Trust the Bible*.[55] Mike knew that confidence is not the same as arrogance, as long as that confidence is anchored in what God has to say rather than what we have to say. Such confidence is in fact an expression of humility, while the refusal to delight in what God has to say, to modify what he has to say or ignore it, is the real arrogance.

Mike's theology was always *deeply biblical*. He loved especially the Gospel of John. Three major pieces of his writing – his masters and doctoral theses, together with his book on the nature of the Father–Son relationship – all contained major sections interacting with the teaching of John's Gospel. His teaching was always *profoundly theological*. Time and again he returned to the nature and character of the triune God, relating all things to him. This was not simply a deliberate theological manoeuvre, it arose from his own unmistakeable delight at God's perfection. As one friend put it, Mike was ever and always a theophile. His theology was always *carefully reasoned*. He sought to help his students and others make connections, to understand that truth has consequences, to integrate the new thing they had been learning into a bigger picture of God and his purposes arising from the pages of the Bible. Mike was careful, at times almost excruciatingly meticulous. If you weren't careful, you could get lost in the detail. And then he would make that mischievous connection which would bring it all together. Mike's theology was *incisively apologetic*. It engaged the world in order to present Christ. He was not afraid of questions and knew that the truth of God addressed the real longings of the human heart. His theology was *wonderfully pastoral*. Mike lived and thought and taught as a pastor, and wrote in order to equip others to live for Christ and proclaim him. In his classes at Oak Hill he was well known for creating pastoral scenarios, penned in Wodehouse-esque style, in order to stimulate his students to think out from the classroom to the church and the world.

Mike Ovey enthused a generation of theological students to take theology seriously. To have the enormous privilege of speaking to and about the living God is something no student of Mike's would take lightly because he did not take it lightly. In the end, with the gifts and opportunities the Lord gave him, he did what all the best theologians do: he pointed away from himself to God, to the God who demonstrated his love for us in the cross of Christ.

Notes

1. An edited form of this lecture is published in M. D. Thompson, C. R. Bale and E. A. Loane (eds.), *Celebrating the Reformation: Its Legacy and Continuing Relevance* (London: Apollos, 2017), pp. 201–218.

2. M. J. Ovey, 'The Gospel "How" of Theological Education.' It is reproduced later in this book (chapter 25), and available online at <https://www.gafcon.org/resources/the-gospel-how-of-theological-education>, accessed 12 September 2017.

3. T. C. Oden, *Classic Christianity: A Systematic Theology* (New York: HarperCollins, 1992), p. xv.

4. M. J. Ovey, 'Is God the Only Theologian? "True but Not Exhaustive"', in R. Cunningham (ed.), *Serving the Church, Reaching the World: Essays in Honour of Don Carson* (London: Inter-Varsity Press, 2017), pp. 37–51 (38).

5. J. Junius, *A Treatise on True Theology*, trans. D. C. Noe (Grand Rapids: Reformation Heritage, 2014), p. 104, cited in Ovey, 'Is God the Only Theologian?', p. 40.

6. Junius, *True Theology*, pp. 104–105, cited in Ovey, 'Is God the Only Theologian?', p. 43.

7. Ovey, 'Is God the Only Theologian?', p. 44.

8. Ovey, 'Is God the Only Theologian?', p. 45.

9. M. J. Ovey, *Hilary of Poitiers: Worshipping the Infinite but Not Solitary God* (Fearn, Ross-shire: Christian Focus, forthcoming).

10. Ovey, 'Is God the Only Theologian?', p. 44.

11. Ovey, 'Gospel "How" of Theological Education'.

12. M. J. Ovey, 'Women, Men and the Nature of God: Equality but Not Symmetry', *Cambridge Papers* 1.2 (Cambridge: Jubilee Centre, 1992). It is reproduced later in this book as chapter 16.

13. M. J. Ovey, 'The Human Identity Crisis: Can We Do Without the Trinity?', *Cambridge Papers* 4.2 (Cambridge: Jubilee Centre, 1995), p. 4. It is reproduced later in this book as chapter 18.

14. M. J. Ovey, 'The Eternal Relation Between the Father and the Son and Its Handling by Selected Patristic Theologians, with Particular Reference to John's Gospel' (unpublished PhD thesis, King's College, University of London, 2005), p. 365.

15. M. J. Ovey, 'A Private Love? Karl Barth and the Triune God', in D. Gibson and D. Strange (eds.), *Engaging with Barth: Contemporary Evangelical Critiques* (Nottingham: Apollos, 2008), p. 217.

16. M. J. Ovey, 'True Sonship – Where Dignity and Submission Meet: A Fourth Century Discussion', in B. A. Ware and J. Starke (eds.), *One God in Three Persons: Unity of Essence, Distinction of Persons, Implications for Life* (Wheaton, Ill.: Crossway, 2015), pp. 127–154.

17. M. J. Ovey, *Your Will Be Done: Exploring Eternal Subordination, Divine Monarchy and Divine Humility* (London: Latimer, 2016).

18. Ovey, *Your Will Be Done*, p. 79.

19. Ovey, *Your Will Be Done*, p. 87.

20. Ovey, *Your Will Be Done*, p. 93.

21. Ovey, *Your Will Be Done*, p. 105.

22. Ovey, *Your Will Be Done*, p. 112.

23. Mike would have delighted at this point in citing the suggestion that we see a causal participle in this verse found in his friend Peter O'Brien's excellent commentary on Philippians; P. T. O'Brien, *Commentary on Philippians*, New International Greek Testament Commentary (Grand Rapids: Eerdmans, 1991), p. 214.

24. K. Barth, *Church Dogmatics* IV.1, *The Doctrine of Reconciliation*, trans. G. W. Bromiley (Edinburgh: T. & T. Clark, 1956), pp. 201, 204. Mike's PhD supervisor Colin Gunton summarized Barth's thought this way: 'it is as godlike to obey as to command'; C. E. Gunton, *Intellect and Action: Elucidations on Christian Theology and the Life of Faith* (Edinburgh: T. & T. Clark, 2000), p. 76. A similar idea had been presented long before Barth in P. T. Forsyth, *God the Holy Father* (1897; repr. London: Independent, 1957), p. 42.

25. M. J. Ovey, 'The Cross, Creation and the Human Predicament', in D. Peterson (ed.), *Where Wrath and Mercy Meet: Proclaiming the Atonement Today* (Carlisle: Paternoster, 2001), pp. 100–135.

26. Ovey, 'Cross', p. 133.

27. S. Jeffery, M. J. Ovey and A. Sach, *Pierced for Our Transgressions: Rediscovering the Glory of Penal Substitution* (Nottingham: Inter-Varsity Press, 2007). This is a collaborative work and it is not always possible to separate Mike's words from those of his fellow-authors (who were two of his students). In what follows I have used the published edition of ch. 3 after comparing it with the first draft of that chapter, which Mike himself wrote.

28. Jeffery, Ovey and Sach, *Pierced*, pp. 101, 103.

29. Jeffery, Ovey and Sach, *Pierced*, pp. 110–111, 117.

30. Jeffery, Ovey and Sach, *Pierced*, p. 117.

31. Jeffery, Ovey and Sach, *Pierced*, p. 130.

32. Jeffery, Ovey and Sach, *Pierced*, pp. 131–132.

33. Jeffery, Ovey and Sach, *Pierced*, p. 147.

34. Jeffery, Ovey and Sach, *Pierced*, p. 147; emphasis original.

35. Unless otherwise noted in this section the quotations are from Mike's unpublished lectures on justification, given at Oak Hill College.

36. M. Luther, 'The Heidelberg Disputation' (1518), in J. Pelikan et al. (eds.), *Luther's Works*, 55 vols. (St. Louis: Concordia; Philadelphia: Fortress, 1955–86), vol. 31, p. 60.

37. M. Luther, 'Lectures on Romans' (1515–16), in *Luther's Works*, vol. 25, pp. 245–246.

38. G. Biel, 'The Circumcision of the Lord', trans. P. L. Nyhus, in H. A. Oberman (ed.), *Forerunners of the Reformation: The Shape of Later Medieval Thought Illustrated by Key Documents* (London: Lutterworth, 1967), pp. 171–172.

39. M. J. Ovey, 'Justification by Faith Alone', in Thompson, Bale and Loane, *Celebrating the Reformation*, p. 206.

40. Homily 3, 'A Sermon of the Salvation of Mankind by Only Christ Our Saviour from Sin and Death Everlasting', in *Certain Sermons or Homilies Appointed to Be Read in Churches in the Time of Queen Elizabeth of Famous Memory* (London: SPCK, 1864), p. 22.

41. J. Calvin, *Institutes of the Christian Religion*, ed. J. C. O'Neill, trans. F. L. Battles (Philadelphia: Westminster, 1960), III.11.2; emphasis added.

42. W. H. Griffith Thomas, *The Principles of Theology: An Introduction to the Thirty-Nine Articles* (repr., London: Vine, 1978), p. 186 (expounding Article XI).

43. Irenaeus, *Against Heresies* 3.18.7.

44. Irenaeus, *Against Heresies* 3.18.1.

45. Mike is quoted in 'Introducing the Cambridge Papers Writing Group', online at <http://www.jubilee-centre.org/cambridge-papers-writing-group>, accessed 12 September 2017.

46. M. J. Ovey, 'The Grace of God *or* the World of the West?' It is reproduced later in this book (chapter 27), and online at <https://www.gafcon.org/sites/gafcon.org/files/resources/files/The_Grace_of_God_or_the_world_of_the_West.pdf>, accessed 12 September 2017.

47. Ovey, 'Grace of God', p. 1.

48. Ovey, 'Grace of God', p. 4.

49. Ovey, 'Grace of God', p. 8.

50. Ovey, 'Grace of God', p. 23.

51. Talk one is online at <https://www.dropbox.com/s/n9vwwepfbe5maai/Being%20Antigone%20-%20talk%201%20%28Autosaved%29.docx?dl=0>, accessed 12 September 2017. Talk two is online at <https://www.dropbox.com/s/uri9gst9db5ztwz/Being%20Antigone%20-%20talk%202%20%28Autosaved%29.docx?dl=0>, accessed 12 September 2017.

52. M. J. Ovey, 'Conference Dinner Talk', online at <https://freedomforfaith.org.au/library/rev.-dr.-mike-oveys-address-at-the-freedom16-conference-dinner-12-august-20>, accessed 12 September 2017. It is in this dinner talk that Mike used the self-description just mentioned.

53. The Nordic Paradox is the puzzling escalation of intimate partner violence in those countries generally considered the most 'gender equal' in the world. Social scientists are still struggling to make sense of a phenomenon which goes against every expectation. E. Gracia and J. Merlo, 'Intimate Partner Violence Against Women and the Nordic Paradox', *Social Science and Medicine* 157 (2016), pp. 27–30.

54. A. Kuyper, 'Inaugural Address at the Dedication of the Free University of Amsterdam', in J. D. Bratt (ed.), *Abraham Kuyper: A Centennial Reader* (Grand Rapids: Eerdmans, 1998), p. 488.

55. D. Strange and M. J. Ovey, *Confident: Why We Can Trust the Bible* (Fearn, Ross-shire: Christian Focus, 2015).

A STEWARD OF KNOWLEDGE: MIKE OVEY 1958–2017

Chris Green, Oak Hill College Vice Principal 2000–2014

A student recently returned a stack of my books from Mike's study. They were a poignant memento, symbolizing so much of what so many miss so sharply. Mike's unexpected death at 58 has shocked a younger generation of evangelicals into concentrating on the legacy of this intelligent, witty, godly, gregarious – and slightly eccentric – man.

Mike was my friend, colleague and eventually my boss, Principal to my Vice Principal. I think I introduced him to Gertrude Himmelfarb, Jean M. Twenge, *Lux Mundi* and Jim Collins. He gave me Isaiah Berlin, Michel Crozier, Jean-Jacques Rousseau and 'The Man from Snowy River'. I never understood his love for Arsenal football club. Each time, he turned ideas into something superbly fresh, always assuming that whatever he'd found had been obvious to me, too. It rarely had been, of course, and he frequently soared over my head. Or he'd sprinkle his conversations with P. G. Wodehouse, Beowulf, James Bond, obscure vampire movies, Flash Gordon, 1960s children's TV programmes – the man was a cultural omnivore. He watched Disney's cartoon *Hercules* on at least four levels (movie, meta-movie, riff on mythology, cultural mash-up), frequently quoting his favourite line 'The son of my hated rival trapped forever in a river of death. . . . Is there a downside to this?'

Mike was undeniably complex. Kind with time and ideas, he could be in angry knots over deception and disloyalty. Loving truth, he deeply hated lies. Loving clarity, he loathed British ambiguity. A graduate of both Oxford and Cambridge, he always felt an outsider in the class system, a grammar-school boy, 'a Cornish Jew – a very small minority'.

In the collection that follows, Mike the intellectual, theologian and educator emerges, but Mike the good friend does not. So to introduce him to those who did not know him, and to provoke memories among his friends, let me take you through my imaginary photo album, each picture clear in my mind.

Photo 1: a wedding, Great St Helen's church, London, 1987

Mike and Heather were married in St Helen's, known for the evangelical ministry of Dick Lucas. Mike, the fresh legal graduate, had met Heather, a physiotherapist, as they had led Bible studies together. The wedding was happy and crowded; it was the first time I had eaten chicken satay with a peanut dip, and I thought it wonderfully exotic.

Mike was born on the Isle of Wight, had become a Christian at school in Southampton, and read law at Balliol College, Oxford. By the wedding, he was working as a Parliamentary Draftsman, preparing legislation for MPs to debate, and his passion for justice, and concern for lawyers, never left him.[1] Solving legal intricacies pleased his classically trained mind. To the end Mike contributed to work in the public square, and one reason he took such care dissecting Isaiah Berlin was that he saw the destructive power of intolerant liberalism; all tyranny, including liberal tyranny, is cruel.[2]

Photo 2: the staff room, an English school, August 1988

Which is a long way from Mike in absurd fancy dress, leading the fun at a summer camp. Such holidays are a staple of English evangelical life, mixing a wonderful holiday for teenagers with clear gospel presentations, and training future leaders. They began in a few private schools, but we were involved in one of the many run by churches for all the teens in their youth groups.

So, early on, Mike and Heather were engaged in evangelism, discipling and training. Even then he could take a Bible verse and make it so transparent that the youngest teenager in the room could understand it, and he would patiently lead a Bible study or arrange individual conversations to develop each person's discipleship. It was almost inevitable that Mike would be challenged to leave his life in the law, and pursue full-time ministry. He headed to theological college, to be ordained in the Church of England.

Photo 3: a croquet lawn, Cambridge, 1990

The Oveys moved to Ridley Hall, Cambridge, one of the Church of England's residential colleges, associated with the university. It is an impressive Victorian college-style building in red brick, organized in a quadrangle around perfect croquet lawns.

It quickly became apparent that Mike found Cambridge a distressing experience, and his friends wondered if it was going to be too much. Mike expected consistency and truthfulness, and he found much that appalled him. The university degree was piecemeal and theologically incoherent, with one tutor, Don Cupitt, openly undermining Christian orthodoxy. The practical aspect of ministry, delivered at Ridley Hall itself, was disconnected from the theology department, internally inconsistent, and required fellowship with some he believed to be false teachers, and others who were immoral in their lifestyle. Contemporaries survived by taking a deep breath, largely ignoring what was going on, and waiting till they could leave. For Mike it was intellectually and spiritually painful; he engaged, but the strain exacted a high price, and he was enormously relieved to begin his ordained ministry in Crowborough, in 1991. The Oveys relaxed. But one pastoral episode crystallized his ongoing tensions: Mike frequently retold how trying to help the leaders of a home group through a marriage crisis made him realize how damagingly he had been sabotaged by his training. His biblical studies taught him to say one thing, his pastoral counselling a second and his doctrine a third; none was a rounded view, and he had no way to integrate the pieces.

Photo 4: a dining table, Newtown, Sydney, 1998

Mike was talent-spotted by Dr Peter Jensen, then Principal of Moore College, Sydney, and invited to join the faculty as a junior lecturer while starting his MTh, on 'Truth in John's Gospel'. He and Heather moved to Sydney in 1995 with a young and growing family, to a small terrace house near Moore, for three cheerful years. My personal photo is of a group of friends celebrating my birthday, with the Oveys thoroughly at home in their new culture.

They quickly slipped into the relaxed Aussie style, and two sets of friendships proved especially formative: Peter and Christine Jensen, and Mark and Kathryn Thompson. Peter and Christine together modelled a pattern of ministry, marriage and family life within a theological college, which Mike and Heather were to use consistently at Oak Hill. Mark and Kathryn were at a similar stage of family and ministry, and as Mike and Mark each later became Principal of their respective colleges, they were deeply influenced by each other.

Within the context of those friendships, Moore influenced Mike as well. Now he experienced integrated theological education, purposefully focused on the delivery of well-rounded pastors, and the faculty to train them. This was more than refreshing – it was transformative, and profoundly inspiring. The connections between theology and educational methodology began to be clarified, and an intellectual process began which would climax in Nairobi, 2013.

But first it meant a move back to London, to become Oak Hill's junior lecturer, in 1988. The new Principal, Dr David Peterson, was a Moore College product, and he was aiming to develop a similar educational model in the UK. Mike was an obvious person to recruit.

Photo 5: a corridor, Oak Hill College, London, 2004

Anyone who visited Mike in his PhD years became aware of a slow but definite movement in the conversations. Initially, we would sit amiably, in a comfortable study, with books and papers cluttered in loose piles. Over time, we stood instead, as the chairs were also commandeered as makeshift filing cabinets. After the carpet was taken over as well, conversations happened in the doorway. Or in the corridor. Then in the small prayer room opposite. In a final surrender to reality, we would meet around the coffee machine in the staff room, or go out for lunch in his preferred haunt, the slightly seedy Buffalo Grill.

Yet we recognized that this chaotic study served a full and methodical mind. Mike's doctoral research into the doctrine of the eternal relation of the Father and the Son in the Trinity[3] was a masterpiece of concise logic, and drilled deeply into both John's Gospel and the fathers, especially his great hero, Hilary of Poitiers. Hilary later featured frequently in Mike's lectures, usually read in a rather dodgy French accent. The PhD developed the hallmark themes of God's truthful self-revelation, his simplicity and his loving justice. Mike's published books, though few, all have this theme, whether on the logic of penal substitution,[4] the clarity of Scripture,[5] or the doctrine of the Trinity itself.[6]

As he became more assured as a lecturer, and matured as a theologian, his key contributions began to show. The stories his students told after his death show time and again Mike's combination of kindness with individuals, and firecrackers in the classroom. Explaining, clarifying and, above all, distinguishing, he modelled a love for the speaking God. Inevitably, therefore, assaults on God's loving truthfulness would cause him not just to think hard, but to feel deeply.

Photo 6: the Beech Room, Oak Hill College, London, 2012

David Peterson retired to Sydney, and in 2007 the Kingham Hill Trustees appointed Mike as his successor. It was a big step up, because he had little experience of daily management in a college, or even a church. But once again, he grew.

My photo this time is of Mike and me, Principal and Vice Principal. The College had been an imposing private home, and the Beech Room was spacious, with stunning views over the grounds. It is now a classroom, hung with portraits of previous Principals, and we would use it on interview days to meet prospective students and explain what a theological education should be designed to achieve. We sat around a long, polished table, which had probably only ever known that room and that view, and Mike would unpack his vision.

Twenty-first-century Britain is fragmented. If it ever shared enough of a single culture to enable easy conversation, that has gone. Drawing small circles on a flip chart, he probed the individualist nature of our times. Furthermore, we are heading into an increasingly fragmented future; and using military shorthand which he had somehow picked up, he described it as VUCA: Volatile (flaring up quickly), Uncertain (difficult to predict where the next issue will erupt), Complex (issues are interconnected, often in multiple and hidden ways) and Ambiguous (difficult to explain with enough clarity). Pastors who evangelize, disciple and lead churches biblically need appropriate skills, such as cross-cultural communication, which mission theologians had been teaching for decades, and which the Theology for Crossing Cultures programme was exploring at Oak Hill. Furthermore, those skills would need to be relearnt and reapplied throughout a lifetime's ministry. Echoing an educationalist's mantra, from his work as a school governor, 'We are preparing students for jobs that don't yet exist, using technologies that haven't been invented, to solve problems that haven't been defined.'

Imagine, he would say, an evangelistic meal. You have laid on a chicken casserole, and to go with it a crisp white wine. To be precise, Mike always insisted it was a Verdelho, a wine he had come to enjoy in Sydney. Now imagine, he said, that your neighbours are Muslim. Does that change anything? Yes, you lose the wine. And the other neighbours are Buddhist, so you have to lose the chicken as well. Your knowledge of your neighbours, their cultures and questions means that you change your communication.

That is easy with other religions, because there are well-identified markers. But all around us are twenty-first-century non-Christians whose assumptions and questions are equally distant, but not obvious. What we need to be able to do, therefore, is to understand both our contemporary context *and* our theological message with sufficient clarity that we can bridge the communication gap. The burden is on us, as Christian evangelists, to understand both so deeply that we can communicate simply.

I was always struck at how personally the issues resonated for Mike. His own theological education had been fragmented until he went to Sydney, and he had felt profoundly ill-equipped by it. No one area of study had been given coherence, and no one had attempted systematic understanding of the whole. The whole experience was broken. And as he looked around contemporary models of theological education he saw the same problem being replicated, because funding pressures meant that pastors were being sent out trained in short-term, pragmatic fads, without the necessary depth to adapt and respond creatively. Even worse, he saw good churches colluding with that disaster, by doing some basic training themselves and then releasing young workers, ill-trained and ill-equipped but thinking they were fully rounded. He foresaw them dropping evangelical ministry in midlife, discouraged or turning heterodox because they had not been trained to be theologically resilient.

Each time he would expound Ephesians 4:11–12, explaining that pastors are God's gift to his church, keeping us healthy, functioning and growing. So a proper theological education is itself the best possible gift we can give a potential pastor.

Leaving the Beech Room and entering the Principal's office, we would find Mike addressing the same issues, but at higher levels. He became involved in a range of discussions, frequently theologically complex, but to which he always brought his clarity. It would now be obvious why he defended penal substitution, because this is God's coherent self-revelation of how he reconciled his love and justice. Assaults on the Trinity, the incarnation, and exploring the dangerous instability of secular thought all seized his attention. These pained him even more when they damaged friendships, but he would not give way on a matter of theological principle, no matter how high the price. At least one projected book, on original sin, was abandoned because he was distracted at the time by dealing with a serious debate, and I suspect he could never revisit a manuscript written in such a painful season.

That familiar, friendly, cluttered study continued, and whatever was top of the pile on the table, whether it was Martin Chemnitz, William Ames, a Ministry Division report or the latest government White Paper, you could always be sure to find Hilary somewhere.

Photo 7: GAFCON, Nairobi, Kenya, 2013

Now imagine Mike, behind a lectern, one hand up, fingers spread as though he were pressing on a pane of glass. It was a characteristic stance, and this time we are in All Saints Cathedral, Nairobi, at the second gathering of the Global Anglican Futures Conference, GAFCON. Fifteen hundred Anglicans have assembled, and Mike is giving the lecture that closes his contribution to this book; in many ways, this paper summarizes all his thought, and he held his multicultural audience spellbound.

Mike was a friend to all kinds of churches and Christians, but was by conviction an Anglican, happiest leading Chapel from the Book of Common Prayer. He revelled in Cranmer's rich, Reformed prayers. But the Anglican Communion is deeply divided; that is no secret. There have been international tensions ever since the first Lambeth Conference in 1867, and they had become increasingly audible over the last decade of the twentieth century, with calls for theologically orthodox leadership from within the Global South. This led to the first GAFCON in Jerusalem, in 2008. Mike spoke there, on theological education, and his papers are also included later. But his real contributions lay in the pre-meetings, and the subsequent theological task group. This was his first experience of international theological discussion, and plunged him more deeply into cross-cultural communication. His clarity and drafting skills became critical, and led him to occupy the platform in Nairobi to give what one experienced theologian called the best single lecture he had ever heard.

Photo 8: the pulpit, Great St Helen's, London, 2015

And finally imagine Mike in that same pose, quintessentially Anglican in cassock and surplice, back in St Helen's, where he and Heather had married, but this time he is in the pulpit.[7] He is preaching at the ordination of some of his students, and the event captures many familiar themes. But retrospectively, there is a poignancy in the words of his sermon, and his friends, colleagues, students will each hear them with particular resonance. Speaking from one generation to another, a battle-hardened soldier to those new to the spiritual front line, he charges them to be ambitious for their Lord:

> We want you to be better than us, we want you to be more faithful than us – we want you, spiritually speaking, to tower above us, so that the cross of the Lord Jesus Christ stands high in this land, and that men and women may know the blessings of eternal life. That is our dream for you, that is our prayer for you, not that you are as we are, but that you are better.

Mike left us on the brink of international significance. God's plan in taking him home so young will have been good, even if his reasons prove hard to discern. But where responsibility for realizing the gospel plan lies with us, it lies with our willingness to rise to Mike's final, ambitious charge.

Εἶπεν αὐτῇ ὁ Ἰησοῦς· Ἐγώ εἰμι ἡ ἀνάστασις καὶ ἡ ζωή· ὁ πιστεύων εἰς ἐμὲ κἂν ἀποθάνῃ ζήσεται, καὶ πᾶς ὁ ζῶν καὶ πιστεύων εἰς ἐμὲ οὐ μὴ ἀποθάνῃ εἰς τὸν αἰῶνα· πιστεύεις τοῦτο; (John 11:25–26)

Notes

1. We could not include Mike's many talks for the Lawyers' Christian Fellowship in this book because they were too difficult to transcribe without losing their spirit, but they are readily available online at <https://lawcf.org/search/app/q/ovey>, accessed 8 May 2017.
2. As chapter 23 shows, Berlin's 'incommensurable pluralism' is the intellectual opposite of Mike's desire to integrate theological truth. They are competing models of how to order morals in the public square.
3. 'The Eternal Relation Between the Father and the Son and Its Handling by Selected Patristic Theologians, With Particular Reference to John's Gospel' (PhD thesis, King's College, University of London, 2005). There is a painful echo in that his initial doctoral supervisor, Professor Colin Gunton, also died surprisingly young, at 62, during this period.
4. S. Jeffery, M. J. Ovey and A. Sach, *Pierced for Our Transgressions: Rediscovering the Glory of Penal Substitution* (Nottingham: Inter-Varsity Press, 2007).
5. M. J. Ovey and D. Strange, *Confident: Why We Can Trust the Bible* (Fearn, Ross-shire: Christian Focus, 2015).
6. M. J. Ovey, *Your Will Be Done: Exploring Eternal Subordination, Divine Monarchy and Divine Humility* (London: Latimer Trust, 2016).
7. See <http://www.st-helens.org.uk/resources/media-library/src/talk/54327/title/ordination-service-sermon>, accessed 8 May 2017.

PART 1:

'OFF THE RECORD' ARTICLES
FROM *THEMELIOS*

Theology in miniature

Themelios is an evangelical peer-reviewed journal, aimed at pastors and theological students, which has been published since 1975. Mike Ovey's brief, punchy pieces, written as consulting editor, served as an appetizer, always modelling his distinctive approach to theology.

1. THE GOLDILOCKS ZONE[1]

'Just right'. This is the key refrain in the Goldilocks story as she tries out the chairs, porridge and beds of the three bears, whose home she has entered (apparently illegally, but nothing turns on that). 'Just right' is also a good summary of a formidable (if not conclusive) apologetic argument for God's existence. The argument suggests that it is staggeringly implausible, if not impossible, for so many finely tuned conditions necessary for human life (size of planet, atmosphere, distance from sun, etc.) to occur without conscious design. Our planet is a Goldilocks planet, with the competing extremes of heat and cold, light and dark, all just right for our existence. But alter the balance, and our life becomes impossible: too close to the sun, and our water is no longer liquid; or if the Earth is too small, it becomes harder to retain its gases.

The Goldilocks 'just right' idea can be applied to theology, too. In fact, I think it must be. One of the most powerful tensions in theology as a discipline is the tension between the local and the global. And here too we need a Goldilocks zone.

By 'local' in this context I mean theology's tendency to drive down into the particular. Thus a theology gets qualified by particular adjectives: liberation theology, Pentecostal theology, black theology, charismatic theology, queer theology, and so forth. The particular adjective readily defines the theology from the viewpoint of those who construct the theology, and it delineates how Christian truth seems to them. There again, the theology can be qualified at the level of subdisciplines, or sub-subdisciplines, as with a study of John's Gospel using the tools of, say, Jungian psychology or Schüssler Fiorenza's liberation hermeneutics. But again, the result is a local theology since one or two particular tools are used out of a complete range, just as one may localize oneself at Palm Beach on Sydney's northern coast rather than the UK's oddly named Bognor Regis. This comparison highlights that a key question is not simply what 'local' tools one uses, but why one has chosen them. Thus Paul's material on the submission due from slaves looks very different if one assumes that all history is really about class warfare.

Now, 'local' theologies have many strengths. Indeed, to some extent such localizations are necessary. The necessity arises because humans are finite knowers, and it is good to recognize that I am a white middle-aged male enculturated into the UK's professional classes. Here, 'localized' theology reminds me of my finitude as a justified yet sinful human creature in this particular society, space and time. Further, I am reminded therefore of my necessary dependence on other local theologies to offset my limitations of race and class, as well as my professional limitations as a systematician who definitely needs the correcting perspectives of other theologians, whether they teach in seminaries and colleges or from the pulpit in local churches.

But 'local' theologies have their perils. A local theology can so stress the particular that what falls outside my own particularity becomes alien to me. Thus the UK does not legally recognize slavery: if I restrict myself to my particularity of white middle-aged professional UK male, then Paul's slavery passages, including the duties of slave owners, seem existentially irrelevant to me. Moreover, precisely because what falls outside my 'location' is alien to me, I can be isolated and deaf to some of what calls me to leave aspects of my location. My choice of 'local theology' can be deeply isolating, or, better, insulating. A way of doing theology that could help me recognize finitude can instead allow me to lock myself into it. Sadly, the focus of local theology can become the 'local' human, not the transcendent God to whom that local theology should refer, an example at worst of theology morphing into anthropology.

Further, it is not just a question of being unable to hear others from different local theologies. Increasingly it may be a question of being unable to speak to them as well. I can become so obsessed with the technicalities of my own field that I both forget and am unable to communicate to those outside it. And sometimes, of course, those outside can play deaf. It might be tempting, for instance, to discount this article because its author is a white middle-aged professional, and so on.

Naturally, I am going to suggest that local theology must be tempered by a more 'global' theology and that we need a theological Goldilocks zone which captures both local and global. However, before I do, we should recall why 'global' theology cannot simply replace local theologies.

By 'global' in this context I am not merely getting at the idea that theologians and ministers can learn truths which go beyond their own local positions, but also need to be heard within other local theologies. A Westerner can have something of permanent value to say to an Easterner, and vice versa. At its best, global obviously gets beyond the local. But adopting a 'global' position can run the risk of suggesting we think we have expressed those truths completely and exhaustively, to the exclusion of other local theologies. It is worth remembering here how easy it is for an apparently local theology to *act* as if it were a fully 'global' theology. That is a significant danger given the way that a particular local theology may seem especially chic.

Two observations are appropriate about global theologies that claim not just truth going beyond the local, but exhaustive truth beyond the local. First, the tendency is to focus on me the theologian as the possessor of an exhaustive truth. Sometimes you do hear evangelicals talking about 'mastering' or 'cracking' or 'mining' a passage of Scripture. The trouble is such language can suggest that that passage has nothing fresh or deeper to say to me. There is profound spiritual danger here for me. I am tempted to see myself as just a bit more like God in my theological grasp than is possible, or fitting, for a human creature. Once again, theology becomes anthropology.

The second observation is that while we evangelicals rightly insist on both the inerrancy and sufficiency of Scripture, at times we seem in more danger of confusing sufficiency with exhaustiveness than we think. And unfortunately it is tempting to indulge that confusion since an ostensibly exhaustive account of, say, Green Christianity can become one which squeezes out any possible alternative view. Exhaustiveness allows my own account of social engagement, for instance, to become final. Postmoderns surely have a point here, that totalizing truth-claims can offer intoxicating power.

By this stage we can see that, perhaps bizarrely, overstressing either the local or the global leads to the same result: the morphing of theology into anthropology. This is why theologians, whether ministers or teachers, simply must stay in the Goldilocks zone, if, that is, they want to be theologians rather than anthropologists.

What does that look like? Older generations of evangelicals would remind us that the knowledge of God is in two broad classes: there is God's perfect self-knowledge of himself (sometimes called archetypal knowledge), and there is the knowledge God has of himself that he has communicated to us (sometimes called ectypal knowledge). God has indeed spoken to us, and his words are true. But we do not hold God's entire knowledge of himself. To have that would entail knowing all of God's perfect attributes completely and in complete relation to each other. Since we believe those perfections to be infinite, it is not possible for a finite creature to know the truth of them in the same way the infinite God does, namely exhaustively. His archetypal self-knowledge is true *and* exhaustive, while our ectypal knowledge is true *but not* exhaustive.

That category of ectypal knowledge gives us space to be rightly local (my knowledge of God from his self-disclosure is not exhaustive) and rightly global (my knowledge of God from his self-disclosure has truths even for those who are not white middle-aged, etc., and I should speak those truths). Consistently seeing my theological knowledge derived from God's self-disclosure as ectypal, not archetypal, helps keep me in the theological Goldilocks zone. In spiritual terms it helps or requires me to be humble before truth (for I am a creature, not God), yet confident in truth (for I am a creature to whom God has spoken and whom God has created to be spoken to). Humility *and* confidence. Evangelicals rightly decry the distorted humility of agnostic theologies which have no confidence that God speaks at all. Equally, evangelicals need to beware an overconfidence that blurs the distinction between ectypal and archetypal. To focus that for myself, maybe I should ask if to my mind when a student or church member disagrees with my sermon or my lecture, it actually counts as disagreeing with God.

Note

1. *Themelios*, Volume 37, Issue 1, 2012, pp. 4–6. Reproduced with permission of The Gospel Coalition.

2. THE RIGHT TO RIDICULE?[1]

'The wisest and the best of men – nay, the wisest and best of their actions – may be rendered ridiculous by a person whose first object in life is a joke.' Thus comments Jane Austen's character Darcy in *Pride and Prejudice* to Elizabeth Bennet. Ridicule is a theme running throughout the novel, and Austen certainly does a fair amount of it herself.

But there are questions about its proper application. Shortly after Darcy's speech, Elizabeth's father remarks about his plans for a future guest, 'There is a mixture of servility and self-importance in his letter, which promises well. I am impatient to see him.' He later amusingly engages this guest in a conversation which displays the guest's servility and self-importance for all to see – all, that is, except the guest. The scene is both entertaining and yet disturbing. For sure, the reader feels that the guest 'deserves' ridicule. But nevertheless Elizabeth's father is determined to bring out the worst in his guest to amuse himself and the more perceptive of his daughters. Elizabeth's father has rightly seen two serious vices in his guest's character, yet encourages them rather than steering his guest toward safer ground.

Elizabeth's father later risks ridicule himself as his weakness contributes to the seduction of his empty-headed youngest daughter, but his final response to this runs, 'For what do we live, but to make sport for our neighbours, and laugh at them in our turn?' His defence of ridiculing others is, if you like, that he is prepared to be ridiculed back. The hint is that if he is prepared to take ridicule, he is in some sense allowed to dish it out.

This takes us to the broader question of the use of ridicule in human engagements, and especially in theological discussion. For the way that a discussion is held and carried forward can be as important as the final conclusion. Thus the basic distinction between a true argument and a valid argument in elementary logic recognizes that a true answer can be reached for inadequate reasons. Similarly, Ephesians 4:15 indicates that truth must be expressed in a particular way – in love (an application of the general New Testament insistence on charitable other-personed love). Luther's reflections on how an externally 'righteous' action can be produced by self-seeking and self-pleasing are very pertinent here. And it is in the context of the *way* Christians should conduct themselves in theological discussion that I want to examine the use of ridicule.

This question assumes renewed force because discussion now happens not just through journals, books and conferences, but through the Internet and its possibilities of blogging, Facebook and Twitter. These possibilities multiply all kinds of discourse, including discourse on serious theological topics. The convention of informality in these possibilities makes it easier for many of us to access these debates. But the informality also allows unsavoury strategies, like trolling, which aims not to advance debate but to disrupt it by provocation and conscious offence. There is an obvious question whether ridicule can cross over into something illicit too.

Yet ridicule has legitimate uses. Strikingly, ridicule can put something into a truer perspective. Isaiah 44:9–20, for example, pursues a strategy of ridicule, and this helps the reader. For the ridicule prods the reader or listener to grasp how vastly incongruous it is to worship something when the other half of it is firewood consumed by the flames. There, ridicule functions as a reality check. It puts things in their true perspective and ultimately has a beneficial and benevolent function for the people of God, helping us see how absurd idolatry is.

There again, ridicule is sometimes a resort for those without power. In *Pride and Prejudice*, Elizabeth Bennet is the family's second daughter, with limited prospects. Her initial internal ridicule of Darcy is partly the response of the weak against the socially strong, and it elicits the reader's sympathy and perhaps admiration that she will not be cowed. She can do little else, but she can ridicule him.

Further, ridicule is very close to the well-tried principle of *reductio ad absurdum*. Here one works through the consequences of a proposition to show, normally, self-contradiction, falsehood or absurdity. Thus a British nationalist of my acquaintance was arguing that all immigrants into Britain should be repatriated. He was also extremely proud of his Norman ancestry. My contention was that on his own reasoning he and myriads of others should be repatriated to France, since they were simply long-standing immigrants dating from 1066. This was

unsympathetically received and perceived as ridicule, although I think it legitimately used *reductio ad absurdum*.

However, there is also a darker set of possibilities with ridicule. Sometimes
ridicule is not the protest of the weak against the strong, but can be a bullying
tool in the hands of the strong to keep the weak weak and to bolster one's own
position. And in the academy, whether theological or not, position and popularity and the power of patronage can make some very strong indeed. Reputation
does seem to me to be a real commodity in the academy, and ridicule, because
it can be so close to demeaning and belittling, can do real undeserved harm to
another.

Thus some blog posts or discussion threads comment not on the argument
but on a writer's alleged intellectual incapacity ('moron'), extreme position
('classic fundamentalist') and possible associations ('on a par with fascists'). Such
rhetoric tends to isolate the writer in question and to some extent demonize
him or her, uniting others against the writer as a person, not simply against the
position he or she has advanced. Such isolation tactics can occur less publicly
but still seriously in a private lecture within an institution. Such isolation tactics
are all too tempting for us, partly because they give vent to our anger at a particular position, but also because they can be a rhetorical shortcut and are easier
than intellectual engagement with the position itself. Such ridicule tactics shade
readily into bullying. I wonder whether the Christian theological academy is
quite as free of bullying by ridicule as it should be.

Further, ridicule is not always used to clarify, but sometimes to obscure or
avoid an argument. The object here is not to cooperate in a discussion by providing something that genuinely tests the strength of an argument but to find
a way of competing successfully in public opinion. Gorgias of Leontini (circa
430 BC) is credited with the slogan 'One must defeat the seriousness of one's
opponents with laughter and their laughter with seriousness.'[2] We rapidly recognize the rhetorical shrewdness and force of this (Gorgias was after all a teacher
of rhetoric). For with this strategy one remains deliberately out of step with
one's dialogue partners, disabling their contribution by always responding in a
different key. To that extent this can be a strategy for silencing a dialogue partner
because the dialogue partner cannot speak in the key he or she chooses.

This underlines how it is possible to engage in dialogue with two very different
models. On the one hand, dialogue can be a cooperative enterprise in which
one meets seriousness with seriousness, laughter with laughter. And here the
point of ridicule is to take the joint conversation further, as a tool of clarification
or restoration of perspective, as I have outlined earlier. This simple but profound
point of dialogue as a cooperative enterprise is taken and developed by H. P.
Grice into maxims for rigorous and respectful conversations. His fundamental

proposition rightly underlines that a conversation has a *joint* purpose, not just a unilaterally imposed one. He writes, 'Make your conversational contribution such as is required, at the stage at which it occurs, by the accepted purpose or direction of the talk exchange in which you are engaged.'[3]

By contrast one can also conduct a dialogue competitively rather than co-operatively. Ridicule wrongly used can feed this competitive strategy. It can become a tool not of cooperation but of asserting power over others by insisting on dialogue in a key that others have neither proposed nor accepted. Hence there are serious questions of holiness to be faced by a Christian scholar who uses ridicule: Am I using it cooperatively, in love and charity for my neighbour with whom I am in dialogue? Or am I using it as a tool of violent domination (because there can be a 'covert thrill of violence' [George Steiner][4] as I ridicule and demean others in the name of truth)? Of all scholarly communities, the Christian academy should be marked by the cooperative principle, with its connotations of charity, fellowship and mutuality. But particularly as I read what we say on the Web and our readiness to ridicule others, I wonder how far our scholarly communities are really distinguishable from the world's. We want truthful, honest, faithful orthodox Christian scholars. We also need holy ones.

Notes

1. *Themelios*, Volume 37, Issue 2, 2012, pp. 182–184. Reproduced with permission of The Gospel Coalition.
2. See Aristotle, *Rhetoric* 3.18, 1419b4–5.
3. Editor's note: H. P. Grice, 'Logic and Conversation', in P. Cole and J. Morgan, *Syntax and Semantics 3: Speech Acts* (New York: Academic, 1975), pp. 41–58 (45).
4. Editor's note: a phrase from George Steiner's 1980 preface to an edition of *Tolstoy or Dostoevsky: An Essay in Contrast* (London: Faber and Faber, 1980; first published, 1959), p. iii.

3. SORROW AT ANOTHER'S GOOD?[1]

One of the most unnerving things you can read is John Milton's great poem *Paradise Lost*. Don't mistake me – I don't dislike the work; far from it. I love it and deeply admire it, but it is profoundly unnerving. Let me explain. It seeks to 'justify the ways of God to men', and Milton goes on to describe the background against which the historical catastrophe of the historical Adam's fall occurs. As he does so, he describes the rebellion of Satan in heaven and starts to draw out Satan's character. And that is where things become unnerving. I'm not sure if Milton has the pathology of Satan's sin correct, but as the poem develops, Milton catches an awful lot about the human heart, certainly mine, and, to be honest, I think others' too.

Milton does not just attribute blame for Adam and Eve's fall to Satan. He describes Satan's motivation:

Who first seduced them to that foul revolt?
Th' infernal Serpent; he it was whose guile
Stirred up with envy and revenge, deceived
The Mother of Mankind . . .

Milton depicts Satan's pride extensively and very powerfully, but what makes his account so telling, I think, is the way he has linked Satan's pride with envy. It is envy of God's supremacy that led him to rebel in heaven in the first place.

It is, further, envy he feels when he sees Adam and Eve in the uncomplicated bliss of Eden in the period of Genesis 2.

Why is Milton's stress on envy so telling? After all, a very strong element of Augustinian accounts of humanity after the fall is the way that in our pride we are curved in on ourselves (humanity *incurvatus in se*). We have a love of self that is disordered, so that typically we think more highly than we ought of ourselves and more disdainfully of others than we ought. Of course, there is debate about whether this depiction of pride can cover issues like low self-esteem and apathy, and I am not going to enter into that here (other than to observe that I think that self-love can be disordered in several ways, of which straightforward arrogance is one form). What interests me here is the connection between envy and pride.

Let me make some observations as we think this through. To begin with, most of us are familiar with the notion of the Ten Commandments as dividing roughly into two connected halves, the first half dealing with sins directly against God and the second half with sins against our fellows. For Luther, all of them are ways of fulfilling the great commandment to love God. It is also rightly said that all of them are ways of breaking the First Commandment.

But what about the Tenth Commandment? In some ways it doesn't fit very easily as a sin against our fellows. Sins of murder, theft, and adultery have very obvious victims in the real world. Covetousness, or envy, does not. Yet it so easily lies behind some of the others. One envies another's wealth and steals it. One envies another's spouse and fornicates with him or her. And so on. Just as the First Commandment can lie behind the others, so to some extent can the Tenth.

Aquinas's analysis makes this even clearer. He comments that envy is a sin against other-personed love because it is sorrow at another's good for no reason other than simply that 'his good surpasses ours'.[2] As such, it is a 'capital' sin which motivates all kinds of other sinful action.[3] To that extent it is not difficult, although still very important, to make some obvious applications. Envy can be present for others in a home group as an attractive loving couple simply sit together on a sofa. Envy can be present as one pastor's preaching is preferred to others' by the congregation. Envy can be present on a college faculty when one teacher receives recognition the others do not, just as it can be in a student body. Envy can take institutional forms, as one college knocks another or one church runs down another. It is not surprising that such settings can feature gossip, backbiting, undermining, factionalism and social sabotage.

Yet Aquinas's comment that envy is sorrow at another's good 'in so far as his good surpasses ours' is hugely suggestive in other ways. Aquinas's point is that behind this sorrow lies a sense of self which suggests that the other should not surpass us in whatever good is in issue, be it spouse, wealth, reputation, or whatever. The lurking assumption is that one is entitled to at least as much of that particular good as the other is.

That word 'entitlement' is highly significant here. Put this way, we start to realize how profoundly important the discussion of envy is for contemporary culture. Social psychologists like Jean Twenge and Keith Campbell argue convincingly that a prominent feature of current Western culture is its growing sense of individual narcissistic entitlement.[4] And such a sense of entitlement, as Twenge in particular notes, equips one very badly to deal not only with one's own failure but also – and this is the point – with somebody else's success.

The sense of entitlement relates very closely to a particular sense of self: whatever good another has, one is entitled to it in at least the same measure. Here an attitude of disordered self-love does indeed form part of the raw material for envy. Intriguingly, though, this kind of entitlement-pride is not necessarily coupled with an overt sense of superiority. Rather, this entitlement-pride can look a lot like a sort of egalitarianism, a perception that 'I'm as good as s/he is', and hence the person in question has no better title to whatever good it is than one does oneself. It is just this sense of 'I'm as good as s/he is' that C. S. Lewis satirizes in his essay 'Screwtape Proposes a Toast'. Put bluntly, it is worth asking whether some forms of current egalitarianism are actually motivated by envy. Entitlement-pride, resentful egalitarianism: envy starts to have a pandemic feel as you look at our contemporary culture.

Envy along these lines is just what Milton's Satan feels. God, he feels, is no better than he is, and therefore no more entitled to the throne of heaven than he is. Satan has a feeling of 'injured merit'. And when it comes to Adam and Eve, again his envy rests on a feeling that they are no more entitled to an existence in bliss than he is: he is as good as they are. Here, though, Milton's Satan trumps Aquinas's original account of envy. For Aquinas envy is something predominantly felt between humans. What is so frightening about Milton's Satan is his envy of God.

This is why Milton's Satan is so unnerving: he seems so truly *human*. After all, consider the temptation of Genesis 3. In part, Eve is prompted to distrust God with the innuendo that God envies humans for their potential to be like him. But behind this lurks the thought that Eve is also being tempted to take the fruit out of envy of God and the wish to have all the goods that God has. In modern terms she behaves as if she feels she is entitled to be like God. The charge of God's envy of human potential looks like a piece of Nietzschean camouflage disguising the truth that in fact the real envy is what she and Adam feel towards God. This is reinforced by the parable of the tenants in the vineyard in Mark 12, where the final reason for the murder of the vineyard owner's son is the tenants' urge to inherit in his place ('Why should he get all this? We're as good as he is'): again a sorrow at another's good 'in so far as his good surpasses ours'.

Now I am used to the thought that I envy my fellow-creatures. It is unpalatable, but familiar. But my envy of my *creator* takes the insanity of disordered self-love to another level, although I reluctantly recognize it as Milton's Satan holds the mirror up to me. Here, though, following Athanasius of Alexandria, another thought strikes us, and we part company from Milton's Satan: the Creator in his generosity not merely does not envy, but takes flesh precisely to redeem the envious.

Notes

1. *Themelios*, Volume 37, Issue 3, 2012, pp. 442–444. Reproduced with permission of The Gospel Coalition.
2. *Summa Theologiae* 2a2ae.36.2.
3. *Summa Theologiae* 2a2ae.36.4.
4. Editor's note: Mike Ovey frequently alluded to two works by Jean M. Twenge: *Generation Me: Why Today's Young Americans Are More Confident, Assertive, Entitled – And More Miserable Than Ever Before* (New York: Free, 2006), and, co-authored with W. Keith Campbell, *The Narcissism Epidemic: Living in the Age of Entitlement* (New York: Free, 2009).

4. COLONIAL ATHEISM: A VERY BRITISH VICE[1]

As I write this, the UK Parliament is considering Clause 1(1) of the Marriage (Same Sex Couples) Bill. It reads, 'Marriage of same sex couples is lawful.' Aside from all considerations about how Christians should respond to same-sex attraction and see biblical teaching reflected in the law of the land, what intrigues me here is one of the background assumptions, namely that same-sex marriage is *possible*. Now, in the UK same-sex marriage has not been a social norm, to put it mildly. And the assumption of the UK government actually boils down to an assumption that, for the geographical entity of the UK, marriage 'belongs' to the UK government. It 'belongs' to it in the sense that it has the right to define and shape it. It has the right to 'name' what is and is not marriage.

Now, you do not have to have the theological acumen of John Calvin to spot that this is in practical terms atheistic. What I want to propose here is that this kind of atheism has a striking quality to it. It is colonialist. It is *colonial atheism*. There are no doubt other dimensions to it, but the colonial quality is important. And while I think it is very British, I do not think we Brits have any monopoly on this kind of colonialism.

Why should we describe some aspects of contemporary atheism as colonialist? The terms obviously suggest that colonial history and contemporary atheism have something in common. But what? The common denominator hinges on the idea of what is now called *terra nullius*, land that belongs to no one. And what I aim to do here is develop a line of thought that came up recently in discussion with the Bishop of St Albans in the UK, Alan Smith ('colonial atheism' is his phrase). It is hugely illuminating.

The idea behind *terra nullius* is quite simple. You declare that some land belongs to no one, so it then becomes available for occupation. Something like this crops up in ancient Roman law, where it gave an account of how, for example, a newly appeared island in the sea could be reduced into ownership (Justinian, *Institutes* II.1.22). This is not unreasonable: it is new land and clearly no one has laid any claim to it, either explicitly or implicitly. But imagine how very different the application is when you come across land where other people are living out their lives and you then declare it belongs to no one, thereby leaving it open to you to occupy for yourself. Now, the provenance of the term *terra nullius* is certainly a point of contention in academic circles just now, but the idea is found in judgments British authorities make in nineteenth-century Australia which relate to the claims to lands lived on by Aboriginal Australians. Unmistakeably, it works to the disadvantage of those Aboriginal Australians.

However, whatever the original intention, there is a 'Heads-I-win-tails-you-lose' sense to *terra nullius* here. This happens in the following way. In order to qualify for recognition as owner, you have to have cultural forms which map onto the culture and practice of the colonial power. If you do have cultural forms which map onto the culture and practice of the colonial power, they are treated *as part of* the culture and practice of the colonial power. They are not treated as having an *independent* validity. The risk then is that your own culture has simply been assimilated into the colonial power anyway. Alternatively, because you retain culture and practice which does not fit the colonial power, you are un-personed in one of the most significant ways a property-owning culture knows: you are a non-owner.

At this point, the *terra nullius* idea goes beyond being simply a 'legal' and 'respectable' way of getting hold of land other people have been living on for generations. It very readily becomes a strategy for un-personing someone else: they either conform to your norms or they are non-owners. But either way, they are not allowed to exist as someone different and other from you. Either way, they have to fit into your scheme of things. They are assimilated or annihilated, but not allowed a real coexistence. Assimilation or annihilation has, tragically, been precisely the experience of people groups who encounter the colonial attitude.

Let us now take one strand of contemporary atheism, of which the late Bertrand Russell is a good example. Asked the question what would he do if it turned out there was a God after all, he responded, 'Not enough evidence, God, not enough evidence.' Now, it is intriguing that Russell's remark has a superficial appeal. How rational, how reasonable, one thinks at first. But in fact the implicit demand is that God conform to whatever rules of evidence we lay down, in the same way that British authorities would only recognize Aboriginal Australian rights if they conformed to British rules of ownership. With regard to God, Bertrand Russell was thoroughly colonial.

Now, to put it mildly, we British had a vested interest in seeing things only in our cultural terms when it came to land ownership and *terra nullius*. In a similar way, humans have a vested interest in un-personing God. Psalm 24:1–2 tells us that the world belongs to God because he made it, all of it, us included. But if we are saying that God does not exist unless he meets our self-interested exacting standards of evidence or behaviour, well, who does everything belong to, then? Us, I suppose. What could be more convenient?

There are profound issues at stake here. If as his human creature I belong to God, then I cannot say my body and mind are mine to do with what I like. My use of my body and the thoughts that I think are not my property. But if I can say God has not made good his 'property title', then why can I not use my body and mind as I wish? All this affects the obvious areas of sex, marriage, social life, but also the intellectual life. If my mind is God's property, what books should I read? What material should I entertain? Do I ever ask if God would have me read such-and-such a book? Or, as a teacher, do I ever ask why I think God would have my students read such-and-such a book?

Of course, it was not just the British who used ideas like *terra nullius* to justify expropriating land other people lived on. Over the years our species has proved frighteningly adept at un-personing other humans, whether on grounds of race, class or belief. But then it is not just atheists who have colonial attitudes to God, because a key part of sin is trying to have God conform to us and our norms, rather than conforming ourselves to God and his. Twentieth-century atheists do indeed have an appalling record of un-personing others, but lest we forget, religious people were involved in the un-personing of God incarnate at the crucifixion. Colonialism: we British didn't start it, but it didn't stop when we left Africa.

Note

1. *Themelios*, Volume 38, Number 1, 2013, pp. 4–5. Reproduced with permission of The Gospel Coalition.

5. FROM MORAL MAJORITY TO EVIL DISBELIEVERS: COMING CLEAN ABOUT CHRISTIAN ATHEISM[1]

People rightly note the way Christians in English-speaking Western culture have moved in a generation from being 'moral majority' to 'immoral minority'. But I wonder whether that really catches the intensity of the dislike and disdain that I see in the two Western societies with which I am most familiar, the UK and Australia. You see, when I read the *Sydney Morning Herald* or the UK's *Guardian*, what I perceive goes beyond a simple charge of immorality (and I'm not talking just about the articles, but the subsequent reader feedback). It has a religious intensity. The same applies to the so-called New Atheism: Richard Dawkins sounds like an Old Testament prophet denouncing Israel's unbelief.

It is important, I think, to understand that our surrounding secular culture regards Christians not just as fools, but also – unconsciously – in a religious sense as evil atheists.

Why? Because our culture practises polytheism. This is a paradoxical polytheism which is *both* a kind of atheism itself *and* which will also see us as atheist. We need to grasp this if we are to respond faithfully in our time and place.

We can explore this paradoxical polytheism using three questions: Is our culture polytheist? How can that polytheism also be atheistic? And why should our culture see Christians as atheist?

So is our culture polytheist?

After all, at first glance this is not how our culture sees itself. But the biblical idea of idolatry sheds a different light. Idolatry has many dimensions, but one key ingredient is that in idolatry we parody the real relationship between us and our creator by using substitutes for God. Substitution is at the heart of the exchange/change language of Romans 1:23 and Jeremiah 2:11.

Tertullian develops this in *De Idololatria* 4 when he points out that an idol stands *pro Deo* (for God). Something can substitute for God either by passing itself off as God and trying to look as much as possible like the real thing (Aaron's golden calves fall into that category) or simply by distracting and obscuring our view of the real God so that we look at the idol and not at God.

I suspect many of our culture's idols fall into that latter category. Our gods are not necessarily gods who create from nothing, are omniscient and are personal. Vitally, they may now be quite small-scale. In particular, we must grasp that idols may be impersonal: wealth is the obvious biblical example of something impersonal that can be treated as a god. For our time, we have many gods, some crass, such as wealth and sexual pleasure, others not ignoble in the right context, like equality before the law and freedom of speech – ideological idols. But the cultural memory that a god should be personal obscures the fact that this is idolatry.

Hence our culture is not only polytheist, in having many small-scale things that stand *pro Deo*; it is an *unaware* polytheist culture. This means that as Christian trinitarian monotheists we are deeply at odds *theologically* with a culture that is polytheist but does not know it.

But why is such polytheism an atheism?

Remember that the patristic theologians were set in a polytheistic culture. Ultimately, their analysis of polytheism was that it became atheism. This sounds odd. Wonderful temples were built, staggering works of art made depicting Zeus, and so on. How can that be atheism?

Athanasius sums it up nicely when discussing the idea of having two gods (*Contra Gentes* 6). He argues that if you have *two* gods, you have *no* gods in the real sense of the word because to be God means you have no rivals who can resist your will. His base assumption here, drawn from biblical descriptions of God as Lord, is that to be 'God' necessarily entails sovereignty. So the multiple impersonal values of our time boil down to this kind of atheism.

But it works the other way too. If you are an atheist in Athanasius' terms, what are you left with? There is no overall coherence, no God who in himself is the sum of all perfections, and so there's no reason not to elevate your own personal values into things which function as absolutes for you, and to accept that others are entitled to do the same. In that way, atheism becomes polytheism where there are lots of small, often impersonal, gods who function as divine in our lives, even if we don't see ourselves as worshipping them. Think of G. K. Chesterton's comment that when people stop worshipping God, they don't worship nothing; they worship anything. Or indeed, everything.

One of Athanasius' followers, Gregory of Nazianzen, is useful here. He commented on the world views that polytheism and monotheism tend to create and noted that there are three ways of viewing the cosmos:[2]

1. A cosmic monarchy (one ruler)
2. A cosmic polyarchy (lots of rulers)
3. A cosmic anarchy (no ruler)

His point was that polytheism involved a cosmic polyarchy, and this in turn became a cosmic anarchy because no one holds things together and integrates them. Atheism and anarchy go together.

But anarchy is unstable. Anarchy is not a self-regulating dynamic equilibrium in human experience, but consistently tends to allow different power-holders to establish themselves at the expense of others. Each power-holder acts and competes against others without restraint – as if absolute. So in the value-anarchy of atheism, each small-scale value can, paradoxically, be treated as if absolute. There is nothing there to restrain it.

But where do Christians fit into a culture caught in polytheism and atheism? This takes us to the third question.

Why should our culture see Christians as atheists?

Again, think back to the early church. One of the more surprising charges made was that Christians were atheists. Why? Because of the number of gods they denied. No Zeus, Hera, Hermes, Mithras, Isis, or whoever. Similarly, we deny our culture's gods.

Take one of the current cultural idols: equality. This is one of those impersonal gods we were discussing earlier. Does the Bible give us an account of equality? Yes, but in relation to other considerations. We have an integrated account of equality, that is, equality is put in proper perspective and place by the whole Bible's teaching, and, crucially, we as creatures are not equal to our creator. In that way, equality is not *the* great overarching theme of Christian thought. But it is one of the gods of the current secular pantheon and pursued with a religious fervour. In the value-anarchy of our time, it competes to be treated as absolute.

So my refusal to accept equality as absolute looks rather like earlier Christians refusing to worship the god Zeus. I am an atheist within that framework of reference.

Hence some of the rage which comes our way on some of the debates of the day. When we oppose same-sex marriage, we are not just discussing different ethical positions; we are demonstrating that we are irreligious atheists because we are denying the 'divinity' of some very popular gods – sexual satisfaction, autonomy, equality, liberty. Of course, what makes it hard for people to see this rage as a religious rage is their self-image as secular people. But then polytheistic idolatry has always had a somewhat delusional, self-deceptive dimension: see Isaiah 44.

There are some further parallels here in the way early Christians were regarded. The Neoplatonist Porphyry famously argues, 'How can people not be in every way impious and atheistic who have apostatized from the customs of our ancestors through which every nation and city is sustained?'[3]

This raises an important dimension. By not worshipping the ancestral 'public' gods, Christians were thought of as atheists who undermined the state. And this is not too far from the way atheist Christians who do not sacrifice at the altar of equality or liberty in personal hedonism can be thought of as atheists who are public enemies, bad citizens. Our assertions of cosmic monarchy destabilize the value-anarchy polytheism of our time.

It's not surprising, then, that Christians in the UK speaking on practising homosexuality as meriting God's condemnation are prosecuted under public-order offences. And such state action is perceived as 'self-defence'. This seems to me to be an extremely important part of the rhetoric the media elite uses against Christians and other cosmic monarchists. It is self-defence because we are thought to undermine a society which is a process of competing and plural forces and persons. The latter half of the twentieth century is replete with arguments that a democratic society can take strong steps in defending itself against those who would overthrow it. In fact, because democracy is so precious (dare one say, such an idol?), security services are justified in taking very extreme action to preserve something so precious.

The rhetoric about self-defence is significant. In an instant the claim of self-defence allows one to present oneself as the victim. And a polytheistic culture may readily see itself victimized by the rhetoric of cosmic monarchists – for we are the atheists.

Notes

1. *Themelios*, Volume 38, Issue 2, 2013, pp. 202–204. Reproduced with permission of The Gospel Coalition.
2. *Third Oration on the Son* 1.
3. Editor's note: Eusebius of Caesarea, almost certainly alluding to Porphyry, although not quoting him by name, in *Praeparatio Evangelica* 1.2. The most likely source of Mike Ovey's translation is R. L. Wilken, 'The Piety of the Persecutors', *Christian History* 27 (1990), pp. 16ff. See <http://www.christianitytoday.com/history/issues/issue-27/piety-of-persecutors.html>.

6. LIBERTY, WHAT CRIMES ARE COMMITTED IN THY NAME?[1]

Does someone have the right to harm his or her own soul? Or if you don't much like the talk of 'soul', do people have the right to do themselves moral harm?

For many years the assumption in the UK has been that individuals do have the right to do themselves spiritual harm. This came to a very visible head in the controversy in the British Parliament this year about laws permitting same-sex marriage, but it had been coming for some time. Thus in immediate post-Second World War England and Wales, it made sense and had public support to have criminal offences of conspiracy to corrupt public morals (e.g. by publishing a directory of call girls), but by the late 1970s this had changed. And the question put rhetorically in the public debate was in these terms: 'Why prohibit victimless behaviour?' More straightforwardly, 'Who other than the perpetrator is actually harmed?'

This line of argument strongly defends the liberty of the individual and has a strong European post-Enlightenment feel to it. In my country it was expressed by John Stuart Mill, the highly influential Victorian essayist, in his *On Liberty* (1859). It is not, though, an exclusively English idea, for Mill drew most of his fundamental argument from Wilhelm von Humboldt's *The Limits of State Action* (1791–2). Mill's point was that the state was justified in limiting someone's freedom to act only if the action resulted in harm to others. In fact, Mill's argument extended to social disapproval as well as state action. He nuanced this by accepting that some societies might not be at a stage where this approach to liberty was feasible. He writes (and this may surprise some), 'Despotism is a legitimate mode of government in dealing with barbarians, provided the end be their improvement, and the means justified by actually effecting that end.'[2]

Similarly, liberty did not apply if the individual was, for instance, a minor. This nuancing clearly resembles Immanuel Kant's claim in his 1784 essay 'What Is Enlightenment?' that since 'we' are now mature, we no longer need others to make our judgments for us but should make them ourselves. Our 'maturity' confers both the *capacity* for and the *right* to autonomy. Mill's point is that this autonomy must in human society be exercised without harm to others.

For Mill, therefore, his own conduct in alienating the affections of Harriet Taylor from her husband and setting up house with her (possibly without consummating until Taylor's death) was not 'harm' to Mr Taylor or the two children she had by him. Logically it should not be subject either to legal sanction or public disapproval. He and Harriet were entitled to do as much harm to themselves and each other as they wished, for they were mature consenting adults whose actions dealt only with themselves.

Behind this position lay a conception of what a human being is. Mill quotes von Humboldt: '[T]he object "towards which every human being must cease-lessly direct his efforts, and on which especially those who design to influence their fellow-men must ever keep their eyes, is the individuality of power and development."'[3] This strong version of individual self-realization rests in turn on this view: 'Over himself, over his own body and mind, the individual is sovereign.'[4]

But while Mill has been hugely influential in my country and elsewhere, he has had critics, both non-Christian and Christian. A lot of that criticism has centred on the idea of harm and how Mill actually smuggles in his own value judgments at that point and covertly imposes them. Take the unfortunate Mr Taylor, for instance. Very few men like being cuckolded, even if the cuckolding is at an emotional rather than consummated level. They experience it as 'hurt' or 'harm' as do wives whose husbands philander. And those of us who are their friends and companions have no doubt that the harm is savagely real.

I think this line of criticism about harm *to others* is important and well taken. But it doesn't tackle the question with which we started. Do I have the right to harm *myself*? Mill's rationale for saying we do as individuals have that right is that we are sovereigns. The image is political with the individual as a little kingdom whose boundaries coincide with our bodies and our thoughts. Within those boundaries, we are rightly independent, little perhaps, but genuinely sovereign entities.

Of course, Christians who are committed to the lordship of Christ immediately sense the difficulties here. How does the lordship of Christ, which shows Christ's sovereignty, interact with my sovereignty over myself on Mill's view? The issue here is cast in *political* terms: two competing sovereignties, one of which may be subordinate and derivative. But at the end of the day, when Christ says I am to use myself (whether it is my body or my mind) in certain ways, do I have the right to say no?

On this political model, where I am my own little kingdom, we readily talk of sin in similarly political terms and describe sinners as 'rebels'. I think this is clearly right, but I want to make two supplementary points about it.

First, sin and the self-harm that it sometimes shows is not just rebellion. It is also *theft*. Second, the language of *theft* helps de-glamourize sin. Let me explain.

First, theft. Why speak in terms of theft? Because this is the necessary implication of passages such as Psalm 24:1–2. The little phrase 'the earth is the LORD's' carries huge freight. The language is that of possession or ownership. This extends our understanding of what it means for God to be the Lord beyond simply a political image ('king') to that of property and ownership. The earth *belongs* to God. It is his *possession*.

This puts a different complexion on my acts of spiritual self-harm. They do affect more than myself, and they affect in other ways than 'political': they compete with God's rights as *owner*. This ownership is grounded in God's creation of all things from nothing, as Psalm 24:2 makes clear, grounding God's claims as owner of all things in the fact of his creation of all things.

On this view, defying God is not just an act of political rebellion; it is a 'property-act' – it is stealing something that belongs to someone else. My use of gifts or talents for purposes other than those for which God gave them is an act of robbery. And when someone commits fornication with another consenting adult, there is the double theft of stealing the gift of sexuality both with regard to oneself and with regard to the other person.

In one sense this idea of sin as theft is implicit in Augustine's famous phrase that sin is 'lust for mastery' (*libido dominandi*), for the Latin word for 'master' (*dominus*) can certainly carry the idea of political power. But it is also strongly used for the right of property, the master who *owns*. Lust for mastery obviously can be manifested in the way I treat others, treating them as if I have rights to ownership. But in view of Psalm 24:1–2, lust for mastery is also something I have with regard to myself. I long to cheat my rightful owner and creator of his rights as my owner and creator. In short, I long not to be a creature.

This takes me to the second point: de-glamourizing sin. Apologetically, speaking of sin as rebellious sovereignty seems to me to risk glamourizing sin in our culture. Given our anti-authoritarian pose in Western culture and our affinity for the rebel, to describe sinners as rebels risks letting people see themselves as heroes. For rebels overthrow governments, and governments are, as a rule of thumb, authoritarian. Aside from Chuck Norris films, few films glamourize upholding order.

But theft is often different. It smacks of deceit and dishonesty, and our experience of it is its sneakiness. In a modern Western society, perhaps more of us have been victims of theft in its various forms than of the ins and outs of political rebellion. Of course, it is possible to glamourize theft too – as the *Ocean's 11* series did. But I find it significant how strongly those acts of theft are cast in terms of stealing from someone who deserves it and who has significant deceit and dishonesty in his or her own life. And it does focus the question 'Did God *deserve* to have me steal from him?'

This article starts with the oft-quoted question 'Liberty, what crimes are committed in thy name?' We are right to say that with respect to God, sedition against him is committed in the name of liberty. But there is another crime that is somehow much more mean-spirited: theft. My allegedly harmless actions towards others can be thefts of those others from God, their owner. And my allegedly harmless actions include stealing myself.

Notes

1. *Themelios*, Volume 38, Issue 3, 2013, pp. 357–359. Reproduced with permission of The Gospel Coalition.
2. J. S. Mill, *On Liberty* (repr., London: Penguin, 1974), p. 69.
3. Mill, *Liberty*, p. 121.
4. Mill, *Liberty*, pp. 68–69.

7. THE COVERT THRILL OF VIOLENCE?
READING THE BIBLE IN DISBELIEF[1]

One of the perils of being a middle-aged parent in England is that you have to attend school plays. By the time your children are in their mid to late teens, they no longer act in dubious juvenile versions of *The Lion King*, but any sense of safety this gives you is thoroughly spurious: they have been told by their drama teachers to do Shakespeare. However, Shakespeare in its raw form gives drama teachers cold feet, it seems. Thus it is that you can find yourself watching *King Lear* or *Romeo and Juliet*, but not in their tragic form: rather Shakespeare's tragedies are played for laughs. The thing is, Mercutio's agonized, dying, 'A plague o' both your houses! They have made worms' meat of me' does not really work as a gag. Trust me on this.

Now I have no doubt that the drama teacher who produced this comic adaptation of Shakespeare's tragedy was doing her postmodern best: 'witty', 'playful', 'imaginative', 'creative', 'rebelling-against-Shakespeare's-patriarchal-authorship', 'the reader-as-empowered-author'. Yet other adjectives seem more appropriate: cruel and violent. 'Cruel' because to treat Mercutio's death in this way is cruel and compassionless. 'Violent' because Shakespeare is not simply being gagged or silenced: he is being made a ventriloquist's dummy and being made to say words of trivial cruelty. George Steiner long ago appreciated that some modern reading strategies had exactly this quality: they had the 'covert thrill of violence'.[2] 'Violence' because the reader makes a ventriloquist's dummy of the author against his or her will, and 'covert' because this is carried out under the cover of 'witty', 'smart', 'playful' and indeed 'scholarly' reading of the author.

Obviously, we see these techniques applied to the Bible too. Equally clearly, I do want to pick up on Don Carson's brilliant book title *The Gagging of God*. Yes, there is a way in which God is silenced, but, going further, there is a sense in which our reading strategies make a ventriloquist's dummy of God, not simply gagging him, but putting our words into his mouth and then treating our words as if they are his.

Why would we do that?

I think Steiner's phrase 'covert thrill of violence' offers a critical clue here. You can read someone *violently*, *violatingly*. A reading strategy can be a strategy for exercising violence. In particular, a reading strategy for the Bible can be a strategy for exercising violence towards God.

Let me explain further by drawing on the thought of the fourth-century bishop Hilary of Poitiers (flourished 360). Hilary was faced by those who denied that the Son was truly son, either by saying that he and the Father were really just masks for the one God (modalists) or that the Son was only a creature (Arians). On either view, the Son was not true son. Hilary feels that the true sonship of Jesus is clearly stated by the Bible, and yet his opponents persistently claim that they find support for their own views in the Bible. He feels he is faced with those who read in disbelief, and has to work through what right and wrong readings of the Bible involve. This leads him to discuss what we would now call presuppositions and the hermeneutics of suspicion.

What, Hilary muses, is this prior commitment which means modalists and Arians read the Scriptures as disbelievingly as they do?

> And yet our disbelief tilts even against obvious truth; we strive in our fury to pluck even God from His throne. If we could, we would climb by bodily strength to heaven, would fling into confusion the ordered courses of sun and stars, would disarrange the ebb and flow of tides, check rivers at their source or make their waters flow backward, would shake the foundations of the world, in the utter irreverence of our rage against the paternal work of God. It is well that our bodily limitations confine us within more modest bounds. Assuredly, there is no concealment of the mischief we would do if we could. In one respect we are free; and so with blasphemous insolence we distort the truth and turn our weapons against the words of God.[3]

Hilary's point is that what humans really want is to do violence to God. Failing being able to do that in a physical way, we do it against what is available to us, his revealed word, because unlike the eternal incorporeal God, his word has physical presence in our world. Our treatment of God's word is the focal point of our violence against him.

This is a kind of hermeneutics of suspicion. Suspicion of both authors and readers can have its place: it is no doubt right and helpful to ask whether I read the Bible and write as I do because I am a person at least partly produced by a particular nation state, in a particular class, in a particular place, of a particular gender and influenced by particular education. But Hilary raises the issue of *spiritual* suspicion. Hilary makes me ask whether I read as I do in my urge to do violence to God. Unnervingly, he makes me ask whether my basic disposition is precisely to want to distort the word of God, just because it is the word of God.

I suspect one response here is that this is too bleak. Certainly human motives can be mixed, including the motives for their hermeneutics, and it is plausible to think that a human being can be both attracted to God and his word and yet simultaneously be repelled. But the point is that this element of repulsion with its dimension of anti-God violence does exist, and this repulsion can be determinative in how we respond. Thus Jesus analyses disbelief in him as arising precisely from the fact that he *does* speak words from his Father (John 8:45). And while he recognizes that those who oppose him and his followers think they do God's will (John 16:2), in fact, he explains, this shows their alienation from the Father (John 16:3) and is in the context of hatred of both Jesus and the Father (John 15:24). Jesus comments that he has been hated 'without a cause' (John 15:25); that is, without good reason. And, finally, Jesus' all too real experience is precisely that humanity, when given the chance by Jesus' physical presence among us in the incarnation, murders God.

Murderers and would-be murderers are not necessarily the best readers of their victims' texts. That is obvious. Why would this not also be so when the one we would murderously love to be the victim is God?

What follows from this? To begin with, we have to expect to fight the battle for the Bible in every generation because it has to be fought in every human heart.

Second, I need to be especially aware of the times when I have so mixed my inner desires and experience with what I claim is God's word, that God's word is merely a ventriloquist's dummy for my own thoughts – making doctrines out of my desires, as Hilary puts it. Perhaps I need to ask myself more carefully whether I *want* something I claim God says to be true. Perhaps I need to ask when God last said something in my reading that I did *not* like or that the world did not already say.

Notes

1. *Themelios*, Volume 39, Issue 1, 2014, pp. 5–7. Reproduced with permission of The Gospel Coalition.

2. Editor's note: a phrase from George Steiner's 1980 preface to an edition of *Tolstoy or Dostoevsky: An Essay in Contrast* (London: Faber and Faber, 1980, first published, 1959), p. iii.

3. *De Trinitate* III.21.

8. PROJECTION ATHEISM: WHY REDUCTIONIST ACCOUNTS OF HUMANITY CAN LEAD TO REDUCTIONIST ACCOUNTS OF GOD[1]

We often associate atheism with a very high, indeed arrogant, view of what a human being is. Thus sometimes God is denied because his existence would threaten the overwhelmingly important value of human freedom. So argues nineteenth-century Russian anarchist Mikhail Bakunin. Sometimes God is denied because a human being argues that his own exacting criteria of proof have not been satisfied and since he is self-evidently so intelligent this indicates God is not there. Thus asserts twentieth-century British philosopher Bertrand Russell.

But what happens to God if we have a very low view of what a human being is?

That's the question I want to explore in this article. There are two background considerations here. First, there is John Calvin's observation that the doctrine of humanity and the doctrine of God are intimately related. Second, there is Ludwig Feuerbach's idea that religion is a projection of our ideals. Taken together, I want to argue that if one thinks a human being is really nothing, this readily leads to atheism.

Let me explain. Calvin famously opens his *Institutes* with the observation that who we think we are and who we think God is are tied very closely together (*Institutes* I.1.1). Calvin notes that this can work inversely: when we see how great God truly is, this engenders humility in us, as we compare his perfection and infinity to our imperfection and finitude. He is great, and we are small. Similarly, if we have a very high view of ourselves, then we may be inclined to despise his goodness and our dependence on him. We are great, so he is not so great. A good example is Immanuel Kant's 1784 claim about the Enlightenment that we humans are 'mature' and therefore do not need to be told by God what to do. Since we are mature, we can work it out for ourselves, and authoritative revelation is superfluous and, indeed, offensive since it treats us like children.

Calvin seems to me quite right, not least because one can see, I think, this inverse relationship at work in Genesis 3 when Adam and Eve both seek to aggrandize themselves and belittle God. Equally, one can see this inverse relationship at work in that particular species of Western modernism which has a vastly inflated view of humanity and can accordingly reduce room for God to the point that one ends up with a world view that has no space for God at all, namely atheism.

However, the relationship between the doctrine of God and the doctrine of humanity is not just inverse. There can be a directly proportional relationship too, whereby an appropriately high view of humanity leads to a high view of God, and an inappropriately low view of humanity leads to a low view of God. This is where Ludwig Feuerbach's projection idea comes in. Feuerbach's basic idea was that God is a projection of the highest human ideals. Thus we have ideas of justice and goodness and charity, and we project them in their perfection onto God.

Now, there's a good deal of truth in Feuerbach's idea in this sense: he is describing one of the ways idolatry works. We attribute to God, or to our gods, the ideals we want to be true. A moment's reflection, of course, indicates that Feuerbach mistakes 'some' for 'all'. Just because some religions are idolatrous projections, it does not follow that all are. After all, a husband may idealize his wife, or a wife her husband, and blindly attribute matrimonial perfection to them; the mere fact the attribution onto the spouse is a mistaken projection does not entail that the spouse does not exist. And, one should add, Feuerbach bypasses the incarnation of Jesus, which is never good.

That said, Feuerbach's case is still valuable as an observation about idolatry. However, we can take Feuerbach further. What happens when we do not have high ideals about humanity, but low ones? Feuerbach's model predicts, of course, that God will be an idealization of these low values (cruelty, exploitation, etc.). But going still further, what happens when we have not just low values among humanity but no value for humans at all?

By talking about no values for humans at all, I'm moving to that area of discussion which sees humans as 'nothing but' conglomerations of organic material governed ultimately by strictly natural, purposeless processes. In this world view, there may be random occurrences but no personal, intentional intervention from outside the system. Humans are 'nothing but' these temporary self-organizing bundles of stuff. The point is often made that this apparently entails that humans have no value and that one of the great inconsistencies of 'naturalist' writers like Richard Dawkins is the lack of any consistent basis for upholding human value in an objective sense.

But what intrigues me is the impact this doctrine of humanity will have on a doctrine of God. Just as Kant's idea of human maturity renders the speaking God superfluous, doesn't the idea of zero-value humanity lead to a zero-value God? After all, if I have denied my own human value by saying my rationality and conscience and soul just boil down to chemical events, is it not easy to project this onto God and deny he has value too? In essence, as I deny my own humanity, I can project this denial onto God too. Descartes notably argued from his own existence to the existence of God: perhaps we have a reverse-Descartes situation in which we project from our own non-existence to the non-existence of God.

Why does this matter? Apologetically, it makes me think about atheism from the perspective of its sometimes being an extreme version of Feuerbach's projection theory of idolatry. It also reminds me of the need sometimes to look at someone's doctrine of who a human being is before I get to discussing with them who God is. I must ask not just who they think God is, but who they think they are. More generally, I am reminded of the consequences of nihilistic world views, because in many ways this is an atheism born of nihilist views of *humanity*.

Pastorally, one is naturally inclined to ask who would adopt this zero-value view of humanity anyway. Is it purely opportunistic, a good way of freeing oneself because one says there are no values anywhere? After all, if I have a zero-value account of humanity, this radically frees me from needing to value others, and that naturally can be quite convenient. Moreover, we have to see this zero-value account of humanity in the light of Jesus' incarnation. Notably, a zero-value view of humanity should include a zero-value for Jesus. And that can be quite convenient too. In fact, is it worth having a zero-value account of humanity precisely as a strategy for applying zero-value to Jesus too?

Or, paradoxically, does the zero-value view of humanity connect with a subtle self-loathing in which human disordered self-love has become so warped that it has become self-harming? Further, this puts the presentation of the gospel in a new light too. We have rightly spoken of God's saving by grace alone. Part of the tragedy of projection atheism is that it is not just saying there is no God to save; it is also saying there is no 'me' to save in the first place. Part of our proclamation problem is not just proclaiming forgiveness of sins to a culture that does not believe there is such a thing as sin, but proclaiming it to a culture that at points has doubts about whether there is even a person there to sin at all.

There is, perhaps, an alluring freedom here, the kind of freedom that comes when people renounce their identity and live in another country, untouched by their old obligations. But this is also very close to despair.

Let me close with another connection. So far we have been talking about projecting from humanity. Greg Beale also argues that in idolatry there is the reverse dynamic – that we become what we worship.[2] This opens up a tragic vicious circle: my zero-value account of humanity can encourage projection atheism. And my atheism can reinforce my zero-value account of humanity. Nietzsche quipped that God is dead and that we have killed him. He asked how we could be worthy of this. One might also ask whether our 'killing' of God does not also kill us.

Notes

1. *Themelios*, Volume 39, Number 2, 2014, pp. 220–222. Reproduced with permission of The Gospel Coalition.
2. G. K. Beale, *We Become What We Worship: A Biblical Theology of Idolatry* (Downers Grove: InterVarsity Press; Nottingham: Apollos, 2008).

9. IS IT A MISTAKE TO STAY AT THE CROSSROADS?[1]

One of Augustine's earliest Christian writings is his dialogue, set in Cassiacum, *Against the Academics* (circa AD 386). It is not, of course, against academic study as such, but against the philosophical school known as the Academics, famous for their commitment to sceptical questioning. For Augustine this was vital ground-clearing work in his nascent Christian faith. He found the scepticism of the Academics powerful and enticing in some respects, and saw its huge significance for any kind of Christian faith, his own included. For the essence of the scepticism of the Academics was to suspend judgment and therefore to suspend commitment. And, noted Augustine, commitment is the essence of Christian faith, for in faith I trust and believe Jesus Christ for who he says he is and what he says he does. Therefore, at some point the scepticism of the Academics makes Christian faith impossible. It kills it – hence the need for Augustine to slay some of his own inner demons in *Against the Academics*.

I want to argue that there are some important parallels between the scepticism that Augustine encountered and some contemporary ways of handling the Bible. I also want to argue that Augustine has given us something of enduring value in meeting those approaches by his analysis of what it is to make a mistake. His point is that when you are on a journey it is a mistake to remain sitting at the crossroads.

Let me begin by outlining the scepticism Augustine meets. By the time he is writing his dialogue, recognizably sceptical philosophy was some 700 years old, with its origins back in the late fourth century BC, with figures like Pyrrho of Elis. In its developed form this is what it asserted by Augustine's time: the wise person assents only to what is definitely true; we cannot prove what is definitely true; therefore we should assent to nothing.

Why should we adopt such an apparently odd position? Well, answers Sextus Empiricus some 150 years before Augustine, this is the way to *happiness*. Sextus comments that the goal of sceptical philosophy is quietude of mind, or freedom from disturbance (*ataraxia*). To achieve this, one must deliver oneself from the existential agony of choosing between different ideas and philosophies, which requires suspension of judgment (*epochē*). To achieve suspension of judgment, one meets every argument with another argument. You do not have to believe this opposing argument or even think it probable. The point is *not* that the arguments are of equal weight but that no argument is wrong beyond *all* shadow of any *possible* doubt. The idea is that for every argument there is at least a *possible* counterargument, no matter how contrived or desperate. At that point you are entitled to suspend judgment and enjoy freedom from disturbance.

I encountered this sceptical technique when taking questions at a university campus in Wales on the historicity of Jesus' resurrection. The objection was that I had not shown in my talk that Jesus was not an alien who had strange powers of self-resurrection after physical death (source critics may identify a Hollywood *ET* debt here). I asked what evidence the objector had to support this. 'Oh none,' came the answer, 'but it's still a possibility.' And of course with this technique comes the claim that one must therefore suspend judgment and therefore suspend any commitment to faith in the resurrection even while admitting the evidence pointed that way – just as Augustine foresaw.

Two quick comments: Obviously this technique can look as though it is intensely intellectually rigorous. Equally obviously this is emphatically not a technique designed to find the truth. Sometimes people assume that sceptical questions are a tool for finding the truth. They are simply not designed for that. Instead, the sceptical programme of questions is designed to ensure that you never have to commit to the truth because on the sceptical view your happiness lies not in commitment to something but in being free from disturbance, that is, in not committing.

But why think sceptical techniques are alive and well in the way we read the Bible? Let me take an example from the last year from the Church of England's Pilling Commission, set up to discuss the issues relating to same-sex relations and marriage. There was both a majority report and a courageous and penetrating minority report. For present purposes let us look at the majority report.

In paragraph 235 the Pilling majority tell us that the Bible is authoritative. So far, so good. However, the meat of the Pilling majority's findings is that they cannot apply or set out what the Bible teaches on the issue of same-sex relations. Let me set out the major factors cited:

1. The sincerity of different opinions must be respected.
2. The scholarship is too vast to be synthesized by the Pilling group.
3. The Bible is not clear.
4. Various members of the Pilling group have heard arguments from those they disagree with but remain unpersuaded by those arguments.
5. The Church of England lacks a magisterium to make a decisive ruling.
6. Not only is there disagreement about what the Bible says; there is disagreement about the hermeneutical approaches we should bring to the Bible.

It is factor 3 that is most pertinent here. The Bible is, say the majority, to be authoritative, but it is also, in the judgment of the majority, not clear. Once you have judged that something is ambiguous or obscure, how can it authoritatively guide your conduct? Put another way, how does the Pilling majority's claim that the Bible is authoritative fit with its judgment that the Bible is unclear?

At this point there is all too readily an argument that runs on very similar lines to the sceptical argument Augustine faced. It goes like this: the wise scholar assents only to an interpretation of the Bible that is definitely true; we cannot prove which interpretation is definitely true beyond all shadow of doubt; therefore, we should assent to no interpretation.

At that point, of course, on the subject in question the Bible is very definitely not authoritative, for we are not using it as a basis either for acting in a particular way or abstaining from acting in a particular way. The statement that one treats the Bible as authoritative has no practical effect. It is purely decorative.

This approach need not be confined to the issue of same-sex marriage or relations. All the theological disciplines are festooned with odd theories here and there. One of my favourites is that it is a misinterpretation of the Gospels to say Jesus ever really existed; rather Jesus never existed but was created as a myth by people on hallucinogenic mushrooms. But let us ask about this theory precisely the killer question that Sextus Empiricus advocates sceptics should ask of any theory: Can we 100% guarantee that no evidence whatsoever will ever emerge that supports this theory?[2] It is pretty hard to claim nothing will ever emerge that could not possibly be construed by someone as supporting the mushroom theory. One hundred per cent guarantees like that are not possible for humans to make. That in turn means that the magic mushroom theory cannot be dismissed. And since this theory is that there is no historical Jesus, how can I make a commitment to him? For I might be wrong – there is an alternative explanation which I cannot completely disprove.

Now how does Augustine help? Among other things he contrasts two different theories of what it is to make a mistake: (1) 'Error is taking as true something that is false.'[3] (2) 'Error is always seeking and never finding.'[4]

The first version of what counts as a mistake is very much that of the sceptics: it prizes the notion that we must not commit to what is false, and therefore to what might be false, and hence we must not commit to anything at all. Similarly, this is the version of mistake implicit in the Pilling majority: we must not commit to an interpretation that is uncertain, and unclear passages can give only un-certain interpretations.

Augustine certainly sees the force of saying we must not commit to what is false. But his second account of mistake (error is always seeking and never finding) opens the door to a subtler and more extensive understanding. After all, if the aim of the game is actually to find something and I spend all my time searching, I still haven't found what I am looking for. I am in the same position as the person who has found the wrong thing: neither of us has the right thing.

Later in the dialogue Augustine develops this line of thought in terms of a journey. Imagine you are on a journey to somewhere, say Kalamazoo: you come to a crossroads. One sign indicates a road leads to Kalamazoo. Imagine you now employ sceptic interpretation: can you be sure 100% this was put up by someone with knowledge? Was it put up by someone who wants to see Kalamazoo cut off from civilized visitors? Was it put up by someone as a postmodern ironic comment on authoritarian authorial statements? On a consistent sceptic basis you cannot exclude these possibilities, and since you do not commit to what might be false, you cannot take the road. You stay sitting at the crossroads. You never arrive at Kalamazoo. That means you are in the same position as someone who actually did follow a false signpost: neither of you is in Kalamazoo.

We can apply Augustine's thinking to the sceptical claim that says, 'Do not commit to an interpretation because the Bible is unclear.' A vital observation is that one thing this suspense of judgment means is that we have not actually obeyed what the Bible says. I am, so to speak, always sitting at the crossroads claiming I cannot be sure what the right interpretation is. And since I have no interpretation, I end up in fact not obeying.

Jack Nicholson, playing the role of Colonel Jessup in *A Few Good Men*, famously shouts, 'You can't handle the truth!' It is a painful moment in the film, and it is painful to contemplate as we think about the interpreter of the Bible who resolutely sits at the crossroads without interpretative commitment. For such an interpreter has a technique which means that she or he never has to handle the truth as such. The Jessup line is understandably iconic. But the less famous close to his speech is even more unnerving: he explains why his audience cannot handle the truth: 'You don't *want* the truth.' Ultimately that becomes the question about the sceptical technique when applied to biblical interpretation: Do we prefer to sit at the crossroads because we do not want to arrive? And is that why we chose to use that particular technique, precisely because it is a seemingly impressive way of never arriving?

Notes

1. *Themelios*, Volume 39, Number 3, 2014, pp. 411–414. Reproduced with permission of The Gospel Coalition.
2. He also notes we can put the killer question round the other way: Can I guarantee 100% that no evidence whatsoever will ever emerge that disproves my theory? Again, humans cannot do this, since it would require omniscience to give such a guarantee.
3. *Error mihi videtur esse falsi pro vero approbatio* (*Against the Academics* I.11).
4. *Nam errare est utique semper quaerere, nunquam invenire* (*Against the Academics* I.10).

10. COURTIER POLITICIANS AND COURTIER PREACHERS[1]

Let's begin with a word in defence of the UK's politicians. We are at the moment in the throes of a General Election campaign, and for some time it has been chic to be cynical about the truthfulness of our politicians. It is a familiar pattern in the anglophone West. One senses the exasperation of citizens who want to be told the truth and feel it is being withheld somehow, whether it is the truth about world economics or the truth about Russia's international intentions. It implies a certain moral integrity on 'our' part (we just want the truth!), and a lack of integrity on the part of our politicians ('they' are somehow conniving to withhold truth from 'us').

Some words of Alexis de Tocqueville make me question this. Writing about American democracy, he observes the way the absolute power of a democracy introduces a 'courtier spirit'. He describes the way that in an absolute monarchy there starts to be a huge problem in how to speak to the monarch. Those who do speak to the absolute monarch risk reactions that are unrestrained and ungoverned. That is the whole point, one might say, of being an absolute monarch – that one can indulge whim and caprice. Hence one addresses an absolute monarch with a 'courtier' spirit. De Tocqueville goes on: just as in an absolute monarchy nobles are reduced to flattering a monarch rather than genuinely advising, so too in a democracy those who want to be leaders are courtiers rather than guides. He writes:

> It is true that American courtiers do not say 'Sire,' or 'Your Majesty,' a distinction
> without a difference. They are forever talking of the natural intelligence of the people

whom they serve; they do not debate the question which of the virtues of their master is pre-eminently worthy of admiration, for they assure him that he possesses all the virtues without having acquired them, or without caring to acquire them.[2]

De Tocqueville's point is not confined to American democracy but applies to any democracy where the democracy is, so to speak, absolute. But de Tocqueville's point is also more subtle than we might initially think. He is not simply saying that democratic politicians have the courtier spirit which does not dare to tell the electorate an unpleasant truth because the politicians are too servile. He is saying this courtier spirit will infuse the people as a whole, and that it is not entirely the 'fault' of politicians that they have become courtiers. The unrestrained nature of the tyranny of the majority in absolute democratic regimes means it will be very hard for a politician to be anything but a courtier. How does one tell the majority that it is not as clever, or virtuous, as it thinks it is, or that a hard truth about itself and its manner of life (whether that is its spending patterns or its morals) must be faced?

De Tocqueville makes us face the way we in democracies contribute to the corruption of our leaders, even though we may also feel cynically that they require little assistance from us in this regard. And he links this to the extreme claims we implicitly make about the ultimately unrestrained competence of democratic power. Thus in the UK an integral part of constitutional theory used to be the competence of the UK Parliament to legislate whatever it liked on any topic. Now, current relationships with the rest of Europe may have limited the UK Parliament in various ways, but in fact the claim to omni-competence persists: it has simply shifted geographical location. Similarly one might observe that even if one thinks the constitutional settlements of the US protect the individual citizen, the settlements themselves remain ultimately vulnerable to the will of the majority, even if one needs a super-majority. That after all, was precisely de Tocqueville's reason for speaking of the 'tyranny of the majority' with regard even to the Constitution.

Given this, de Tocqueville would, I think, analyse our situation in modern Western democracies as having just the formula of absolutist democratic power, and would predict that we would be afflicted with the courtier spirit which dares not tell the truth. The reason in part why our politicians do not tell us the truth, he would say, is that they dare not because we handle truth so badly. It is not simply that we have the leaders we deserve; we have made them so.

This broadens into a more general question about how we can tell unwelcome truths, and here I want to move to the question of shifting theologies. Over the last twenty-five years we have seen church leaders shifting their ground over God's sovereignty and knowledge of the future (Clark Pinnock), God's wrath

(Steve Chalke), universal salvation (Rob Bell), same-sex relations and the nature of Scripture (Steve Chalke again) as well as the essence of Christianity (Brian McLaren).

These shifts take place against a backdrop where even the way we argue and discuss things is shifting. Conservative evangelicals do get criticized in Web chatter for arguing in a cold and unfeeling way, and for an underlying harshness. No doubt there is some truth in that on occasion, and no doubt it is not a sufficient response to suggest that there is a fair amount of harshness coming back the other way.

What does interest me is how I am supposed to communicate an unpleasant reality under these conditions. Let us suppose, just for a moment, that God is genuinely angry at the UK's abortion policy on the grounds that an unborn baby is indeed a human being from conception. What would be an appropriate way to tell the truth about that, given that the numbers of unborn babies killed since our laws were liberalized in 1967 now run into millions? Just how angry might God be? If I point out that the UK has passed Hitler's Holocaust in numbers terms and is fast catching up on Stalin's terror famines in the Ukraine, would that be seen as distasteful hyperbole or simply fair comparison? I strongly suspect that this would be seen as distasteful hyperbole not just in the wider secular culture, but in mainstream churches too.

Why is this so? No doubt because we are seeing 2 Timothy 4:3–4 being fulfilled in our time as the itching ears of the Christian community demand particular approaches and accordingly reward particular teachers with celebrity status. In other words, just as our democratic political culture incentivizes the courtier politician, so our church culture incentivizes the courtier Christian preacher. Of course, we are going to find God's wrath denied or same-sex marriage defended and encouraged. We send out too many messages that we will not accept hard truths for anything else to happen.

What 2 Timothy 4:3–4 opens up for us is an unhappy co-dependence between pastor and people: the pastor who cannot afford to tell the truth to an over-indulged people, and an overindulged people who are deprived of truths that might bring them to repentance. After all, the courtier cannot afford to tell the absolute monarch the truth, and the absolute monarch remains in blissful ignorance that an enemy is at the gate. But unfortunately to the outside and untutored eye this will look like a remarkably successful church, where pastor and people hold each other in high regard. It will probably be rich, conscientious and passionate about those causes the congregation finds acceptable (fashionable good works), attractive to decent non-believers since it does not disturb, well-regarded even, since it blends so effortlessly into the surrounding culture, offering God's therapy but not God's forgiveness of sins, and an inclusion that bypasses anything so demeaning as repentance and amendment of life. A beautiful church with beautiful people and nothing so ugly as a God who demands things from us that we do not already wish to give. Such churches will thrive (dare I say, are thriving?) in the modern UK, and, for all I can see, elsewhere in the cultural West. And at that point we realize the courtier preacher has helped fashion a courtier church, not a light on a hill, nor salt for the world.

Viewed this way, it is not at all surprising that we have seen the theological shifts we have among self-identifying evangelical leaders. And while I disagree profoundly with the shifts I have referred to above, I think de Tocqueville would remind me of what makes for a courtier spirit. And he would also remind me that if I do not want to be on the receiving end of a courtier spirit, I must dare to let people tell me truths I do not want to hear. And at that point as a modern Christian teacher, I must confront my own appetite both to be on the receiving end of the courtier spirit (it is nice to be flattered) and to offer it, because courtiers do get rewards. In this life, anyway.

Notes

1. *Themelios*, Volume 40, Issue 1, 2015, pp. 10–12. Reproduced with permission of The Gospel Coalition.
2. Alexis de Tocqueville, *Democracy in America*, trans. Henry Reeve, 2 vols. (repr., New York: Langley, 1841), vol. 2, p. 291. See <https://archive.org/details/democracyinameo1tocq>.

11. CAN *ANTIGONE* WORK IN A SECULARIST SOCIETY?[1]

No doubt about it, the British Broadcasting Corporation is plain quirky. Excellent sports coverage, but the most depressing soap opera ever. Then it covers itself with glory by broadcasting Sophocles' great tragedy *Antigone*, but has it introduced by someone (a sort of current affairs journalist) who misses Sophocles' point by a couple of parsecs. But then I reflect that for a secularist institution like the BBC the true nature of the *Antigone* tragedy simply does not exist. You have to make the play say something different. Let me explain.

Sophocles' play from the Athens of the fifth century BC is set in mythical Thebes. Before the play starts, the king, Oedipus, has left power after discovering he has killed his father and married his mother. He has had several children by her and, after his fall, two of his sons have fought each other for the rule of Thebes. One had allied with foreign powers in order to seize the throne. Both sons have died fighting each other, and a new king, their uncle Creon, now reigns. At the start of the play Creon has decreed that no one is to bury the body of the son of Oedipus, who invaded his own homeland. For his crime against his country he is to lie unburied, a horrific breach of the law that says relatives owe a duty to bury their kinsfolk. The young woman Antigone, daughter of Oedipus, decides to defy Creon's law and bury her brother in obedience to the laws of the gods. This means her own death, and Creon's own son, Haemon, her betrothed, kills himself in grief. Creon's wife, Eurydice, kills herself at this turn of events, leaving the grieving, lonely, isolated figure of

Creon lamenting, 'Now I believe it is by the laws of heaven that man must live.' The chorus concludes the play by saying that the law we learn when we are old, as we see 'the stricken heart of pride brought down', is the wisdom to hold the gods in awe, which Creon in his arrogance has not. This is certainly tragedy – but for both Antigone and Creon. In fact, you could argue the real tragedy is finally Creon's.

Now, the BBC voiceover makes this a play about the individual versus the state; individual liberty as against state oppression. In other words, it makes this a contest purely at the human level between human nodes of authority, individual rights and collective responsibility. This airbrushes out the true nature of the tragedy.

Sophocles is not opposing two human claims, individual versus collective. He is seeing how the laws of the gods and the laws of human beings can intersect and conflict, and in particular the tragic act of hubris or arrogance by which a human *knowingly* makes a claim that contradicts the laws of the gods, albeit with the best of motives. In this, Sophocles is reflecting the great Sophist debate of fifth century BC Greece, as the Sophists contrasted the claims or laws of Nature (*physis*) against the claims or laws of human convention (*nomos*). We humans set the laws of *nomos* but we cannot make or alter the laws of *physis*.

Now the difficulty of the BBC's presentation is that it makes the play *Antigone* a tragedy about the conflict between two types of *nomos*, two *human-originated* claims, one collective, the other individual. It is not a conflict between *nomos* and *physis*, between the laws we humans set and the laws above us of the gods that we do not set. It is, for the BBC, not a divine–human conflict, but only a human–human conflict. This airbrushes out several things.

First, it airbrushes out quite how right the young woman Antigone is. She is not right because she is a courageous individual (although she certainly is that). She is right because she has elected to obey the laws of the gods. In terms of character, Sophocles portrays her as difficult, angular and stubborn, but as right. Her rightness is not her rugged individualism and her defiance. Her rightness is her *obedience*. You would never guess that from the BBC's commentary.

Second, it airbrushes the true wrongness of Creon. If we think of things purely at the human level, Creon has an excellent case. Oedipus' son has betrayed his country, levying war against it for his own selfish power-interests. Why then should he be interred in the earth of the homeland he betrayed? He does not deserve it, and this serves as an excellent deterrent against future coup leaders. But in fact, Creon has lifted his hand against the gods by daring to make a human decree (*nomos*) which he knows conflicts with the laws of the gods (*physis*). At that point he is not merely a heavy-handed ruler; he is a human arrogantly setting himself against the gods – he has forgotten what he is. He is guilty of hubris, setting himself against heaven, not just guilty of oppressing other humans.

Third, as it airbrushes out the hubris of Creon, it airbrushes out the extent to which this is Creon's tragedy as much as Antigone's. Creon is brought down by his hubris: he is judged by the gods for it. We are not just being told by Sophocles that some human power claims are hubristic; Sophocles is also warning us that this does not work, and not because Creon will be overthrown by popular acclaim. He is brought low by the gods. Sophocles tells us that we disdain *physis*, the laws of heaven, at our peril.

Why does this matter? After all, it is not very surprising that a secularist institution cannot see this as a divine–human conflict rather than a human–human conflict. And the BBC message of 'beware of oppressive state claims' is well worth hearing.

It matters because it reveals what a secularist society cannot see, where its blind spots are. A secularist society simply cannot have the framework to comprehend truly Antigone's actions as actions of obedience to God rather than of rugged individualism. Antigone is emphatically not anti-social, but she does want Thebes to be a society based not on Creon's laws, nor indeed her human laws, but on divine laws. She does, however, appear to Creon (and to the BBC) as though she simply puts the individual before the collective. So too with us. As Christian Antigones we will look like selfish individualists to a secular society that has no vocabulary for obedience to God. If we do defy the state over various matters (such as public preaching of the uniqueness of Christ), we will, unfortunately, not look like heroes.

There again a secular society cannot see Creon's actions for what they are. In a secularist culture hubris is simply impossible because there is no heaven against which to rail and in practice no God whom we displace by our power claims. To state the obvious, the hubris of Genesis 3 is impossible in this secularist setting. There is no framework within which to express it or understand it. In this sense sin as hubris becomes a nameless crime within a secularist society. Such a society can recognize arrogance towards other humans, but not in its primary form, which is towards God. As a nameless crime, hubris will instead have a certain aura of terrible innocence. A secularist culture will literally see nothing wrong with hubris in its most basic sense. This in turn means that secularist analysis of what is wrong with the human condition is condemned to being superficial, always looking to the human–human level, rather than the divine–human conflict from which our human–human problems ultimately spring. This does not mean such analysis (or its treatments) will be altogether useless. But it does mean it can look only at symptoms and not causes.

This brings us to a final dreadful irony. In a secularist, individualist society we will reverse Antigone and Creon. For we will think the people who set up their own laws in defiance of others are expressing an Antigone-spirit, that they are free-spirited individuals, whereas in fact their spirit is that of Creon, deciding what is right in their own eyes, no matter what anyone else says, including God. Sophocles meant his play to humble our Creon-like spirits with our hubris and to warn his audience that divine judgment brings people like Creon low. The BBC's take in our secularist individualist culture unconsciously tends to endorse just that Creon-spirit of hubris, but adds to it the sanctifying sense that we are heroic figures like Antigone. We will think we are righteous when we have committed a crime for which we no longer have a name. We will certainly have no fear that our hubris brings down judgment, for who could condemn such Antigone-like people as us? And there we have reached one of the most characteristic and spiritually troubling aspects of our secularist society: our invincible self-righteousness. No wonder we think we do not need God. And no wonder we have to rewrite *Antigone*.

Note

1. *Themelios*, Volume 40, Issue 2, 2015, pp. 198–200. Reproduced with permission of The Gospel Coalition.

12. IS THE WRATH OF GOD EXTREMIST?[1]

We have had enough, proclaims re-elected UK Prime Minister David Cameron, of 'passive tolerance'. By 'passive tolerance' Cameron means the tolerance that puts up with what people say provided it remains within the law. No matter that traditional definitions of political toleration would have majored precisely on leaving people alone if they obey the law, Cameron's point is that this tradition is inadequate. For we can no longer be content with passive tolerance because there are those in the UK and the West who radicalize others, especially the young, by teaching and preaching that which carefully remains within the law but which erodes commitment to, in the UK's case, 'British values'. People who do that kind of teaching are extremists. And extremists are dangerous. Cameron's preferred term is 'non-violent extremists', but even a non-violent extremist is dangerous.

Just to be clear, Cameron is not talking about speakers who incite or encourage others to criminal acts. What is dangerous is opposition to 'British values', an inclusive term covering democracy, the rule of law, human rights. But since this is an inclusive term, no one quite knows how much wider this may go. You don't have to advocate violence yourself, you just have to have said something which can contribute to the radicalization of someone else towards violence. You have provided, so to speak, the ideological bricks from which a terrorist ideology can be constructed, even if you have not incited such violence.

It will no doubt be tempting to see this as a purely British problem. In fact, it seems to me symptomatic of something deeper in Western culture at the moment, certainly in its European form and I fear incipiently in its American form.

At root, Cameron and others are reflecting the idea that religion is dangerous – toxic – although this is not openly voiced. The character Dr Maxted in J. G. Ballard's superb dystopian novel *Kingdom Come*[2] catches this sentiment well as he says of Islam and Christianity that they are 'vast systems of psychopathic delusion that murdered millions, launched crusades and founded empires. A great religion spells danger.' Maxted's words ring bells with Europe's chattering intelligentsia.

Now, in a sense this is nothing new. The case has been argued that mono-theism is inherently violent, given that the totalizing implication of monotheism means that the dissident non-believer can, so the argument runs, only be demon-ized. Less extreme versions are found in Jürgen Moltmann's contention that our views of God (is he hierarchical or egalitarian?) will work their way through to how we organize church, family and state.[3] Where does patriarchy come from in those institutions? Not least from a patriarchal idea of God, Moltmann argues.[4] Moving wider, the argument is also made that the idea of God found in the medieval Islamic thinker al-Ghazali (circa 1058–1111) helps explain some of the political currents in Islam and why violence can have plausibility to Muslims worldwide.[5] For al-Ghazali is an extreme divine voluntarist in the sense that the divine will is God's sole primary attribute and is not constrained by any external norm, nor, it seems, by any internal nature. God's will is so free that he can will something as good at one point and then will the opposite.

Then comes the awkward moment. I can quite see that al-Ghazali's divine voluntarism takes you logically down a line of thought that says arbitrary political or other rule is not necessarily bad. I am, though, also clear that al-Ghazali did not have in mind how extreme divine voluntarism could reinforce arbitrary political rule at the expense of democracy. Do I think al-Ghazali is responsible for some of the worst currents in Islamist ideology? In a sense, yes. This is one of those cases where a religious idea – even if it was originally peacefully advocated – is dangerous, given its logical consequences. And I wonder if we are not ethically bound to think through as far as we can the logical consequences of our arguments.

Now obviously some would say that a Calvinist like me has the same kind of understanding of divine power as al-Ghazali does. God can do what he wills, and what he wills, happens. However, conventional Calvinists do not think the divine will is God's only primary attribute. We think his will is primary, but then too are his goodness and love. God cannot stop being good, and to that extent his goodness is not contingent and not merely a product of his will. Athanasius made just this point in the Arian debate (*Contra Arianos* III.58ff.).

Can I then smugly sit back and let contemporary followers of al-Ghazali take the heat for the 'religion is toxic danger' fear? Not really. For there is another line of argument to bear in mind, this time about God's wrath.

Some years ago the English emergent church leader Steve Chalke argued that those talking about penal substitution were 'telling the wrong story about God'.[6] For they were talking about an angry God, and this was in part because they were angry people. However, the idea of an angry God then reinforced their own anger. Thus there was a sort of feedback loop between human anger and the idea of divine anger.

At this point an obvious line of argument appears. I should not preach about an angry God because this is dangerous. It is dangerous because it reinforces anger in myself and those who listen to me, and our anger can all too readily lead to violence. Hence even if I do not advocate violence and possibly even speak against it at one level (Cameron's 'non-violent extremism'), at the deeper level my teaching about God's wrath puts public order and safety in danger. What is more, if I think al-Ghazali is at some level responsible for some of the outcomes of extreme divine voluntarism, then why should I not be held responsible if someone does become enraged on God's behalf as I describe God's anger at sin? After all, as I write this, I can at least foresee the possibility. Perhaps I genuinely have not taken responsibility for what I teach and how people may not just hear but *mishear* it as seriously as I should. Perhaps when I foresee a *deservedly* criminalized act as the foreseeable outcome of my utterances I should be far more careful and circumspect and qualified. Perhaps sometimes I might even consider being silent.

There are, though, a number of other features about the argument that religious ideas are toxic and dangerous which bear reflection.

To begin with, this affects the current chic claim that the secularization thesis has been disproved and religion is thriving. The secularization thesis, crudely put, predicted the demise of religion in modern society, but in fact religion thrives, although it does so pluralistically in a modern state. It is not the case, so the argument goes, that modern society is anti-religion. Notably, the comparatively slow growth of dogmatic atheism is sometimes cited as a comforting factor in these debates.

This, though, mistakes what is happening. Here Cameron's antipathy to 'non-violent extremism' comes to the fore. It may well be true that dogmatic atheism is not winning as many converts as it might want (not surprising since its arguments are actually frequently quite poor). But dogmatic atheism was insisting religion was not *true*. Cameron and others are not adjudicating on truth: their misgiving is not whether a religious idea is true or not, but whether it is *dangerous* to public order. Something can be true and 'dangerous'. In that way, the 'religion is toxic danger' argument is as anti-religious as anything David Hume came up with. In fact, I wonder if in the long run it is not more dangerous. At least we can read Hume's argument on miracles, analyse it and then demonstrate rationally why it is not true. Showing my words could never be *dangerous* is far trickier than showing they are *true*.

Second, the Cameron approach I have outlined sounds extraordinarily illiberal in a political sense to a Christian. We do not plan to break the laws as we teach about God's wrath and don't want others to do so. Why then treat us the same as those who do? However, secular Western ears will be tone deaf to the illiberalism, for it has framed the question to itself essentially as an application of the 'harm' principle set out by John Stuart Mill in his influential essay *On Liberty*. The state foresees harm in the long run from a set of ideas in terms of people being more inclined to violence: to avoid this clear 'harm', the freedom of speech of some (the religious) must be constrained.

Third, it is no surprise the argument about what one can say is framed in this way about danger. Zygmunt Bauman persuasively argues that if a society is full of 'liquid' relationships (relationships which are infinitely malleable according to the will of the individual involved), then there are consequences.[7] For sure, constructing and changing my relationships may be exciting and an expression of autonomy, but it is also destabilizing: it is no wonder, Bauman suggests, that ours is an anxious society, worried about diffuse threats and dangers precisely because so much is liquid and uncertain. Hence, in part, why legislation and rules proliferate in what is theoretically an increasingly liberal society. Paradoxically, the urge to control 'dangerous' speech can be related to the same urges to control and regulate dangerous substances like coffee that is served too hot.

And the tragedy here in current Western discourse is that some speech is indeed dangerous. And Cameron's inability to draw the line rightly about where danger falls should not blind me to my own ethical duty to make intellectual arguments that are not only true and honest, but logically thought through and carefully expressed precisely so I am not a 'danger to others'. Conceivably this will make me less attractive and charismatic as a speaker and writer, as my words lose the thrill of being transgressive for my audience. Conceivably, though, I will be presenting only the same kinds of dangers to the public good as the apostles did, but who were still charged with turning the world upside down (Acts 17:6). I must continue to provide that kind of danger, but labour to provide no more.

Notes

1. *Themelios*, Volume 40, Issue 3, 2015, pp. 389–391. Reproduced with permission of The Gospel Coalition.

2. J. G. Ballard, *Kingdom Come* (London: Fourth Estate, 2006).

3. E.g. Jürgen Moltmann, *History and the Triune God*, trans. J. Bowden (London: SCM, 1991), p. 2.

4. Moltmann, *History*, p. 2.

5. E.g. Robert R. Reilly, *The Closing of the Muslim Mind: How Intellectual Suicide Created the Modern Islamist Crisis* (Wilmington, Del.: Intercollegiate Studies Institute, 2014).

6. From an address at a symposium on penal substitution held at London School of Theology, July 2005.

7. A point Bauman makes in several places but at length in *Liquid Times: Living in an Age of Uncertainty* (Cambridge: Polity, 2007).

13. THE ART OF IMPERIOUS IGNORANCE[1]

Earlier this year I found myself lured from the secure theological fastnesses of north London to a consultation on one of the hot topics of our day. One delegate listened to the contributions about what relevant biblical passages meant and then commented that he or she still did not know what the passages meant, and the explanations offered just didn't do it for him or her. The passages were unclear. I was surprised in one way, because I thought the explanations had been nothing if not clear. Unwelcome very possibly, but not unclear. The response, though, was not a disagreement in the sense of offering an alternative explanation which should be preferred for better reasons. This was not direct disagreement but something much more oblique. It was a disagreement that took the form of declaring that the passages were not clear.

Of course, in another way this is no longer a surprising response to attempts to explain passages from the Bible or synthesize them – over the years one has heard it in regard to God's knowledge of the future, predestination, God's changing his mind, same-sex marriage, the role of women, and so on. The Bible is unclear, it is said, and so we must be content not to know. We must be ignorant. In that sense I think we are observing an argumentative move that is perhaps increasingly common.

In this article I want to argue that the claim to be ignorant on the grounds that something is unclear is actually quite ambitious. More than that, it can be an imperious claim that exercises power over others without, at times, the inconvenience of reasoned argument. No wonder it is so popular.

Please note, I am not suggesting this is always the case and that every claim of unclarity is manipulative and power-driven, but it is worth thinking through how such claims can be.

By way of illustration, take the pro-Arian Creed announced at Sirmium in 357, which marked a new phase in the Arian controversy as Arian opposition to Nicene trinitarian theology became more overt. For our purposes the relevant part of the Creed comes just after it outlines a prohibition on using the terms *homoousios* (one and the same substance) or *homoiousios* (of a similar substance). The Creed states:

> Nor ought any exposition to be made of them [the terms *homoousios* and *homoiousios*] for the reason and consideration that they are not contained in the divine Scriptures, and that they are above man's understanding, nor can any man declare the birth of the Son, of whom it is written, *Who shall declare His generation?* For it is plain that only the Father knows how He begot the Son, and the Son how He was begotten of the Father.[2]

Does this not sound very pious and indeed very evangelical to avoid using terms that are not in the Bible and remember that the generation of the Son is too wonderful to declare (*enarrare*) so no one should declare (*enarrare*) it? In other words, it is not clear and we do not know, so we should not speak of the generation of the Son. How would you have reacted to this if I had not already primed you that Sirmium 357 was 'pro-Arian'? I suspect that many of us would be struck by what could be a humble, pious caution in speaking of God.

Yet Hilary of Poitiers, Athanasius of Alexandria and other supporters of the view that the Son is truly a son hit the roof over Sirmium 357. Hilary describes it as *Blasphemia*, blasphemy. Why does a profession of ignorance generate such an extreme reaction? Among other reasons, in Hilary's case, precisely because of the claim of ignorance.

Hilary decodes the claims of Sirmium 357 for us. First, there was the element of compulsion. For him this was an *ignorantiae decretum* – a *law* of ignorance, aptly translated 'Compulsory Ignorance Act'.[3] The language repays attention: *decretum* implies a serious binding decision; that is to say, not just a confession of one's own lack of knowledge but a decision that others do not know either. The term has legislative connotations. To that extent the framers of Sirmium 357 were not just saying they did not know about the Son's generation; they were saying no other human being could either. What initially sounds like a pious caution emerges as coercive.

Second, Hilary notes an absurdity in the idea that one tries to compel people not to know something. He comments scathingly of the *decretum*, 'just as if it could be commanded or decreed that a man should know what in future he is to be ignorant of, or be ignorant of what he already knows'.[4]

The absurdity here is in attempting to legislate the internal knowledge of others. It is one thing to demand silence, but quite another to demand ignorance.

Third, Hilary sees that the law of ignorance actually stops a particular proposition being made. Because we are bound to be ignorant about the Son's generation, we cannot declare that the Son is 'of God',[5] and if we cannot speak at all of the Son's generation, then how do we say the Son really and truly is a son, since generation is inherent to the relation of fathers and sons. At root, by preventing us speaking of the Son's generation, the framers of Sirmium are preventing us from speaking of the Son as truly son. Coercive ignorance masks a positive theological position – that one does not have to say the Son is truly a son. This, of course, opens the door to admitting Arianism with its view that the second person is a creature rather than truly son as being just as orthodox as Nicene theology which insists the Son is truly son. A little ignorance can go a long way.

Two things emerge quite painfully from Hilary's observations on the Compulsory Ignorance Act of Sirmium 357. First, the coercive nature of the claims to ignorance or unclarity. There is something strongly unilateral about the claims of Sirmium 357: Why should something that is, allegedly, subjectively unclear to me be judged by me as unclear for you too? Second, there is the way those coercive claims were far from value-neutral but actually carried strong agendas of their own.

However, there are other elements in play in the declaration of ignorance or unclarity that make it an extraordinarily attractive move in today's debates. Naturally it plays well with a postmodern mood that tends to value scepticism, but more than that it can offer the attraction of not needing to have a reason for my position. At its worst, I can declare something unclear and then pursue my own line without needing to provide reasons for it – after all the issue is unclear. Declaring something unclear can maximize my freedom of action because it tends to remove an issue from the field of common debate. In its way, it is strongly individualist.

More than that, some of the claims about unclarity or ignorance leave unspecified what counts as being clear enough for actions to proceed or decisions to be made. It is sometimes quite revealing to ask 'How clear do things need to be?' or 'What would make things clearer for you?' But without knowing what counts as 'clear enough' or what considerations would clarify, the task of discussing something with someone claiming ignorance or lack of clarity becomes remarkably thankless. Again, the tendency here is to remove an issue from discussion.

Yet most attractive of all is that the claim of lack of clarity or ignorance allows one to pursue one's own position quite dogmatically while appearing to be very undogmatic. After all, the claim of ignorance looks as though it advances no position, but vitally it tacitly asserts that one's opponent's position cannot be decisively asserted – it is for ever only a possibility, not a certainty on which one could base action or decision. There is something very rewarding in being a closet dogmatist while appearing to be the reverse.

This in turn raises two questions, one more philosophical, the other more theological. Philosophically, how do I move from my observation about my own understanding that I find something unclear (fundamentally subjective) to the proposition that something is unclear for everyone else too (something universal)? After all, I frequently have the experience that a text from my children is subjectively unclear to me, but laughably clear to others versed in the texting argot of today's youth. Of course, it can be a mark of genuine epistemic humility to recognize one does not know something or that something is unclear to one. But it can be an important mark of epistemic humility too to concede that others may have understood something that I have not, rather than insist that if I do not see something no one else has or even could either.

Theologically, however, even more is at stake. Thus the claim of John 1:18 is that God has been made known by the incarnate Son and Word. This looks very like a claim that God has actually made himself known and at least at the objective level revealed himself. Given this, what should I make of the claim that knowledge of God is unclear and uncertain? After all, for the uncertainty claim to work here, I have to tread very close to the proposition that God did not successfully reveal himself. Do I think God tried to reveal himself and failed? Or do I think God never revealed himself? Here again the claims of ignorance seem extraordinarily imperious – after all, the kind of knowledge I would need to support the claim that God has failed to reveal himself or that God never revealed himself seems to be that I have an independent non-revealed knowledge of God and therefore can weigh the claims of revelation. This, of course, was one reason why Hilary and Athanasius thought the Arian claims of 'ignorance' they encountered were in fact simply arrogant. Perhaps I should be more ready to adapt another of Hilary's thoughts, that when faced with God's revelation in the Bible, I should point less to a defect in the text (lack of clarity) but more to a defect in my understanding (subjective limits). Perhaps we should be less certain that parts of Scripture are 'uncertain'.

Notes

1. *Themelios*, Volume 41, Issue 1, 2016, pp. 5–7. Reproduced with permission of The Gospel Coalition.
2. Hilary of Poitiers, *De Synodis* 11.
3. *De Synodis* 10.
4. *De Synodis* 10.
5. *De Synodis* 10.

14. THE ECHO CHAMBER OF IDOLATRY[1]

One of the most helpful books I have read over recent years is Greg Beale's *We Become What We Worship*.[2] Beale takes up the biblical themes of idolatry (notably passages such as Ps. 135:15–18) and notes that idolatry changes us – 'we resemble what we revere'.[3] This is a kind of satanic parody of real sanctification in which we become more like Christ.

One of the reasons this is so pastorally helpful is that it has a certain predictive power. As someone who from time to time does Christian apologetics, I want to know what makes my interlocutor tick and also what trajectory he or she is on. I want to see the way my culture (or some of the subcultures constituting my 'culture') is going and Beale's identification that we are like, and become increasingly like, our idols is really helpful for getting a glimpse of what may be coming. It also reminds me that when I encounter an idolater (as humans naturally are after the fall), I am not just encountering what someone thinks, but at one level, who someone is and who they are becoming.

You can see some of this line of analysis about a resemblance dynamic in Vinoth Ramachandra as he works through some particular examples:

[I]t is not surprising that those who worship technology eventually develop machine-like personalities: emotionally under-developed, shallow in their relationships, driven by a desire to control and quantify every human situation, unable to appreciate beauty and value in anything outside the artificial. Those who worship sex, on the other hand,

are incapable of trust and commitment in their human relationships and hide a lonely
existence behind a mask of superficial 'adulthood'.[4]

This catches some modern personality types painfully accurately. Of course, it
also builds on a strong line of Reformed thought which, following Calvin, sees
the human heart as an idol-making factory, in which in particular we want to
make a god according to our own personal specifications.[5] All this makes the
question 'What do you worship?' extraordinarily important in evangelism and
apologetics. After all, until we know what the idols are that we worship it is difficult to see how or why we should repent, as Acts 17:30 tells us God commands,
notably a call to repentance given in the context of the Athenians' idolatry.

However, I want to blend this theme of the resemblance dynamic from
the idol-making human heart with another ingredient from Calvin, along with
a soupçon of Albert Schweitzer and indeed some duly crumbled Ludwig
Feuerbach for extra flavour. (My culinary metaphor may be getting out of hand
here.) As well as drawing out the compulsive designer-deity-making nature of
our hearts, Calvin emphasizes right at the start of the *Institutes* that our doctrine
of humanity and our doctrine of God interrelate.[6] Changing one will in all
likelihood change the other. Indeed, coming to resemble what we worship is
one outworking of this.

One implication of Calvin's suggestion is that the reciprocal relationship
between the doctrines of God and humanity means that a change in how we
view ourselves readily engenders a change in how we view God. Schweitzer's
rightly famous comments on scholars searching for the historical Jesus are very
much to the point here.[7] Scholars look into the well of history and see their
own reflections. In a sense Schweitzer was observing how close to the mark
Ludwig Feuerbach was with his projection theory of religion, that humans
absolutize their own ideals and virtues into a deity. On this view, no wonder an
aristocratic Bronze Age warrior culture comes up with a set of deities such as
you find in Homer's *Iliad* who would in a more bourgeois society be by rights
in and out of jail like yo-yos.

This has several consequences for evangelism and apologetics. First, alongside the predictive power of an idol → human resemblance dynamic, there is
also a human → idol resemblance dynamic. We make (whether consciously or
not) gods in our image, even as idols make us in theirs. This helps with the key
question 'Who do you worship?' because I can start to analyse what God will
look like for someone when I understand who and what they think they are.
There is a predictive power in looking at what someone thinks of himself or
herself for envisaging what his or her god will look like. The two questions
'Who do you worship?' and 'Who/what do you think you are?' are related.

Second, precisely because the resemblance dynamic is two way – idol ↔ human – the resemblance dynamic will tend to be self-reinforcing. Here I want to modify Schweitzer's image of seeing one's own reflection to that of an echo chamber. In an echo chamber I hear my own voice back. I speak and the echo appears to be someone else saying the same things I do. Except in this case the echo is clothed with a higher authority than I think I might possess. I mistake the echo of my own voice for the voice of God/god and am therefore encouraged to make my own voice louder because the echo has agreed with me and reinforced me. My own louder voice produces a louder echo still, which encourages me to be still louder in my own assertions, and so the process goes on.

Third, the echoes will not always tell the same story. We should remember that modern Western culture offers different and sometimes inconsistent pictures of who the human self is: for example, is one a sovereign autonomous individual inventing oneself or a self that is shaped by the sovereign voice of the majority consensus? Both versions are vigorously sold. But if I do not have a coherent account of myself, then my echo will not simply return one voice to me, but many voices. Of course, the modern cultural West looks polytheistic: it is not just that people from London have different values from people in Ohio. It is that the person in London and the person in Ohio do not have an internally consistent view of themselves to project outwards as God. Feuerbach does have something to teach in his account of projection, but we have to modify what we learn from him by bearing in mind that the self who projects is both inclined to be individualistic and has an unstable, non-coherent individuality. This complicates the 'Who are you?' question. Frequently it may become 'Who are you in which setting?'

Fourth, let me mix a little Luther into the pot (to return to the culinary metaphor). Luther's view of our claims to righteousness is that our good deeds are even more dangerous than our obviously bad ones. Our 'good deeds' delude us: while they may be relatively good or count as 'civic righteousness', they mislead us into thinking we can do absolute good. I wonder if when we Christians think of the idols of our culture we think of the deities of sensuality and pleasure and power. I think there is much truth in saying these are contemporary idols and they are awful ones. But Luther would also have me look at what look very much like civic virtues – democracy, toleration, the rule of law and duly enforced individual rights. These tend to be our culture's 'good deeds' in Luther's terms, and when I hear spokespeople for this culture, these seem to me to be the things that are to the front of what they absolutize and project. Of course, sensuality, power and pleasure may be there, but I suspect these idols are 'backgrounded' rather than foregrounded.

This suggests that as I look at the idol ↔ human resemblance dynamic and ask 'Who do you worship?' and 'Who are you just now?', I remember that one of the effects of the echo chamber is not just to give me something to worship, but also to guarantee my own self-righteousness. And unless we tackle our culture's sense of self-righteousness and the dynamics that sustain it, how can we bring it to hear the call to repent?

Notes

1. *Themelios*, Volume 41, Issue 2, 2016, pp. 214–216. Reproduced with permission of The Gospel Coalition.
2. G. K. Beale, *We Become What We Worship: A Biblical Theology of Idolatry* (Downers Grove: InterVarsity Press; Nottingham: Apollos, 2008).
3. Beale, *We Become*, p. 22, where he notes this is the 'primary theme' of his book. See also on this theme Edward P. Meadors, *Idolatry and the Hardening of the Heart: A Study in Biblical Theology* (New York: T. & T. Clark, 2006).
4. Vinoth Ramachandra, *Gods That Fail: Modern Idolatry and Christian Mission*, rev. edn (Eugene, Ore.: Wipf and Stock, 2016), p. 112.
5. *Institutes* I.5.
6. *Institutes* I.1.1ff.
7. 'But it was not only each epoch that found its reflection in Jesus; each individual created Him in accordance with his own character. There is no historical task which so reveals a man's true self as the writing of a Life of Jesus.' Albert Schweitzer, *The Quest of the Historical Jesus: A Critical Study of Its Progress from Reimarus to Wrede*, trans. W. Montgomery (London: Adam and Charles Black, 1910), p. 4.

15. CHOOSE YOUR FEARS CAREFULLY[1]

> The defining feature is the belief that humanity is confronted by
> powerful destructive forces that threaten our everyday existence.
> (Frank Furedi)[2]

'Terror is the order of the day' – so decided the Convention in 1793 during the
French Revolution, meaning that opponents of the Revolution would face
terror. Looking out over Western Europe you wonder whether fear has not
become the order of the day. Secular and Christian writers alike have been
commenting for over twenty years that Western culture has an ambience of
fear, as well as an air of brash self-confidence. It predates the attacks on the
Twin Towers, although those terrorist crimes undoubtedly accelerated and
inflamed it, and it has been only too evident in the cultural West over the last
year. My own country, the UK, has opted to leave the European Union, but the
manner of its doing so has been striking. Whether you were Exit or Remain,
both sides in the referendum campaign invoked our fears. The issue could have
presented as 'Which fear do you prefer?' Going back to the Scottish independence referendum of 2014, again fear played such a large part, whether it was
fear of going it alone or fear of Westminster. Western Europe more generally
so often sees the plight of the refugee through the lens of fear of the other,
and where fear can almost legitimate racist violence and fertilize the growth of
far-right groups in mainland Europe. One of the dominating notes of our discourse about public safety and security in the UK is fear of so-called non-
violent extremists, prompting a government that was none too sympathetic to
liberty for dissident voices anyway to propose levels of surveillance that would
have been unthinkable thirty years ago. We are fearful to let our kids walk home

from school let alone go out after dark. And as a European I look bemusedly at an American election where one candidate complements his extraordinary choice of hairstyle with a ruthless playing on the fears of 'the Other' in US life as immigrant and potential terrorist, while his opponent plays on the fears this candidate inspires. The list of fears is extensive: our pensions, the level of the dollar or euro or sterling (take your pick), whether our children will be able to afford a house or repay their student loans, terrorism, whether what we have been eating turns out to be carcinogenic, and the list just goes on.

This 'environment' of fear, as Paul Virilio calls it,[3] has some important features. First, it is exacerbated by the speed of movement of our culture,[4] which heightens a sense that we do not know what is coming next, but – whatever it is – it is coming quickly and will be followed equally quickly by something else. Such speed cuts down our time to analyse, react and cope.

Second, that speeding, accelerating culture is also a very liquid culture and that, as Zygmunt Bauman remarks,[5] reconfigures our relationships: How do I have long-term relationships with you when you are a liquid and shifting individual and so am I? Relationships can have their edge of anxiety and fear – no wonder the film *Four Weddings and a Funeral* became so iconic when it included the theme of a commitment-phobic generation. The tragic trajectory, no matter what that film's closing scenes suggest, is that in that kind of 'liquid mass individualism'[6] we cut ourselves off both from loving others and receiving love from them.

Third, this environment of fear relates to a more general sense of powerlessness. Somehow we have become a society open to the 'blows of "fate"'.[7] Bauman goes on, '"Fate" stands for human ignorance and helplessness, and owes its awesome frightening power to those very weaknesses of its victims.'[8]

This impression of powerlessness stands closely with the perception that the blows of 'fate' are random, creating a cumulative picture of an environment where huge, unknowable, unmanageable forces afflict us haphazardly and randomly, both as individuals and as collectives. Oddly enough, there is a parallel here with the Hellenistic principle of *Tychē*.[9] While *Tychē* is certainly something ineluctable that grinds remorselessly on, she is also deeply connected with randomness and the way someone can be lifted up one moment and cast helplessly down the next. L. H. Martin aptly comments on *Tychē*, 'Embodied in a single image, the goddess' ambiguity or capriciousness, her double nature, positive and negative, is her most characteristic trait.'[10] *Tychē* at the end of the day is irresistible and unpredictable but also literally implacable. One may fear her, but it does little good.

In terms of Christian analysis, the view that fear relates to lack of power is central for Thomas Aquinas. He writes, '[W]hatever is entirely subject to our power and will, is not an object of fear; and . . . nothing gives rise to fear save what is due to an external cause.'[11]

To this extent, our fear rises directly in proportion to our perceived lack of power to deal with whatever the threat may be. Fear can of course therefore be a good thing in that it leads one to recognize a situation or person one cannot control. But it certainly also does help reveal our perceptions. This in turn prompts some intriguing reflections.

First, the earlier list of what our culture fears has one conspicuous absentee. Our culture does not have fear of God on its worry list. Neither, come to that, does an awful lot of what passes for Christianity in the UK and mainland Europe. That is not necessarily because of full-blown commitment to atheism. But if one looks at Aquinas's account of fear to the effect it reflects my perceived lack of power, then my lack of fear readily reflects my perceived ability to 'handle' whatever the threat may be. The underlying logic is that God is not a threat in the way that global economic downturn is, or a random encounter with a road-rage driver.

Unfortunately, such a lack of fear of God is ultimately despairing. Think of the list of fears as one considers the terrorist incidents over the summer: is there not the feeling that even if we cut out 99 out of the 100 bomb plots, it only takes one bomb on the subway or metro line to terminate us? Ultimately our culture has no answer to its fears, does it? With all those health and safety measures, accidents still happen. Some things remain beyond our control. And when we ceased to fear God, we ceased to have someone who could actually finally save. A God I need not fear is a God the terrorist need not fear either.

In fact, one way or another, the assumption is that we need not fear God because we can deal with him: perhaps we think we have earned security before him, or that we are simply entitled to it or that he will never do anything we would find uncongenial. Of course, the more we articulate this assumption, the more problematic it appears. If God is God at all, then, as the Beavers remark in C. S. Lewis's *The Lion, the Witch and the Wardrobe*, he will not be 'safe', as in controllable by us. He may be good, but he is not tame or domesticated.

This has two consequences. First, it takes us back to the instructions God gives his people through Jeremiah and other prophets (e.g. Jer. 10:1–16). We are not to fear the idols and elemental principles that people without God do fear. We need not fear them because the God who is infinitely more powerful than us can deliver where we cannot. One current challenge for us is whether we fear God enough so that we need not fear the things that 'the nations' do. What we fear reveals a lot about where we think power truly lies. What, exactly, do we fear and in what order?

Second, one way of reading the environment of fear is that our culture would rather fear our modern version of *Tychē* with her grinding, ineluctable randomness than fear a God who providentially controls human affairs with purpose. I think it is indisputable that so many in the culture do prefer *Tychē* to Jesus of Nazareth: but why?

Notes

1. *Themelios*, Volume 41, Issue 3, 2016, pp. 410–412. Reproduced with permission of The Gospel Coalition.
2. Frank Furedi, 'The Politics of Fear', 28 October 2004, <http://www.frankfuredi.com/articles/politicsFear-20041028.shtml>.
3. P. Virilio, *The Administration of Fear* (Los Angeles: Semiotext(e), 2012), p. 19.
4. Virilio speaks of a 'dromosphere' created by this phenomenon (*Administration*, p. 16).
5. Z. Bauman, *Liquid Love: On the Frailty of Human Bonds* (Cambridge: Polity, 2003).
6. Combining Bauman's theme of liquidity with Virilio's comments about mass individualism.
7. Z. Bauman, *Liquid Times: Living in an Age of Uncertainty* (Cambridge: Polity, 2007), p. 6.
8. Bauman, *Liquid Times*, p. 10.
9. *Fortuna* in Latin. Fate/Fortuna in her capricious, irresistible aspects is hymned in the medieval poetic cycle *Carmina Burana* as *Fortuna imperatrix mundi* (Fortune, empress of the world).
10. L. H. Martin, *Hellenistic Religions: An Introduction* (Oxford: Oxford University Press, 1987), p. 22.
11. *Summa Theologiae* 1a2ae.42.3, <http://www.newadvent.org/summa/2042.htm#article3>.

PART 2

THE *CAMBRIDGE PAPERS*

Theology, politics and culture

The *Cambridge Papers* are produced by The Jubilee Centre, aiming to stimulate readers to develop a Christian perspective on contemporary issues.

Mike Ovey's papers therefore range widely, both through theological history and contemporary thought, and from Plato to Disney. And because he was identifying trends, the underlying ideas remain relevant even though the occasional item in the news has faded from view.

> Feminists of the Jewish and Christian faiths are faced with a basic
> dilemma. Are they to be faithful to the teachings of the Hebrew
> scriptures and the Christian scriptures, or are they to be faithful to
> their own integrity as whole human beings?
>
> (Letty M. Russell)[2]

Presuppositions matter in any debate. This chapter looks at a presupposition sometimes held in the debate over women's ordination, that God could
not by his nature restrict certain roles in churches to men. In the light of the
relationship between God the Father and God the Son, it will argue that
this presupposition is mistaken. The full humanity of women is a heart-cry of
feminist theology today, and rightly so. But as this quotation indicates, this
legitimate concern has sometimes been perceived as hopelessly inconsistent
with commonly held biblical interpretations of women's roles. It is suggested,
for example, that we must choose between accepting restrictions on women's
teaching authority and accepting the full humanity of women. The two are
mutually exclusive, it might be said, because to exclude a person from a particular
function amounts to denying that person's full humanity.

Humanity in the image of God

The idea of 'full humanity' is obviously central to this position and has far-
reaching consequences. Thus Margaret Farley remarks that the full humanity
of women implies two principles: first, equality (women and men are to be
treated as equally human and valued as such) and second, mutuality (humans
are relational as well as autonomous and free).[3] Biblically, full humanity is rooted

in the creation narrative of Genesis 1 and 2 in which both women and men, uniquely in creation, are made in the image of God (see especially Gen. 1:27). This truth is vital because our own uniqueness in creation as humans is bound up with the image of God: to understand ourselves fully as humans we must understand what it means to be made in the image of God. Only then can we answer the question 'What does it mean to be fully human?' Without answering that question it is extremely difficult to see how to evaluate any distribution of authority, whether between the sexes or otherwise.

This chapter, therefore, takes the widely held starting point that women share full humanity in the light of Genesis 1:27 and must be valued as such. The next step is to look at what the image of God involves. The Bible teaches that God has revealed himself to us not only in the Word of God written but also within creation. To a limited extent the image can be seen in human experience. However, as a result of the fall of Genesis 3, sin mars that image. Just looking at ourselves, or meditating on what we find within, does not give us an authenticated picture of what the image of God means. Our own experience, therefore, cannot safely be used either as a source or as an absolute criterion of religious truth. Christians of whatever persuasion face this predicament.

The image of God in Jesus

Instead, we have to look at Jesus. For the biblical teaching is that he is the image of God. He is the image both in his divinity and in his perfect humanity. Seeing him, we do not need to ask to see the Father, for we have seen him in Jesus (John 14:9), who reveals him to us since he is equally divine. Jesus is uniquely the image, for he is divine. At the same time he is the image in that he is the perfect human, for he is sinless, the Adam who did not fall. As such he shows us what it means to be fully human, human as God intended. In him the image of Genesis 1 and 2 remains intact and unmarred. Jesus' humanity is normative humanity: he teaches us, both men and women, how to be fully human.

All this is important for the debate over women's roles due to the implications it may have for traditional interpretations of biblical texts relating specifically to women, such as Ephesians 5 or 1 Timothy 2. Of course, many committed to the supremacy of Scripture have concluded that those traditional interpretations are incorrect: the texts simply do not say what these interpretations suggest. Others accept the interpretations as accurate, but feel that the texts themselves simply cannot be of God because they say something inconsistent with the nature of God. God, so it is said, simply could not say these things, because he is not like that. This chapter is concerned with examining this latter position. To assess its strength we must find out what God is like from elsewhere in the biblical witness, in order to see what could be in accord with the divine nature. The significance of Jesus in this is that he reveals to us both the nature of God and the nature of full humanity. In this way, looking at the nature of God may illuminate what could or could not be conceivable for a humanity made in his image.

These two aspects of Jesus as the revealed image of God are the concern of what follows: first, the divine nature of Jesus in relation to God the Father, which is a question of the eternal character of the triune God; and second, the perfect humanity of Jesus in relation to other humans.

Jesus and God the Father

It is bedrock orthodoxy to see Jesus as fully divine: as divine as the Father is. Nevertheless, Jesus and God the Father remain distinct persons. This is particularly clear in one aspect of their relationship: the obedience of Jesus. John's Gospel, which has such striking incidents as Thomas's confession ('My Lord and my God'), also stresses the sonship of Jesus: he is the obedient Son of God, the one who does his Father's will. This is poignantly clear in his prayers in Gethsemane, 'not my will but yours . . .' This Son–Father language points to distinct persons in the Godhead, as the church fathers observed. Moreover, because it is language of submission to another's will it points to a 'subordination' between Father and Son, yet without derogating from the full equal divinity of Jesus. As the church fathers also found, it is difficult to capture in words this relationship between Father and Son. The word chosen here is subordination, which must be understood, following the fathers, as pointing to a subordination of function and not a subordination of being. Further, the Son–Father language appears to capture the eternal dynamics of this trinitarian relationship. The primacy of the Father neither derives from the Father's enjoying a higher order of being than the Son nor confers such a superiority. The Word always has been and is equally divine.

This means there can be a permanent relationship between beings who have equal value but asymmetrical roles, for the Son obeys the Father's will and the Father glorifies the Son. There is equality but not symmetry. Reference was made earlier to Margaret Farley's remark that full humanity involved equality and mutuality. So here with full divinity: there is the equal value and mutuality of two persons but their roles are not symmetrical. Yet since the triune God is a perfect being, this must be a perfect relationship. It is, moreover, not incompatible with a relationship of love: the love of God the Father for the Son and the Son for the Father is a continual biblical theme. It is worth stressing that in the biblical view the Father's relationship with Jesus is one of both primacy and love. The Godhead, therefore, shows us that relationships can exist between equals involving subordination but without being necessarily immoral or unloving.

The relevance of 1 Corinthians 11:3 – headship as 'source'?

For many, a central text to support this view comes in 1 Corinthians 11:3. '[T]he head of every man is Christ, the head of a woman is her husband, and the head of Christ is God' (RSV).

A crucial question in construing this passage is whether or not the word for head, *kephalē*, imports a note of authority or whether it should simply be taken as meaning 'source'. Some scholars, including some evangelicals, take the view that source is the appropriate sense in that passage.

However, the source translation is not taken here, for a number of reasons. It is certainly true that in extra-biblical literature *kephalē* can simply mean 'source', but when the Old Testament was translated into Greek, *kephalē* was used at times to import authority. The frequency of this usage is disputed, but the word can have that sense. The question, then, is whether it bears that (some would say unusual) sense in this instance.

The most obvious area of misgiving comes in the implications which the source idea has for the person of Christ. In what sense would Christ be equally divine if the Father was his source? In the other two relationships mentioned in 1 Corinthians 11:3, the head is the source in a temporal sense. There was a time when men were not, and when women were not, but there came a point when their existence was derived from their 'heads'. But to use headship in this way with respect to the Father and the Son makes the Son into a lesser derived being – it would mean that, once, the Son was not, rather similar to Arian thought. This is at odds with other elements of the biblical witness which endorse the idea of the Son's obedience and submission to the Father.

Some would say, perhaps, that Paul is referring to the Son's being eternally begotten of the Father, but this has been understood to refer not to an inferiority of being between the two but to the Son's eternally existing relationship with the Father, one of eternal willing submission to the Father in which the authority notion is clearly present. Others would say, possibly, that the words of 1 Corinthians 11:3 refer to the sending of the Son in the incarnation. But the authority idea certainly is present in the incarnation. The Son on earth does the Father's will and it is not orthodoxy to believe that the Son ceased to be divine during the incarnation. If he did, it would suggest that divinity is not an essential attribute but is rather like a snake's skin, something which can be sloughed off, leaving the same essential being behind. This would create the paradox that the incarnate Jesus was rightly executed for blasphemy. For he was claiming to be divine during the incarnation, when he had ceased to be.

Moreover, in Ephesians 5:21–24 Paul uses the head idea in the context of the church's submission to Christ – this seems particularly clear in verse 24 (again, this interpretation is disputed). This text suggests *kephalē* as importing authority would not be unparalleled in the Pauline corpus.

Furthermore, in terms of the headship relationship between the man and Christ, a note of authority would by no means be out of place. It does not follow from this that authority would therefore have to be the sense, but it does show that *kephalē* as importing authority fits two out of the three pairs of relationships well, whereas in at least one of the pairs (God–Christ) to take *kephalē* as source is definitely inappropriate.

For these reasons the traditional interpretation of *kephalē* in 1 Corinthians 11:3 is preferred here, so that the headship relationship between God the Father and Jesus the Son, and therefore also between husband and wife, is seen in terms of authority rather than simply source.

Father and Son are equals in an asymmetrical relationship

Looking at the relationship of Father and Son within the Trinity shows that having different roles in a relationship does not imply necessarily an inferiority of being, even where that difference relates to authority and submission. To say that it necessarily does would logically falsify the eternal trinitarian relationship of Father and Son. That in turn would suggest that Jesus cannot give us accurate information about God and therefore casts doubt on him as the incarnate God.

In addition, relationships between equal beings without symmetry of function exist elsewhere than between women and men. Complementarity underlies Paul's discussion of the church as a body with different parts, yet there is no hint that one part is inferior to others. For Paul, different roles do not entail diminished value. Moreover, Paul enjoins obedience to church leaders and those in civil authority. In neither case is it suggested that leadership derives from or confers a superiority of being; rather, what is at stake is God's right to delegate a degree of authority to others, and his delegates are not chosen because they are higher beings. We do not obey them because they are intrinsically higher beings (although their qualities may make obedience easier) but because of our quite independent obedience to a third party, God.

Is this simply endorsing 'hierarchy'? The Father–Son relationship within the Godhead does indicate a 'hierarchy' of sorts but, crucially, not a hierarchy of being; rather, of voluntary submission by an equal to an equal. Nor is it a hierarchy of exploitation but of perfection. It shows there can be 'hierarchies' involving authority where the authority is not intrinsically evil. It is to the question of the nature of authority that we now turn, and it will be examined within the framework of Jesus' relationships with other humans.

Jesus' exercise of authority

The Gospels show Jesus as a person of authority, able to command nature, demons and, of course, people. His relationships with others are certainly 'mutual' in that they are personal. They involve responsiveness and care, but also authority. However, this is not a domineering authority. Jesus does not lord it as Gentile rulers do, and he instructs his followers that their pattern of authority is to be similarly distinctive too. The model for the exercise of authority is that of a humble servant, strikingly illustrated when he washes his disciples' feet. Christians are in a relationship of submission to Jesus, and yet his promise is that in this relationship we enjoy not a stunted life but life in all its fullness. In that sense, being subordinate, far from diminishing human experience, actually fulfils it. Authority as normatively revealed by Jesus is a relationship not of exploitation but of benefit, since authority is given for serving others, not aggrandizing self.

At this point men, and indeed the church, must recognize that the texts on submission of wives have often been cited to justify authority which has been sinfully perverted from its servant purpose to enforce service on others. This is something that cries out for repentance. If men want to be biblical, then they must live out John 13 rather than simply expecting their wives to observe those parts of Ephesians 5 that they as husbands find most congenial. That in itself forces a re-evaluation of stereotypical roles: part of the thrust of the foot washing in John is that Jesus assumes tasks which are genuinely menial. His authority is not used to try to make sure someone else does them. In terms of our present social structures, this servant ideal is no doubt as unwelcome to men as the authority idea is to women: it forces them to look again at things like distribution of domestic labour, or the proper place for their career ambitions ('Do I genuinely want that promotion for the sake of my family?'). Furthermore, if one accepts the principle of 'equality but not symmetry', then that equality must be recognized and defended in, for example, the workplace.

The general failure by men to use authority as God intended calls for repentance and change. But is this not one feature of the general human tendency to pervert authority, a tendency also found in the way men treat men or women treat women? This does not mean that every authority relationship is intrinsically evil or sinful and should be abolished. Rather, we should strive to purify those relationships which involve or require authority.

Concluding remarks

This chapter has not dealt with all the usual texts discussed in connection with the role of women. It has, therefore, not dealt with the question 'Has God actually established equality but asymmetry between the sexes?' Rather, it has looked at the question 'Could God conceivably establish equality but asymmetry between the sexes?' Given his eternal nature as the trinitarian God, and given humanity in his image as shown to us by Jesus, it is clear that God could indeed establish asymmetry without denying the equality of the sexes. Indeed, since we are made in the image of this trinitarian God, equality and asymmetry in our relationships need not be surprising. (Gal. 3:28 is not a bar to this, since its context is not church order or the wider social order but the universal availability of salvation through Christ, and we know that Paul did envisage sexual distinctives being preserved after salvation: marriage, for instance, continues.)

This is obviously relevant for the debate over women's ordination. Space precludes discussing all the relevant texts and issues – for example, what exactly ordination involves, or whether the same considerations apply to 'sacramental' and pastor-teacher ministries. But it is clear that we cannot assume that God, by his very nature, must inevitably be in favour of ordination for both sexes in order to maintain their equal value, as some seem to assume. This means that in answering the question of ordination of women we cannot say, for example, that the traditional interpretation of 1 Timothy 2, confining ultimate responsibility for teaching in the church to men, is so wildly out of character with other parts of the biblical witness that we can safely disregard it. Whether that interpretation is in fact correct is, of course, a separate question. The fear is that in the present climate an erroneous presupposition controlling what God 'must' say about ordination obscures what he actually has said.

It should also be stressed at this point that the traditional interpretation of 1 Timothy 2 is not a blanket ban on women's ministry. It deals with only one aspect of ministerial work. The contribution of women already made and to be made in the future in ministry should not be allowed to disappear from view in the present debate, nor be devalued. On this point, again, men need to reconsider and repent.

We all agree that women and men are made 'in God's image', but our understanding of this phrase must be controlled by God's self-revelation. At this point, far from being trivial the ordination debate touches on the most fundamental ideas about God's nature. Further, taking the image of God as the starting point throws into sharp relief the question 'What is the kind of God you believe in?' Perhaps one of the dangers in this debate is that inadvertently we create our own image of God which conforms to our own cultural presuppositions, rather than ensuring that our image of God is conformed to what Jesus reveals.

Notes

1. *Cambridge Papers*, Volume 1, Number 2 (Cambridge: Jubilee Centre, June 1992). Reproduced with permission.
2. Letty M. Russell (ed.), *Feminist Interpretation of the Bible* (Oxford: Blackwell, 1985), p. 137.
3. Margaret Farley, 'Feminist Consciousness and Scripture', in Russell, *Feminist Interpretation*, p. 45.

17. DECONSTRUCTION: GAGGING THE SPEAKING GOD?[1]

Scholars have been thrilled recently at discovering a hitherto unpublished fragment of Lewis Carroll's work about Alice. It goes like this:

> 'When I use a word,' said Humpty Dumpty scornfully, 'it means what I want it to mean, neither more nor less.'
>
> 'My dear old thing,' said the March Hare, 'there's more to it than that. When you say or write something, you've got to reckon that you can't keep tabs on it. Other people may take what you say quite differently from how you meant it. It's like setting a bird free. Once it's gone, it flies where it wants.'
>
> 'I'm afraid he's right, Humpty,' chipped in Alice, passing him his tea. 'If you want to get through to us, you've got to use words in ways that we'll understand.'
>
> 'Absolutely,' the March Hare agreed. 'There's no ultimate reason why we shouldn't call that teapot over there by the name "hot water bottle" instead. But if you were the only one who did call it "hot water bottle" you'd be in for a shock come teatime.'
>
> Alice continued, 'Of course, you could start a new fashion, and if you did it frequently enough then at least all your friends could get the hang of it, and we'd know "hot water bottle" meant "teapot".'
>
> The Mad Hatter had been listening to all this with mounting displeasure. 'What tommy rot! You're both talking as though Humpty could use language to communicate something.'
>
> 'He's not as thick as that,' objected the March Hare defensively.

'Not just him – anyone,' the Mad Hatter came back, splattering bits of muffin over
the tea party in his intensity. 'Language doesn't give me access to what Humpty thinks.
How could I know he was using language in the same way I was? When he says, "I'm
having a nice time here" he might mean by "nice" what I mean by "nasty". And we
could never find that out, because all we have to say is that what we mean by "nice"
and "nasty" are other words. It's all just words. It's as though each one of us is inside
a little bubble, all on our own, and every now and then we float close to each other,
but we never know what's going on in the bubble next door.' He paused for breath
and turned to Alice. 'Another cuppa, please, Alice pet, three sugars.'

'Pet, eh?' said Alice from between clenched teeth. 'That sounds like an offensive
socially conditioned sexist term.'

'Only to you, Alice dear, just your subjective reaction,' said the Mad Hatter, taking
his tea and sipping it. 'Blinking heck, I asked for sugar, didn't I?'

'So sorry,' said Alice sweetly. 'In my language "three sugars" means you don't
want any.'

'You know jolly well what I meant . . .' the Mad Hatter accused as the tea party
broke up in disarray.

In this 'fragment' the Mad Hatter adopts an approach to interpretation very
similar to deconstructionism. Deconstructionism itself is a new and potent
player on the interpretative stage, applying to many fields and disciplines. As
such it already features in the courses of many of our students, especially the
humanities. One Christian student remarked after a year studying deconstructionism that there was simply no point in studying the Bible any more – it could
communicate no truth: such were the implications of deconstruction.

This was an understandable reaction. Thus P. Miscall, utilizing deconstructionist approaches, observes that questions of interpretation are insoluble: 'The
reader encounters ambiguity, equivocation, opposed meanings and cannot
decide for or establish one or the other.'[2] Hence Miscall's reaction to 1 Samuel
17 and David's combat with Goliath: it is impossible to determine what David's
character is[3] and hence what the incident is to teach.

To that extent, deconstructionism tends to eliminate our dependence on the
Bible, and indeed the doctrine that God reveals himself. It is, therefore, vitally
important to examine it.

The background

Before plunging into deconstructionism, it is as well to set the scene. Several
schools of thought have grown up in recent years about how language works

and whether words, and literature in particular, can be a vehicle for truth. This is strikingly relevant for the Christian doctrine that God reveals himself in and through the Bible. Whatever else it is, it is also a collection of written words, employing human language.

Some of those schools of thought are represented, albeit in cartoon form, in the literary fragment above. Humpty Dumpty starts with the importance of the author. In the early years of the twentieth century, recovering the author's intention was indeed greatly emphasized: What did Isaiah mean in chapter 53? And so on. This emphasis obviously appeals to biblical Christians. If God has inspired human authors, then *we* long to recover that authorial intent.

However, in the years after the Second World War this 'intentional fallacy', as it was dubbed, came under fire from the so-called New Criticism, which asserted the difficulty/impossibility of recovering authorial intent. Rather, we should accept that a text created by an author becomes, so to speak, independent of the author, as the March Hare's opening remarks suggest. An example of this is the way a legal agreement may be construed in a way the solicitor drafting it never anticipated. So, for this school, we must focus attention on the text, not the author.

Structuralism also concentrates on text. It builds on the work of the great linguist Saussure, who pointed out that there is no essential, intrinsic link between the word which signifies and the thing which it signifies. (Alice and the March Hare recognize this conventional, arbitrary aspect of language in their discussion of what to call a teapot.) This means that what a word signifies depends on the place that word has in the overall language system, its structural position. For the structuralist, therefore, it is tremendously important to discover the structure, and accordingly context becomes vital, both the immediate context of a word or phrase in a literary work and also the context of the total language usage of a particular society. In a way this is, of course, a systematic presentation of the old maxim of construction in English law, *Noscitur a sodis* (a thing is known and understood by the company it keeps).

However, other schools would criticize the New Criticism and the type of structuralism described here for implying that meaning in language is objective. That objectivity would be called an illusion. Instead of concentrating on the text, they would suggest a reader-centred approach. Meaning is only what the reader decides the meaning is. The Mad Hatter plays with this when provoking a particular response in Alice by his use of the term 'pet'. Reader-response theories are already employed in some feminist and liberation theology readings of certain texts.

The Mad Hatter has another string to his linguistic bow, deconstructionism itself. He takes the line that language is outsideless (a formulation adopted by Don Cupitt, for whom orthodox religious language is non-realist, that is to say, does not refer to anything real). 'Outsideless' refers to the idea that we cannot transcend language and its limits. A crucial claim here is that language is simply self-referring. Thus any word, any phrase can be known only from other words and phrases. They, in their turn, derive their significance from their structural position with respect to still more, and so on. As language is essentially self-referring, there is no guaranteed 'real' meaning. We are in fact in an endless labyrinth. Language therefore deconstructs. Further, as the Mad Hatter continues, it is not even clear whether as individuals we are in the same linguistic labyrinth. I claim to speak 'English', but is this the same 'English' as the man next door? Could I show they are part of the same linguistic system?

This way of putting the deconstructionist case means language disappears as a sure vehicle for transmitting objective meaning between persons – an earth-shaking claim.

What we gain from modern literary theories

Some modern theories are of great use in reinforcing and expanding traditional concerns in interpreting the Bible.

Structuralism, for example, serves both to warn us and to provide incentives for study. By stressing the importance of context it reminds us of the very real danger of 'proof-texting'. It is not a legitimate use of the Bible simply to find a form of words grammatically capable of supporting a particular position. Rather, we are driven to rigorous examination of our texts within the context of the book that contains them and ultimately the canon as a whole. The structuralist view encourages us to beware of an over-atomistic reading of the Bible and to take extremely seriously the principle of looking to the whole counsel of God.

Structuralism pushes us in other directions too. Paul's letters are rooted in the Greek of the Near East of the first century. That puts a value on investigating other uses of the language to rebuild the linguistic context of that particular time. Moreover, it reinforces the usefulness of an informed social history of, say, first-century Corinth.

None of this is strikingly new. But what structuralism does underline for us is the importance of these tasks if we want to arrive at what the text says rather than what we assume it to say.

Text-centred and reader-centred theories can be suggestive in other positive ways. Evangelicals stress the Bible as a living rather than a dead text. It can and does address us in our present-day lives. As we study a passage like Ephesians 4:29 with its instructions about the edifying use of the tongue, we may see it directly applying to us in a current situation. Yet it scarcely seems that Paul could directly have had that in mind. It therefore seems illegitimate to say that the human author 'intended' to address us in that situation (although he might have wanted to had he thought about it). At that point it is clear that *one* way of putting the 'authorial intent' view, far from protecting the Bible, tends to render it a dead letter by restricting it to the particular human author. This does not, of course, entail accepting extreme reader-response views. To say all interpretations are equal distorts our relationship with God (see the theological objections to deconstructionism, below). Rather, the point made here is that text and reader-centred theories can redress certain overemphases in author-centred theories of meaning.

Text and reader-centred theories are also suggestive in approaching another puzzle in our doctrine of revelation: the way that prophecy, for instance, can have a meaning different from the one the original human author had in mind. One example is Matthew 2:15, with its application of Hosea 11:1, 'Out of Egypt have I called my son' (RSV). Another is Paul's application of Deuteronomy 30:12 to Jesus in Romans 10:6–7. In neither case does it seem apparent that the human author had Jesus himself in mind. As such, one is conscious that 'authorial intent' defined simply and solely as human authorial intent seems inadequate to draw out the full meaning of Scripture.

Both these instances deal with New Testament applications of Old Testament texts. As such, they may be said to form God's footnotes to his own earlier word, and such use of the Old Testament could be said to be no longer possible (we are not apostles) or at least be practised with extreme caution because of the risks of subjectivity. We are nevertheless reminded that human authorial intent does not exhaust the text's meaning. Nor, come to that, do the efforts of generations of interpreters of Hosea before the birth of Jesus.

In this way biblical Christians need not write off all the interpretative theories that have arisen recently as being irrelevant or completely unhelpful. There are congruencies and resonances with traditional doctrines of revelation and they can be useful in helping us to present a properly nuanced account of what inspiration and revelation really involve.

However, the development of deconstructionism has a strong tendency to undermine the doctrine of revelation, with fatal effects elsewhere in our theology. To the consequences of that theory we now turn.

Deconstructionism

At first glance, deconstructionism could appear to be simply an extension, possibly extreme, of some of the approaches outlined above. Is it, in fact, essentially harmful?

The demolition of a personal relationship with God

The most serious casualty is what Martin Buber called an I–Thou relationship between humans and God, by which is meant the idea of a relationship between persons in which each encounters the other as a person and communicates with them as a person. This is in contrast to an I–It relationship, where I may indeed encounter other persons but do not treat them as such nor communicate with them as such.

Deconstructionism tends to destroy an I–Thou relationship with God by denying communication. If language is not a possible vehicle for God to use in revealing himself to us, then the Bible cannot give us direct knowledge of God. Nor can we avoid this by using the notion of 'direct encounter' with God (through prayer, meditation, thought or ecstasy). The results of such encounters ought in principle to be capable of some kind of verbal description. But if verbal description is inherently and totally inadequate, then it is difficult in the extreme to know what kind of relationship there is, what contours it has, what content there is to it. If I cannot say the relationship is pleasant or unpleasant, worthwhile or pointless, then what in fact do I know about it? In what sense is it genuinely an I–Thou relationship?

It may be justly pointed out that the words are not the relationship. Those sympathetic to the deconstructionist view may cite John 5:39 with Christ's warnings about those who scour the Scriptures but do not find Jesus, the person. Yet the thrust of those words (in the context of John) is that the words of Scripture do point to Jesus and that the scribes and others are at fault for not seeing that. C. S. Lewis points out that while Scripture may only be a 'map', and not itself the country that has to be navigated, navigation is nevertheless possible only with a map. This is equally applicable to our relationship with God. If deconstructionism is correct, then a certain type of relationship, I–Thou, disappears.

Momentous consequences follow from that.

First, God's personal sovereignty over us necessarily disappears too. God may be the creator and ruler of the universe, but we are capable only of conformity and not of obedience. We may fall in with God's wishes through good fortune, but obedience presupposes knowledge of another's will. That in turn depends on communicating that will, which is just what deconstructionism rules out. Naturally, with obedience goes disobedience. It is really extremely difficult to say I am answerable to God or responsible to him if his will is unascertainable. Sin becomes meaningless: the concept of rebellion which is central to sin (Rom. 1:18ff.) is not applicable in that context. That in turn removes the need for Christ's redeeming death.

Second, God's love becomes problematic. If God cannot express this, how can we know we are loved? We might have a sensation which we think is from

God, and which we imagine is produced by his love. But we cannot know this if he cannot tell us.

This in turn throws our entire relationship with him into serious doubt. Logically we can only remain unsure of our status with him and thus insecure. Even if I were right about those feelings (perhaps they were only self-serving delusions?), how can I be sure that they will last for eternity? A very serious casualty of deconstructionism is our assurance of salvation (as well as our assurance that being saved is worthwhile).

The demolition of other personal relationships

Naturally this demolition of personal relationships extends logically to relationships with each other as well as with God, although here, of course, we experience strong empirical resistance (see 'The demolition of the ego?', below). This leaves us in a kind of linguistic solipsism: we are left only with ourselves because we have no access to others. This may well be attractive to a highly individualistic culture, with its prospect of apparent freedom. Part of its attraction, indeed, may be that it tends to diminish personal responsibility to others.

The demolition of the ego?

Yet it is worth questioning whether even this solipsism can be sustained. If even my own language deconstructs by its self-referential nature, can I describe myself, even to myself? And if I cannot describe myself, who is the 'I' of whom I so glibly speak? In that sense the ultimate casualty of deconstruction may be the individual ego.

Given these momentous consequences it is vital to see if deconstructionism is correct.

Objections to deconstructionism

These can be grouped under three headings.

Theological

Deconstructionism, if it addresses the question of God at all, seems to rest on an implicit doctrine of God. But the God implied by this view is not the God of orthodox Christianity. After all, that orthodox God enjoys the advantages of both omnipotence and omniscience. As such he is surely a competent linguistic performer, able to find apt words to express his meaning even to fallen and finite beings. The 'distance' which exists between the minds of author and reader, the problems created by the difficulty of any individual getting 'outside' his or her own linguistic code, would surely be obviated by these attributes of the orthodox God, who knows the minds of author and reader and can act in the minds of both (although this should not be taken as an endorsement either of a 'dictation' theory of inspiration or a 'dictatorial' theory of reading).

Of course, there are traditional constraints on God's actions: but using his omnipotence to communicate does not seem inherently evil. Nor does it seem self-contradictory (as when one might say that God cannot make both an immovable object and an irresistible force). Rather, it seems that one is simply being faced with the assertion 'Even God cannot use language to communicate.' This assertion seems highly problematic because it involves considerations of the nature of God as well as of the nature of language. Deconstructionism here seems to be saying, indirectly, something about God. But, on deconstructionism's own premises, how can we know that? Is there, in fact, an assumption within deconstructionism that God simply *cannot* be the God of orthodox Christianity? This is why radical employment of the technique of deconstruction is properly termed an 'ism'. It carries an ideological position that takes it beyond being a 'neutral' tool.

In fact, of course, it is just those attributes of omnipotence and omniscience that the biblical God does claim to have.

A second theological objection to a certain kind of deconstructionism (and a certain type of reader-response theory) also arises. It could be said that any response by a reader to Scripture is as valid as any other. Thus an interpretation of feeding the five thousand as a sermon on sharing community wealth is as valid as the one that Jesus has miraculous powers. It is said that the Bible is polyvalent (conveys a number of different meanings), and that the *sensus plenior* discussed above ('What we gain from modern literary theories') recognizes this.

Yet it is one thing to say the Bible is polyvalent, with many meanings; quite another to say it is omnivalent, that it can mean *all* things. This is, however, where these extreme views end up, that the text can 'mean' anything. If it were so, God would indeed be a God of inconsistency (since one could respond to a text with two mutually inconsistent reactions about his character: but both would be true). By saying all things, God would be saying nothing. Moreover, this God would be shaped essentially by us and by our reactions, rather than what he discloses himself to be. Indeed, this is one of the greatest objections to seeing God in I–It terms, that it encourages idolatry.

Theologically, deconstructionism involves us by its assumptions with a 'dark, dumb, idol'. Yet it is precisely that point which remains to be established.

Philosophical

It is extremely hard to rescue deconstructionism from self-refutation. The case is advanced using language and discussed using language. Its proponents write books, apparently expecting to be understood. It seems there is at least one privileged, communicable, objectively true proposition, namely the deconstructionist thesis. But if so, there are two alternatives:

1. If the proposition is true, then language in at least one instance communicates truth. But the words and concepts used to express this proposition are not severable from the rest of the linguistic structure: they are part of it. In which case, does not the entire system receive some kind of grounding from this proposition? If deconstructionism is true, why does it not apply to the proposition itself? In which case we could ignore it, because it could never be communicated to us.
2. If the proposition is false, then it can be ignored anyway.

Moreover, it is far from clear whether deconstructionism faces us with a correct set of alternatives. It appears to assert that we have a choice between absolute understanding and deconstructionism. But, as has often been observed, there may be other options, such as an understanding which we accept as true but is in principle open to falsification and which we concede is not exhaustive. Thus we understand 'God is love' as indicating that God has a disposition towards us describable as love because it bears an affinity to love in our own lives. We accept that this understanding of the text is *in principle* falsifiable, although falsifying it would involve such a massive shift in our understanding of other texts too that it seems *in practice* inconceivable. We also accept that we have not exhausted what this love means – human love is not a perfect exemplar of it.

However, there is no need to dismiss this knowledge just because it is provisional, and true but not exhaustive. That point could equally be made of my knowledge of the physical world (human senses may be deceptive), but most of us nevertheless find provisional limited knowledge of the world around us useful.

Empirical
Deconstructionism faces a massive difficulty in explaining the successful use of language in the everyday world. True, misconstructions do occur. But the fact that they are occasions for comment or for humour or for irritation reveals how overwhelmingly successful language seems to be. If language is so unreliable, why do we so readily assume it is a viable means of communication?

Part of the answer, no doubt, is the public nature of language. If I use words in an unusual way, others remark on it and correct me. There is a pervasive pressure towards using language uniformly, and with sufficient uniformity comes the possibility of transmitting information. It is doubtful whether the deconstructionist model takes sufficient account of the social pressure created by the public nature of discourse.

This is related to the point that deconstructionism oversimplifies by claiming that language is self-referring. Clearly, language is more than a mere 'nomenclature', but words are often used with respect to physical phenomena ('This knife is sharp'). If I 'misuse' language to convey that, for example, 'This knife is blunt,' the fact that words are being used with respect to physical phenomena provides an opportunity for my use of language to be corrected and brought into conformity with others' usage of 'sharp' and 'blunt'. The physical world is a shared world and a public world, and the fact that language is at times used in respect of it suggests that the slogan 'language is self-referring' is not the whole truth. And at that point one is aware that although language may sometimes be a complex maze, it is not quite accurate to say it is simply an endless labyrinth.

Conclusion

Deconstructionism is a curious thesis. In a way it takes the Babel story a stage further. Instead of the multiplicity of languages and the confusion it creates, we are left, as it were, with no language at all, either in which God could speak to us or in which we can address each other. As such it would deprive us of the knowledge of God as well as any rationale for evangelism.

Its influence, however, is pervasive. Since so many academic disciplines employ language, they are all potentially affected by deconstructionism and our students already have to reckon with it in their courses, sometimes with grave effects for their spiritual lives.

The tragedy is, of course, that there is no compelling (or even ultimately persuasive) reason for adopting the thesis. This should not hide how attractive we may find it in some ways. The serpent now no longer has to say, 'Did God really say ... ?' (Gen. 3:1, NIV). Instead, he may only have to remind us 'God can't really speak anyway ...'

Notes

1. *Cambridge Papers*, Volume 2, Number 4 (Cambridge: Jubilee Centre, December 1993). Reproduced with permission.
2. P. Miscall, *The Workings of Old Testament Narrative* (Philadelphia: Fortress, 1983), p. 2.
3. Miscall, *Workings*, p. 73.

18. THE HUMAN IDENTITY CRISIS: CAN WE DO WITHOUT THE TRINITY?[1]

'Mirror, mirror, on the wall, who is the fairest of them all?' The Stepmother from *Snow White and the Seven Dwarfs* is an unlikely place to start a discussion of the Trinity, but there is something fascinating about her question. It is not enough for her to have her own opinion about her beauty. Above all she craves objective knowledge of herself, something which only someone other than she herself can provide. The mirror in the tale witnesses truthfully to who she really is, and accordingly she needs it to know her place in the world. On her own, she lacks, so to speak, definition.

The problem of who we are

Perhaps unflatteringly, we share this question with the Stepmother. Of course, this is a perennial question since it deals with a permanent human problem. Yet the end of the twentieth century poses it exceptionally acutely. It is worth reflecting which features today make this so. Two are of particular interest here.

Individualism
One of the most striking aspects of modern life is the place of the individual. The individual is often increasingly isolated as communitarian dimensions to life become more difficult to protect. Naturally, this has its attractions, since the

burden of responsibility is often lessened as the social bond dissolves. This offers very considerable freedom of action, but what we observe goes beyond the simple fact or phenomenon that late twentieth-century life is individual: it is also individualist. The fact is ideologically justified – individualism is a creed.

In practice, this creed means I am ultimately answerable to myself, not others. My first duty is to my own self, an attitude resonating with a market-oriented culture. But there is a price: others too owe a duty to themselves in the first instance; they are not primarily accountable to me. In that sense individualism is a lonely creed.

Uniformity

Paradoxically, a trend to uniformity coexists with individualism. Modern lifestyles have tended to create a global, mass culture in which differences are gradually eliminated. You can have McDonald's fries in New York, Moscow and Bangkok. Even languages, those badges of human cultural diversity, are becoming extinct as a global culture puts a premium on relatively few languages. However, in such a climate it becomes increasingly difficult to see what makes any given human individual unique. He or she has so much in common with such huge numbers of others that they seem interchangeable. Indeed, twentieth-century culture, with its drive for efficiency and convenience, has a vested interest in uniformity. Interchangeability among the workforce can seem highly desirable to an employer, and having the 'standard' customer makes for streamlining.

The causes of our problem

Of course, no factor is solely responsible for these features of life. It is possible only to scratch the surface of what has contributed to our present situation. But a number of different factors require comment.

Modern lifestyle

A combination of trends and developments makes modern life distinctive and contributes to both our individualism and our uniformity. Whatever the original intention, our patterns of work and leisure in large, fluid and anonymous cities can make us remote from extended family. Close friendships can become temporary. This tends to create isolated and atomized individuals. Moreover, family breakdown and a careerist ethic can so focus attention on identity as a function of work that broader questions about the individual are submerged.

As work emerges as the central function for an individual's life, and since that work is often far from unique, the differences between individuals can sink from view. It is no surprise to see the individual becoming merely one of many in a mass, global culture. Personal relationships tend to become dispensable and the individual can become insulated from others and, indeed, insular.

Reductionism

Our understanding of the mechanics of our universe has increased and we are more and more able to 'reduce' events by providing explanations in terms of more and more basic scientific laws. This type of reduction is, of course, a perfectly proper part of the scientific method. Yet with this has also come a different type of reductionism, an ideological tendency to say that philosophically 'all' we are is nothing but a collection of organs, or a collection of atoms: our existence has no transcendent or metaphysical dimension. This type of reductionism is the ideology of 'nothing buttery'.

This reductionism takes many forms. At a popular level psychology has been seen as reducing human beings to a bundle of instincts, conditioned reflexes and neuroses, a crude behaviourism, in which it is redundant to talk of a coherent 'self'. More radically, others argue that we are simply biological machines for propagating our genes. Going still further, we could be analysed as conglomerations of subatomic particles whose activity is governed by the fundamental laws of physics.

Reductionism of this type could be criticized on several grounds, but for present purposes it is worth noting that it 'levels' humanity: there is nothing intrinsically different between different members of the human race. Indeed, there is no intrinsic difference between us and the rest of the universe. The significance of this for twentieth-century attitudes is profound. It provides a reason, in fact something like a moral justification, for treating individual human beings as essentially interchangeable. One is very much the same as another, since all can be reduced to the same basic constituents. It legitimates the uniformity of our culture.

Western philosophical tradition

Some aspects of mainstream Western philosophy can also prove less than beneficial. There has been a tendency to seek answers to human identity by looking at individuals as individuals, self-contained and self-existent, with no necessary contact or communion with others.

This is deeply rooted. Boethius is an example, with his assertion that a person is an individual substance of a rational nature. This stresses the individual both as self-contained and also as purely rational. Descartes continues this approach in stating, 'I think, therefore I am.' This is clearly ego-centred since all enquiry starts with me, the thinker, and that enquiry needs no external input.

A successor in this tradition of the self-existent 'I' is Kant. Kant was attempting to meet David Hume's scepticism about our knowledge of the physical world. To do this, he investigated the faculty of human reason, which involved looking at how 'I' perceive the world and my abilities and my limitations in doing that. But in starting there, Kant finds it difficult to verify that the human mind can indeed scrutinize its abilities and limitations correctly. If this were verifiable, then of course the Stepmother in *Snow White* would not require the external aid of her mirror: she would know herself. If only she had read her Kant . . .

Disconcertingly, this philosophical tradition provides an ideological underpinning for both individualism and uniformity.

Thus if the self is approached in terms of a self-contained, self-explaining entity, then others are in some ways irrelevant to that self. Indeed, verifying the existence of other 'selves' is problematic. I know that I am rational since I can observe my own mental processes (following Boethius) but I cannot observe others in the same way.

This tends to justify me in holding myself accountable only to myself: after all, I can speak only for myself as definitely being an individual. Tragically, though, this has a corollary: as an ideological individualist I can have no call on others; I have conceded they are unaccountable to me.

However, this philosophical tradition can also legitimate uniformity when developed slightly differently. If I assume that what makes me 'human' is my rationality and that others actually do exercise rationality, then what makes me different from all of them? One Apple Mac computer is very like another. Others share my 'human' faculty almost indistinguishably.

What is so potent about these three influences is not their individual impact. Rather, they form a cocktail of influences, in which social facts and ideology combine and reinforce each other to produce a culture in which individual definition becomes extremely problematic and in which human identity becomes, in practice, epiphenomenal: something that, if there, is secondary and not an essential part of the basic model.

The results

Civic relationships: fragility of human rights
Given these twin features of individualism and uniformity, the basis for human rights to be enjoyed by all starts to become fragile. After all, on an individualist level, if I am a self-contained, self-existent ego, why should I bother with your

rights at all? My world is complete without you, and respecting your rights or invading your rights are equal options, dependent on my personal sovereign choice alone. What is more, on a uniformity basis, there is nothing in you which cannot be replaced by another creature from the global community: your value is undercut.

We naturally resist such conclusions, and historically have attempted to ground rights pragmatically: I demand and assert certain rights but am willing to accord reciprocal rights to others in exchange for those rights so that society can function. The difficulty here is our inclination to freeload, to demand our 'rights' while trying to withhold the 'rights' of others. And pragmatism cannot ultimately provide a moral framework to say this is wrong.

Transcendent relationships: the exclusion of God
Naturally, a society that has bought heavily into ideological individualism puts the self at the centre of the universe. This means that God cannot be treated 'as God' (Rom. 1:21), because to treat God as God must include seeing him as the centre of existence rather than ourselves. Moreover, reductionism tends to deny either the existence of God or the necessity of relationship with him: if I am truly 'nothing but' atoms and molecules, it seems farcical to demand that it is necessary for me to know God and enjoy him for ever.

Dispensing with the Trinity?

At first glance the doctrine of the Trinity appears to deal with a completely different area of thought: the nature and person of God rather than the character of being human. The only thing in common, some would argue, is that trinitarian doctrine is equally an 'add-on', a non-essential: an epiphenomenal dogma.

In recent years several considerations, even though hardly Christian orthodoxy, push us in this direction.

First, there is the sheer difficulty of explanation. The old joke is that in mathematics one plus one plus one is three, while in theology one plus one plus one is one. And it is argued that something so difficult to believe and comprehend makes evangelism more difficult. Moreover, it may make us dishonest as we insist on something that we do not clearly comprehend ourselves.

Second, there are the demands of interfaith dialogue. The Trinity is such a distinctively Christian doctrine that it prevents cooperation with the monotheistic religions of Islam and Judaism, and with monist streams in Hinduism and Buddhism too. And, the argument runs, we could happily jettison the

Trinity as a non-essential, or refrain from mentioning it in polite interfaith company.

Third, the doctrine stems from a view of Jesus as fully and uniquely divine, which can only separate us from a secular world which would like to embrace Christian ethics, and from other faiths which, like us, want to oppose the materialism and inhumanity of modern life.

Fourth, it is said that the doctrine is a post-biblical development, only one of a number of theological 'options' available on the biblical material.

Nevertheless, dispensing with the trinitarian doctrine of God has a very high price tag.

The personhood of God

If God is not trinitarian, but is still the sole God who is uncreated and eternal, and therefore without any existing personal relationships within his own being, then we end up having to say some very odd things about his nature. One of two things must be true.

On the one hand, we could say that he simply does not have personal relationships. He did not have them before creation and creation has not altered this: whatever his relationship is with creation, it would not be personal. He is in fact incapable of personal relationships. Rather, his relationship with creation resembles that of a giant supercomputer towards the objects of its thought or that of electricity towards the object it affects. However, this creates unpalatable consequences. If we are capable of personal relationships, this means we have a capacity, not inherently immoral, which God does not, a bizarre result for an omnipotent God. Or we could conclude that, since we are in God's image, our own claims to personal relationships are in fact as illusory as his.

On the other hand, we could say that God is only potentially personal. Before creation he had no personal relationships and only started to have them when he embarked on creation. On this view God is having to find out about relationships as he goes along (scarcely an encouraging thought). But this view leaves us with an acute dilemma:

1. *If God was self-sufficient before creation* (as the major monotheistic traditions maintain), then personal relationship is not essential for him; he does not need it: it is epiphenomenal, and at rock bottom God is impersonal, which leaves us with a picture which differs little from the first option above.
2. *If God was not self-sufficient before creation*, but was essentially personal, and had to create the universe in order to complete himself, then our relationship with him is obviously not what, for example, Paul depicts

in Acts 17:24–27, where Paul insists on God's complete independence of creation. He becomes a God who needs us and depends on us in order to fulfil himself. That would put us in a position to bargain (we will love him if he drops the adultery clause from the Decalogue).

Whichever non-trinitarian course one takes here, we are left with a lesser God, because we are left with a God for whom personhood is unsatisfied in his essential being before creation.

That in turn creates other tensions. John (one of the most explicitly 'trinitarian' of the New Testament writers) speaks of God as love (1 John 4:8). And in this he is speaking of God's essential being. But it is hard to see how this could be true if God is either impersonal or not essentially personal. Moreover, the love of the biblical God towards us is free and gracious. Indeed, our salvation depends on that very quality (Rom. 5:6–8), and it is one we are called to imitate. Yet the character of God's love, if there at all, changes if God is not trinitarian: it becomes self-seeking and conditional, because God needs our love in order to complete himself.

However, it is not just God's loving character that is affected. Other fundamental aspects of God's character become problematic, too. For instance, the Bible stresses God's faithfulness. But faithfulness is possible only within an existing personal relationship. The same arguments apply to both faithfulness and love. A non-trinitarian God means either a God for whom faithfulness is irrelevant, since he is not personal, or else a God who is finding out about faithfulness as he experiences personal relationships with his creation for the first time. This is devastating since it means we do not actually know now that God is permanently faithful – he might turn out not to be. That doubt eats away at the assurance of our destiny with him.

Similarly, Broughton Knox remarks in *The Everlasting God* that God's character as just also becomes questionable under a straightforward non-trinitarian monotheism.[2] To be just, Knox argues, requires that there be someone to whom to be just. It certainly is hard to see how a self-existent, not essentially personal, being can properly be described as 'just'.

A diminution of humanity

If God is not essentially personal, then we too are affected by that. The biblical claim is that we were made in God's image. But as we have seen above, a non-trinitarian God is at best only potentially personal. In that case, personhood ought only to be potential and non-essential for us too. On that basis, personhood really is only epiphenomenal for us, just as it is with God. That again would have implications for the values of personal identity: they cannot be as fundamental as all that. Rather, it would be more accurate to say that God has created a universe that is sublimely indifferent to these things. That is scarcely desirable since it undermines the importance of maintaining both the rights of individuals and the dignity of the race as a whole. These things we are so keen to protect would merely be interesting accidents of creation, but nothing more.

The relevance of the Trinity

In fact, the Bible presents a picture of God which inevitably pushes us in a trinitarian direction. God is consistently portrayed as personal (to love and to be faithful are personal qualities). But he is also portrayed as complete in himself, needing nothing from creation, us included. For this to be true, his nature must be such as to enable those personal attributes to be actual before creation and not merely potential.

This is indicated in passages like John 1:1ff., Hebrews 1:1ff. and Colossians 1:15–20, which speak of the *eternal* coexistence of the Son with the Father. The existence of the other person enables these personal qualities to be actual: following Augustine, love requires an object, and the different persons of the Trinity fulfil that. Moreover, as Richard of Saint Victor noted, the fact that there are three and not two persons in the Trinity gives an extra dimension to the personal relationships involved: the Son and Spirit *join* in loving the Father and doing his will. The Spirit and Father *join* in loving the Son, and so on.

As regards God, therefore, the Trinity underlines the *personal* perfection of God: we need this as a guarantee of the perfection of his personal character-istics and of our own security with him. However, we also need the doctrine to underwrite our own identities and value. For we are made in the image of God, and therefore an essentially personal God indicates both that we too are created to be personal beings, and also that this aspect of our existence is not epiphenom-enal and dispensable. We are given a vital basis for our claims to personhood, and this helps us answer the individualism and uniformity of our own time.

Individualism
In terms of God himself, Father, Son and Spirit, the Trinity means that we do not have a monist or 'individualist' God. For God, personal identity is found in relationships rather than in the kind of self-contained, undifferentiated unity that tends to underlie Boethius, Descartes and Kant. We 'locate' the Father by reference to his relationships with the Son and the Spirit: he himself as Father is, in a way, defined by where he stands with respect to the other persons of the Trinity (Calvin raises this in his *Institutes of the Christian Religion*, Book 1, chapter

13, section 6). In that way, personal relationships are essential and not optional extras. And this implies for humans made in his image that we know ourselves truly in relationship, not in isolation.

Trinitarian doctrine provides a rationale defending individuality without degenerating into individualism. We can justify the common value of each member of the human race without depending on the notion of the self-contained ego, with the problems that entails.

Uniformity

This trinitarian understanding also guarantees diversity rather than uniformity. The Son and the Spirit have distinct roles within the Godhead, mirrored, for instance, by the way the Spirit acts as a pointer to the achievements of the Father and the Son (Acts 2:1–11) or the way the Son supremely obeys the will of the Father (e.g. John 17:4). Although equally divine, there is a diversity between the persons: they are not mere clones, nor simply interchangeable. Equality of value does not mean symmetry of role.

It is for this reason that some recent developments of trinitarian doctrine seem rash. It has been suggested that there is a symmetrical, mutual submission between the persons of the Trinity. This makes the Father completely inter-changeable with the Son and the Spirit in their relationships. That in turn starts to eliminate the individuality of the persons of the Trinity since they are a common coin. Obviously that is not the way the persons appear in salvation history. (Biblically, the Father does not submit to the Son: in fact, 1 Cor. 15:24 makes it clear that the Father is the final monarch after the general resurrection and the conquest of evil.)

This suggestion is disastrous, both for our doctrine of God, because it tends to make the persons of God contingent and not essential, and also for our doctrine of humanity, because we would be persons in the image of a clone-type God who could not guarantee our unique value as human individuals. (As it happens, this argument emerged during the ordination discussions in order to safeguard the value of women. Ironically, it undercuts their value as human beings.)

However, orthodox trinitarian doctrine gives a rationale for seeing ourselves as unique individuals rather than as essentially uniform, interchangeable clones. With God, we find that relationships are, as it were, constitutive of us as persons, and our very diversity of relationships indicates a diversity of persons enjoying them. Accordingly, I am not simply substitutable by any other member of the human race in my relationships: someone else could not straightforwardly replace me as friend or parent or spouse or child. Rather, they would form different constitutive relationships in their own right.

In this way the Trinity gives an account of human uniqueness which tends to compel respect for the dignity of each individual. This in turn implies an objectivity to human rights and responsibilities, and the significance of that in a world so often lukewarm to both is obvious.

Conclusion

This means that the trinitarian account of God is necessary for us. We need it to understand and value both our relationship with him and also our relationships with one another. The Trinity is a uniquely Christian doctrine and underlines what Christian belief contributes to understanding ourselves, our God and our place in his world. In fact, in a world struggling to validate human values, it could be presented as one of the most attractive features of our faith to those outside, a tool for evangelism and a feature of our apologetics, not a disability for which we apologize.

Notes

1. *Cambridge Papers*, Volume 4, Number 2 (Cambridge: Jubilee Centre, June 1995). Reproduced with permission.
2. D. Broughton Knox, *The Everlasting God: A Character Study of God in the Old and New Testaments* (Sydney: Lancer; Welwyn: Evangelical Press, 1988).

19. DOES ATHENS NEED JERUSALEM? A CHRISTIAN CONTEXT FOR SECULAR THOUGHT[1]

> There is no longer a Christian mind. The Christian mind has succumbed to the secular drift with a degree of weakness and nervelessness unmatched in Christian history. It is difficult to do justice in words to the complete loss of intellectual morale in the twentieth-century Church.
>
> (Harry Blamires)[2]

Three questions: the leaders of a church ministry team want to find more fruitful ways for the team to work together. Should they use the Myers-Briggs personality-type tests? A committee of elders is considering church growth. Can contemporary organization theory be used? A Christian parent is reading a feature in the Sunday paper by a secular child counsellor on raising children. Can she adopt the ideas?

These examples relate to secular thinking or learning about the world. That is to say, an understanding of the world or some part of it, whether based on experience, experiment, intuition or rational reflection, but not consciously arising from God's revelation in the Bible. Such secular learning raises a perennial question for Christians: How does secular thought fit with being a faithful Christian who relies on the revelation of God? 'What indeed has Athens to do with Jerusalem?' demanded Tertullian circa AD 200,[3] as he insisted that 'Jerusalem' did not need 'Athens', that Christian thought did not depend on secular thought. But how, then, do Christian and secular thinking relate? The explosion of knowledge, or at least information, over the last three hundred years makes this question particularly acute now. Do we deny secular thinking? Or endorse it? Or respond critically and charitably to it? And if the last, on what basis?

Frameworks for thought

Frameworks in the Christian community

'A text without a context is a pretext.' That motto has served Christians well in handling God's Word. It reminds us we must locate any individual phrase or sentence of God's revelation correctly in the overall framework of what he has said. This helps minimize distortion and misrepresentation. Our knowledge of God and his will is seen holistically, coherently. It is properly contextualized. Unfortunately it is far from clear that Christians take similar care with their knowledge of their world. This is not least because we tend to mirror our culture in compartmentalizing our lives into 'public' and 'private'.[4] Christians may well have sufficient learning to take part intelligently in this public, secular square, but this is not related to their belief in Jesus as Lord of all. Since this learning is not put into the larger context of Christian belief, it seems, in practice, func-tionally separate from faith. In that sense, Blamires's point (cited above) hits home. Furthermore, when Christians contribute as Christians in the public square, it can seem like an intrusion into an independent arena. This does, though, raise a question for Christians: Just what is the context for our thought about our world?

Frameworks for thought in the secular community

Secular thinking does not necessarily provide a workable alternative context. Our culture seems increasingly unable to locate its wealth of information in a viable context or framework, to put a piece of information in its appropriate 'place'. Modernism once claimed – vociferously – to provide just such a context for our knowledge: the overarching power of objective human reason to find truth, not with external help from God, but by dispassionate enquiry. Mankind has come of age, claimed Immanuel Kant, implying that humanity had come into full possession of its powers. Yet those powers have subsequently proved less universal and objective than imagined, as thinkers like Polanyi showed that human knowing has an irreducibly personal, subjective, element.[5]

Yet postmodern understandings offer little more. For the mood is one where a complete account of our condition (a metanarrative in the jargon) seems implausible, so that any context for our thinking seems fractured and partial, unable to account for why we know what we know or what the real significance of our learning is. This loss of context or framework presents a real difficulty for us: How can we rightly value and use our learning without a full context within which to see and understand it? A piece of information without its full context threatens to become information without full significance. Our current culture has an ocean of facts, but finds navigation increasingly difficult.

A biblical case for secular thinking?

Does Christianity after all provide a viable context for thought, whether Christian or secular? Two very different groups feel uneasy: secularizing thinkers and some Christians. For many secularists Christianity has no contribution to make, either because bringing Christian belief to bear puts the search for truth in danger by biasing dispassionate enquiry (a modernist objection), or because the claim to a unique or exclusive, or 'total', truth which evaluates (or 'judges') other perspectives is oppressive – such claims are 'totalizing', even totalitarian (a postmodern objection).

Christian misgivings about Christian engagement

Christians can be wary of such engagement with secular thinking, and not merely because of other-worldly blindness. Some weighty theological arguments are at stake. It is argued, quite rightly, that Romans 1:18–23 describes how sin affects the mind, as well as other features of the human person. Everyone, Jesus excepted, sins (Rom. 3:23), and hence suffers from a corruption of the mind. It is the work of the Holy Spirit to overcome this, at any rate in relation to knowing the truth about Jesus (1 Cor. 12:1–3). To insist, therefore, on the need for rational argument on secular topics with secular people, even from a Christian position, seems dubious for several reasons.

It seems dubious, first, because of the impact on the doctrine of God's revelation. Such purely 'rational', or rather rationalist, argument can suggest that mere rational discourse, on its own, without God's Spirit, conveys God's truth. This implies that we can adequately understand God independent of his revelation. A related point is that some secular thinking simply appears to be in conflict with biblical teaching, and an undue exaltation of secular thinking can create the impression that we can choose which bits of the Bible to reject and which to accept.

Second, this approach also affects the doctrine of salvation by God's grace alone. For, if mere rational discourse, on its own, can convey God's truth, then sin seems not to be genuinely enslaving. If one can, without God's grace, think with purity, then why can one not ultimately act with purity? That would mean, this argument suggests, that we have forgotten that salvation is by grace, not works.

Third, and perhaps most obviously, there is the fear of 'drinking impure water'. For, if we start meeting secular thought in this kind of way, even though much is harmless and even useful, eventually we imbibe some idea that is genuinely wrong and dangerous. Moreover, because secular ideas are not located in their proper theological framework, it is harder to deal with such foreign bodies.

Thus basic theological hygiene requires minimal traffic between theology and secularized disciplines.

This is all somewhat ironic. Theology was once called the queen of the sciences. But the sciences have long been republican, while even some faithful theologians advocate abdication.

A Christian knowledge of God and the world

The Christian argument outlined above is not negligible, but still needs supplementing with further biblical considerations, which affect the picture considerably. Romans 1:18–23 is predominantly concerned with the knowledge of God, and is not a general account of all human knowledge. Verse 19 suggests a contextual limitation – 'what can be known about *God*' (RSV; emphasis added). And the discussion then proceeds on the basis of fallen human suppression of the truth about God, so that, to quote Calvin, 'they wantonly bring darkness upon themselves'.[6] The futility of thought here is in the first instance about God, although its effects may ultimately go wider.

In fact, other biblical material suggests fallen humans can genuinely know things other than God without special revelation. Job 28:1–11 brings this out. It uses the example of mining, and human ability to uncover and use the resources of the natural world. This is a particularly telling example in a book much concerned with what lies hidden – the reasons for Job's suffering. Humans can, however, come to know their world and therefore direct it. This lies very close to the creation mandate of Genesis 1:28–30, and clearly knowledge helps humans exercise dominion in God's world. What is more, this position of responsible dominion, albeit impaired, is retained even after the fall (Gen. 9:1ff.). If dominion is kept, it is no surprise that knowledge is too.

However, part of the fascination of Job 28 is that after the celebration of human ability and knowledge with respect to created things, verses 12–28 speak of the human inability to discern *wisdom* independently. This is what human ingenuity cannot uncover. Now wisdom in the Old Testament is certainly complex, but it does include the idea of an overarching framework within which to view life in God's creation. It is, so to speak, knowing creation in its fullest context.[7] Unfortunately for creaturely knowledge, only the Creator knows that kind of ultimate context. Hence for the creature, the only route to knowing creation in its fullest context is to turn to the God who created. This is indeed the perspective of Job 28: God alone knows wisdom in this sense (v. 23), but in his mercy communicates it (v. 28).

This, then, suggests a nuanced account of sin's effect on knowledge. Much depends on the object of knowledge. Fallen humans do not adequately or savingly know God our creator (Rom. 1:18–23), but may usefully, although with limitations, know objects within his creation (Job 28:1–11). The Bible gives an integrated account of fallen humans as knowers, the objects of human knowledge, and even why there is something that humans cannot know without special revelation. However, even our knowledge of creation is shorn of its ultimate purpose and meaning, for it is removed from its final, fullest context: it is decontextualized knowledge, although not without value.

Workable secular thought in a Christian framework

Where does this leave secular learning? Three things follow. First, secular thought is possible, but ultimately decontextualized, because it is ignorant of our triune creator. The problem with any decontextualization is that, while it may be harmless, it can also be highly misleading. Theology, the queen of the sciences? Yes, for only so can the sciences find their fullest meaning: she is a benevolent monarch.

Second, secular knowledge works with capital borrowed from the doctrine of creation. The borrowing takes place on several levels: there is the created capacity for thought and learning that relates to humans as holders of dominion over God's creation, and the knowability and coherence of a cosmos created for that dominion. Secular thought works – without acknowledgment – because of a Christian creation. It works not because of secular presuppositions, but despite them. Indeed, secular thought can work very well and may therefore have much to teach on many levels. One can use a gift without recognizing the giver. Conversely, the more explicit and consistent its denial of a Christian creation, the less its thinking coheres, for the gift itself is then being denied. Jettisoning any working capital, even borrowed capital, can lead to bankruptcy. The queen of the sciences, though, to extend the metaphor, is a benevolent monarch providing viable working capital for thinking, whether her subjects acknowledge it or not.

Third, this suggests something about the relationship between secular and Christian thought. Secular thought 'works' through its unacknowledged borrowed capital from a Christian creation. This, though, suggests that common rational discourse between Christian and secularist is not taking place on the secularist's territory, nor on some 'neutral' meeting ground, but on Christian territory, on which the secularist, unconsciously, stands. For a Christian, meeting secular thought on the basis of common rational discourse is a match played at home. But the Christian too must recall that secular knowledge is to be set in its fullest context, its theological context, and weighed within it. When the Christian does this, she or he is most able to evaluate that secular contribution effectively and constructively, winnowing out what is falsified, but gratefully and humbly accepting what the fullest context endorses. In this way the primacy of God's written revelation is preserved.

Modernist and postmodernist responses

Now, it will be objected that this is a Christian answer to a Christian objection. We turn then to secularists. For the modernists, one naturally sympathizes with their defence of rationality, for a Christian account of creation stresses this too. But modernist rationalism is indefensible. Scientists, to take the paradigm profession of modernism, apparently obtain coherent results. They also have, however, personal commitments, even at work, which are also apparently inescapable and whose contours they themselves seem unable to determine definitively. Clearly, then, commitment is not necessarily fatal to learning. The point has often been made but bears repetition: it is not so much having a perspective which creates problems, but which perspective one has. And there are good reasons for accepting that Christianity does provide the right perspective, the fullest context.

For the postmodernists, one appreciates both their emphasis that human knowers are not 'neutral' and their stress on what relativizes thought. However, our problem is worse than they think. A nostalgic aroma of modernism clings to some postmodern thinking, for it has not grasped the full depth of what relativizes and skews our learning: not just time, place, race, gender, class, among others, but our rebellion against our creator. And it is that supremely relativizing factor that makes one sceptical of dismissing the Christian context as 'totalizing'. Humans have a clear self-interest in dismissing such a claim. And the question is not simply, is Christian discourse 'totalizing', but rather, is it true?[8] For a Christian, without that understanding of the sinful relativity of our thought, it is difficult either to demonstrate the validity of postmodern contributions, or to challenge and supplement their views where that is necessary. Moreover, the Christian context proposed here does not automatically dismiss secular thought but asserts its potential contribution. It is to an example of this that we now turn.

Secular knowledge in context: a postmodern case study

The French sociologist Jean Baudrillard has contributed to postmodern thought in several ways, but particularly regarding 'virtual reality' – the reality our computer and television technologies construct. The impact of these technologies is real enough. Some did become clinically depressed over the death of the Princess of Wales, despite meeting her only through television. For some the story of a soap opera can appear more important than their own personal relationships. It is problematic whether the Gulf War was a genuine war or a lavish piece of entertainment for CNN's viewers. How should we understand this? Baudrillard suggests we have developed a 'simulacrum' society ('simu-lacrum' in the sense of an image which is a deceptive substitute). For we are a culture that revolves around the image and he notes successive stages of the image society:

1. The image reflects a basic reality.
2. The image masks and perverts a basic reality.
3. The image masks the absence of a basic reality.
4. The image bears no relation to any reality, but is its own simulacrum.[9]

Now Baudrillard is by no means the clearest of writers, but on one interpret-ation the image has moved in our culture from being something which represents something else to being itself primary and needing no 'validation' by anything external to itself. It is, so to speak, self-referring. And this world of image, in Baudrillard's view, now encroaches on the reality to which it originally referred. For Baudrillard, Disney and the corporation succeeding him exemplify this, especially with their Disney 'worlds':

> But the Disney enterprise goes beyond the imaginary. Disney, the precursor, the grand initiator of the imaginary as virtual reality, is now in the process of capturing all the real world to integrate it into its synthetic universe, in the form of a vast 'reality show' where reality itself becomes a spectacle, where the real becomes a theme park.[10]

A commonsense response is that the real world remains real and the world of image always remains image. However, Baudrillard has captured something of value. He recognizes a world where, at least for some, the image has become more real than reality and these virtual realities have an overwhelming power. In fact, there is an aura of inescapability here: Baudrillard speaks of our having gone beyond history to entering 'into pure fiction',[11] so that we are 'forced to abide in our present destruction'.[12]

However, this raises a double question: first, how far should a Christian endorse Baudrillard's analysis, and second, if Baudrillard is anything like right, how can one avoid the nihilism that Baudrillard himself apparently thinks inevitable?

Humans as manufacturers and captives

A key point of contact is the view of people as those who manufacture images to stand for reality. Baudrillard himself notes that humans construct images, icons, of God. In fact, he uses the icon as one of his examples of the successive stages of the image culminating in the simulacrum. Now Baudrillard's description of the successive stages of the image shows the image coming to *displace* that for which it originally stood. However, in Christian theological terms the displacement of God by that which is not God is idolatry (Rom. 1:25). The point is often made that a crucial feature is not so much the physical presence, say, of an image, but the way that in idolatry the true God is displaced by something out of human imagination (Acts 17:29). In this way, we can speak of idolatrous ideologies, and even idolatrous theologies.[13] Yet Baudrillard gives us an enriched account of the range of our own culture's idolatry. For he has brought to our attention the way our technologies have enabled us to inhabit a new virtual reality which seems overwhelmingly 'real'. At this point it is not simply that one particular object is being given inflated value, a statue perhaps. Our capacity to manufacture has far surpassed that. Rather, it is the entire virtual world humans are coming to live in. On this view, present idolatry is on an engulfing scale because it is the entire 'world' modern humans inhabit, not just one item within it, and this simulacrum world is difficult, even impossible, to transcend. Two things follow:

1. God is occluded or eclipsed, and thereby displaced. For the world of image does not permit us to see through to him. He is not necessarily explicitly denied, but is functionally irrelevant. Keyes comments of an idol, 'We become increasingly attached to it until it comes between us and God.'[14]
2. We are enmeshed in a fictive reality: it claims to be more real than it is. To quote Keyes again, 'The idol deceives both about what it is and what it does,'[15] echoing the biblical evaluation of the idol as lie (e.g. Isa. 44:20; Jer. 10:14). But this fictive reality is on a vaster scale than the fictive claims of one particular idol. This fictive nature is also binding, enslaving, as Isaiah 44:18 indicates.

God as Creator
What is, of course, missing from Baudrillard's description is exactly the contextualization of this human manufacturing activity. When it is seen in the context of God the Creator and humans as created, a number of additional factors come into play:

1. The point about the 'original' reality which human constructions mirror, represent and attempt to replace is that it is a reality established by God. Baudrillard notes a certain inevitable conflict between 'reality' and simulacrum, but he implies the victory of the image when he speaks of images as 'murderers of the real, murderers of their own model'.[16] But this underscores that in his thought God tends to be passive, an

object of which images are made, and not an active person. This disallows the way God himself is insistent that in the conflict between idolatrous lying realities and himself, he will be vindicated. For Isaiah 40 – 55 in many ways revolves around the vindication of God as against the idols as the only true God. The assumption therefore that the simulacrum will win against this active creator God is indeed a leap of faith.

2. It is perhaps a natural human temptation after the fall to prefer our idols to the living God. Certainly Baudrillard most often appears as a describer of this overwhelming virtual reality rather than as a critic of it. But again the full creational context alters this value-neutral view of the simulacrum society. If the simulacrum really is idolatrous and occludes God, then it has to be ethically evaluated, and the biblical testimony is clear that such activity is wrong. It is just here that the shoe pinches for those Christians in the 'developed' world. We may be far more implicated in idolatrous living than we realize, because of our everyday participation in our culture's constructed 'world'.

3. Last, the creational context is liberating. Baudrillard himself seems at the least resigned to, or even accepting of, the victory of the simulacrum society, the 'Disneyfication' of culture. Others feel less sanguine. The difficulty, obviously, is how humans could extricate themselves from virtual reality once having bought into it. This difficulty parallels, but even surpasses, that of the idolater of Isaiah 44 whose reason is so blunted that he cannot escape his idol. And where an entire culture is to a greater or lesser extent implicated in a fictive, virtual reality, the difficulties of escape seem all the more. At this point it is indeed vital to recall that the Creator is not enmeshed as we are, and that he remains graciously concerned for his creatures. Baudrillard drives home (unconsciously) in a new way the force of Athanasius' insight that only the Creator can redeem.[17]

On this basis, then, Baudrillard's analysis has something to teach Christians, making us aware of the potential for idolatry in our current cultural climate, and more acutely aware of our need for another to deliver us. But it is also an analysis that needs the Christian context, for it is that which provides both ethical framework and justified hope.

Epilogue

'What indeed has Athens to do with Jerusalem?' The foregoing indicates that Jerusalem does not depend on Athens, but nor can she simply ignore Athens.

Instead, Jerusalem is obliged to bring what Athens suggests into the context of the full biblical revelation. This is an onerous task for Jerusalem and probably unwelcome for Athens, but it remains the best way, ironically, to understand, value, employ and even preserve the very learning which Athens claims to desire and prize.

Notes

1. *Cambridge Papers*, Volume 9, Number 1 (Cambridge: Jubilee Centre, March 2000). Reproduced with permission.
2. Harry Blamires, *The Christian Mind* (London: SPCK, 1963), p. 3.
3. *Prescription Against Heretics* 7.
4. See e.g. D. Wells, *God in the Wasteland: The Reality of Truth in a World of Fading Dreams* (Grand Rapids: Eerdmans; Leicester: Inter-Varsity Press, 1994), pp. 9ff.
5. E.g. M. Polanyi, *Personal Knowledge: Towards a Post-Critical Philosophy* (Chicago: University of Chicago Press; London: Routledge & Kegan Paul, corrected edn, 1962).
6. *Institutes* I.4.1.
7. Cf. L. G. Perdue, *Wisdom and Creation: The Theology of Wisdom Literature* (Nashville: Abingdon, 1994), p. 341.
8. To dismiss all truth questions as irrelevant is itself a form of tyrannical 'totalizing' discourse.
9. From the essay 'The Precession of Simulacra', in *Simulations*, trans. P. Foss and P. Patton (New York: Semiotext(e), 1983), pp. 1–79.
10. J. Baudrillard, 'Disneyworld Company', in *Libération*, trans. F. Debrix, 4.3.96.
11. J. Baudrillard, 'Pataphysics of the Year 2000', in *L'Illusion de la Fin*, trans. C. Dudas (Paris: Galilee, 1992), p. 1.
12. Baudrillard, 'Pataphysics', p. 1; Baudrillard is quoting Elias Canetti.
13. Where one insists on God as one would like him to be, rather than as he reveals himself.
14. R. Keyes, 'The Idol Factory', in O. Guinness and J. Seel (eds.), *No God but God* (Chicago: Moody, 1992), p. 33.
15. Keyes, 'Idol Factory', p. 45.
16. E.g. in 'Precession of Simulacra', *Simulacra and Simulation,* trans. Sheila F. Glaser (Ann Arbor: University of Michigan Press, 1994), p. 5.
17. Athanasius, *On the Incarnation* 7.

20. IDOLATRY AND SPIRITUAL PARODY: COUNTERFEIT FAITHS[1]

> Your man has been accustomed, ever since he was a boy, to have a dozen incompatible philosophies dancing about together inside his head. He doesn't think of doctrines as primarily 'true' or 'false', but as 'academic' or 'practical', 'outworn' or 'contemporary', 'conventional' or 'ruthless'. Jargon, not argument, is your best ally in keeping him from the church.
>
> (C. S. Lewis)[2]

So writes C. S. Lewis as the experienced demonic tempter Screwtape. He is chronicling the difficulties of discussing spiritual matters in terms of truth. Many Christians have indeed tried to speak in terms of truth as against false-hood, sometimes employing the biblical vocabulary of idolatry for this. An idol lies about God in some way. Thus idolatry has been a very significant tool in attempting to witness faithfully to God. But several reasons are urged for discarding this archaic-sounding tool:

1. *The tool of idolatry seems irrelevant.* If idolatry is merely the worship of a physical object, most Westernized people do not bow down to such physical objects.
2. *The tool of idolatry breeds spiritual blindness.* Some interfaith advocates fear that the tool of idolatry dismisses religious experiences outside Christianity. This, the argument runs, excludes spiritual insights, engendering godlessness, not godliness.
3. *The tool of idolatry breeds bigotry and arrogance.* Dubbing something as an 'idol' can demean the idol worshipper, thereby facilitating religious intolerance and discrimination.[3] Our cosmopolitan world cannot afford such divisions or the tools that create them.

Such reasons, the argument suggests, mean that idolatry has rightly had its day as a category or way of analysing beliefs about God or the cosmos.

Yet this is premature. Improper use of a particular analysis does not automatically mean it produces a false diagnosis. Historically, when faced with a strongly pluriform religious culture where political control lay clearly in non-Christian hands, the Christians of the Roman Empire made enormous, and unembarrassed, analytical use of idolatry, seeing it as theologically fundamental. Tertullian could write:

> The principal crime of the human race, the highest guilt charged upon the world, the whole procuring cause of judgement, is idolatry. For, although each single fault retains its own proper feature, . . . yet it is marked off under the general account of idolatry.[4]

Why disregard this central aspect of their work while studiously preserving closely related material such as Nicene trinitarian theology[5] and Chalcedonian descriptions of Christ?[6] Why was idolatry so useful analytically?

Most important, though, is the biblical data. In using the tool of idolatry, the early church applied not simply Old Testament but New Testament material: thus 1 John 5:21 retains the warnings against idols, and 1 Thessalonians 1:9–10 describes salvation itself as turning from idols and being delivered from the coming wrath. Is then idolatry fundamental to describing the human condition?

The biblical scope of idolatry: idolatry and creating

The first objection to using idolatry analytically is its irrelevance, since today's Westernized cultures do not use physical idols. This misunderstands how the New Testament in particular uses the concept. Paul well knows that a physical idol is 'nothing' (1 Cor. 8:4). Yet his Areopagus address of Acts 17:22–34 illustrates concerns beyond physicality alone. A dominant thought is that the creator God needs no humans to serve or provide for him. To act as though he does reverses the true relationship in which he provides for humans. The true relationship is that of uncreated creator with created.[7]

However, the relationship is denied if the uncreated creator is treated as created, as a being who is somehow dependent, rather than independent and self-existing.[8] Making physical objects of worship certainly does deny this. But behind such manufacture lie someone's art and imagination, depicting God, or the gods, as he or she sees fit (Acts 17:29). The uncreated Maker is treated as something made, conceived by human thought. So, reducing something to

physical form is not of the essence of idolatry. Hence the remark that covetousness is idolatry (Col. 3:5). One can idolize an abstract thought, as in classical
Marxism, or a lifestyle, as in the leisured and pleasured West. Therefore the
redundancy objection to the analytical tool of idolatry fails, because idolatry
does not require a physical idol.

The relationship is equally denied, though, when what is created denies its
dependency and contingency towards its creator. This robs the Creator of his
glory (Rev. 4:11 glorifies God since creation is sustained by his will). In classical
mythology this denial occurred by attributing human existence to the making
not of God but of Zeus, but there again the fact of createdness itself can be
denied, as with the Epicureans' insistence on human life as random, not created.
Atheism itself is idolatry in this developed sense, and is thus pervasively present
in today's culture in the objective randomness of some existentialists and some
'creedal' versions of evolution. Furthermore, a culture, like ours, so insistent
on prioritizing its pleasures also appears idolatrous: we accept a 'dependence'
on what is not God. Such denials so elevate a human construct (a story about
Zeus, a human theory of randomness, a view of human well-being) that it
displaces God considered as creator.

The early church deployed this developed sense of idolatry. Idolatry, insists
Tertullian, occurs when something is elevated 'in place of God, against God',
and needs no physical idol.[9] It matters not whether the 'something' is physical,
or an abstract idea, or a lifestyle, or a political party, or even a conception of
God originating purely in human imagination. For something originated has
been elevated in place of the unoriginated.

Humans, remarked Bertrand Russell, are born with the 'cruel thirst for
worship'.[10] Russell observes that people elevate something, anything, in their
lives, but passes by the biblical perception that while all equally may worship,
not all worship is equal. Strikingly, God uses idolatry terminology to distinguish
himself from other objects of worship, and to provide a fundamental description of the human condition. Romans 1:18–32 is the classic example, and
highlights 'exchange': people exchange the glory of the immortal God for
images (v. 23), and they exchange the truth for a lie (v. 25). Genesis 1 – 3 and
Jeremiah contribute greatly here.

The reader of Genesis 3 approaches it with two repeated lessons from
Genesis 1 and 2. First, when God speaks, it is so. His word is utterly effective
and sovereign. Physical reality and word correspond. Second, God is a benevolent creator: creation is created good and he blesses his creation. The
serpent's words in Genesis 3:4–5 provoke incredulity, for they tempt the woman
to deny God's word is effective ('you will not die') and his goodness ('God knows
. . . that you will be like God'). The serpent disputes not God's existence, but

his character as creator. Taking the fruit denies God's sovereignty and also his character. Man and woman act on a false view of God and indeed exchange the truth about their creator for a lie.

Jeremiah deals less with denying God's character than attributing that character to something other than God. In chapter 10 the Creator–created distinction is pervasive: what distinguishes God is that he creates (vv. 12–13) while the idol is created (vv. 3b–4, 9) and so is not a creator (v. 11). The idol has no life in it, but only the form and place its makers give it. It therefore has no power to speak, instruct, save or judge.

Nevertheless, what idolatry offers is highly attractive. By reversing the relationship of humans in the image God confers, humans have a god of their choosing, a designer deity.

Idolatry and lie

This reversal of relationship involves idolatry as telling a 'story' about God, but a fictitious one. The 'making' is a 'making up'. The Bible strongly develops this motif that idolatry is human fiction as 'lie' (Isa. 44:20). The idol lies about God by likening something to the unique uncreated God. Thus Isaiah 40 – 55 insists the 'nations' are idolatrous and proclaims God is incomparable to anything within the created order.[11] This contrasts with depicting him as a golden bull, something created (Exod. 32:4). But idolatry equally lies about God by asserting what is not true of him – for example that he requires human sacrifice.

Alternatively the fiction may attribute divine characteristics to something we create (divine rights of judgment to 'the Party', or divine omniscience to 'the Market'). A subtler version of the latter obtains where God is 'written out' as a speaking character. A culture whose views on morality and meaning are so strongly shaped by the media risks writing God out, since it chooses others than God as its defining truth-tellers. The first and second commandments reflect these forms of fiction (no *other* gods, and no *made thing* to be worshipped, even if it allegedly represents Yahweh).

Such idolatrous lies falsify a person, obscuring and distorting who the person is. The lie destroys true relationship as humans stop relating to God as he knows himself to be, instead treating him as they have fashioned him. Idolatry strongly expresses human sovereignty, but sovereignty at the expense of true relationship. God is treated not as a person we encounter (a 'Thou' in Martin Buber's terms), but as an object (an 'It');[12] indeed, a plastic, malleable one. Buber writes 'The *Thou* meets me.'[13] Imposing identities on other persons risks not 'meeting' them

– preventing them being a 'Thou'. The biblical God reveals he is not infinitely plastic and malleable. To treat him as that involves counterfeit, not true, relationship with him. The price for being makers of God, albeit attractive, is that the God we make is not real. The true God is hidden, because we attempt to reduce him to an 'It' of our choosing. Buber notes, 'This self-hood . . . steps in between and shuts off from us the light of heaven.'[14] Thus the Bible does not primarily condemn pre-exilic Israel for materialism (or secularism), but for idolatry. This matters. First it helps us recognize secularism and other avowedly a-religious or atheistic belief structures not as non-religious, but as covertly religious. The pressing question becomes 'What eclipses the true God?' That might be express worship of 'another' god. It might be ascription of ultimate, God-eclipsing, worth to particular values, such as the inspiring mottoes of European secularists ('liberty, equality, fraternity' or 'truth, beauty and freedom'). More darkly, it might perhaps be the minimal position of 'eat, drink and be merry for tomorrow we die', born of the false belief that God is absent or indifferent. These self-proclaimed a-religious systems carry a religious weight.[15] Thus a primary apologetic and evangelistic question concerns a person's particular idolatry: What has eclipsed God for them?

Second, the concept of idolatry provides the biblical framework for analysing explicitly spiritual beliefs, doing so in the context of truth and falsehood. This contrasts with the Romantic influence on European culture, which stresses the subjective force and immediacy of experience, and its consequent authenticity. The Bible endorses that paganism may provide 'spiritual' experiences,[16] but the criterion of evaluation is not intensity of experience or emotion, but attestation to the God revealed by Jesus Christ.[17] The shift is subtle, but enormously significant. Christians in early centuries met many religions in a world hungry for religious experience and they normally evaluated these things within the framework provided by the analytical tool of idolatry. For their pains these Christians were dubbed godless and irreligious, indeed atheists, the counterpart of today's charge that Christians are spiritually imperceptive.

Christians then did not, of course, succumb to the view that spiritual experience was largely self-authenticating. They sought to uphold the truth about God, and were aware that by losing the concept of idolatry, which implies that one can lie about God, one loses the ability to tell the truth about God. And truth mattered. Abolishing the concept of lie abolishes the concept of truth, including the truth that humans are sheep without a shepherd, which motivates compassion, and hence evangelism. The concern for truth is not simply calculating, rational and cerebral. Biblical love and biblical truth go hand in hand.[18] A biblical love for the lost cannot be divorced from awareness that idolatry is possible. Without idolatry, there are no lost. Thus the second objection noted above, that the concept of idolatry breeds spiritual blindness, is unfounded. The concept of idolatry opens up spiritual perception regarding being truthful to and about the God who is worshipped.

However, the wish to discard idolatry as an analytical tool is unsurprising. Idolatry necessarily introduces truth and falsehood, a highly threatening distinction for fallen humanity. Humans do not by nature desire the truth about God. Jesus describes the opposition of his antagonists in John chapter 8 as arising not from simply failing intellectually, either to know the facts or to grasp his case, but from just the fact his teaching is the truth (8:45). This tendency continues within the redeemed community: people, Paul predicts, will prefer teaching they like to teaching that is true (2 Tim. 4:3ff.).

Despite great criticisms, then, the analytical tool of idolatry is central for today's church, for examining both our general culture, and also our own practices. We are strikingly prone to evaluating services on whether they make those who do not believe 'at home'; evangelistic tools on the acceptability of content to non-believers and simple numerical 'results'; sermons on whether people 'felt guilty'; and pastoral work as 'successful' because the person counselled felt there was empathy. Such things may be highly desirable. Yet making them final criteria of judgment departs from the category of true/false on which idolatry concentrates. Whether our teaching and practice is idolatrous should be a primary question, especially since indwelling sin makes it so naturally one of the last.

Idolatry and harlotry

Idolatry, then, counterfeits the true relation between worshipper and worshipped. Old and New Testaments portray that true relationship as marriage: Yahweh to Israel and Christ to the church. The marriage imagery conveys intensity (especially because of the sexual dimension), highlighted in Hosea 1 – 3. This impression of intensity is confirmed elsewhere, notably in the Song of Songs, whose refrains warn of the power of human marital love[19] and celebrate its mutuality.[20] Holy marriage also involves a conformity between bride and groom. In Hosea 2 and 3 Israel is expected ultimately to conform to Yahweh's conception of marriage, not hers; and in the New Testament, Christians pattern themselves on Christ, and indeed are expected to conform their lives to the Trinity's mutual life.[21]

Thus the worshipping relation involves profound attachment and conformity between worshipper and worshipped. It is therefore enormously important that idolatry is so strongly depicted as harlotry. Physical adultery or immorality parodies marriage, as gifts God intended for marriage are perverted. Spiritual harlotry likewise parodies holy marriage, as Israel becomes embroiled with other gods. She displays quasi-marital devotion to them (e.g. Hos. 2:5) and two considerations about this adulterous parody of marriage are particularly pertinent. First, the sexual imagery (e.g. Ezek. 23) suggests the idolatrous relation is compulsive, carrying insatiability and addiction. Second, there is the developing conformity between worshipper and worshipped: in Ezekiel 22 Israel's standards are increasingly those of the idols. A people become like their gods, predictably, given the addictive, compulsive nature of the relationship. Outside the biblical material, just this aspect of relationships is emphasized by Buber: that as an 'I', that with which I am in relation shapes me.[22]

This is bleakly suggestive in several directions. First, S. P. Huntington suggested that with the end of the Cold War, conflict would now occur on a 'civilizational' level.[23] In biblical terms one might describe such conflicts as battles between conflicting idolatries. This is illuminating, because it explains that commitment to a 'civilization' is not always going to be 'voluntarist' or explicable on purely 'rational' bases. In the context of Huntington's model the addictive and conforming elements imply a further dynamic, even an intensification, to civilizational conflict, despite globalization.

The third objection above, that the analytical tool of idolatry breeds bigotry and arrogance, is answered by the positive contribution the tool makes in a cosmopolitan setting, recognizing spiritual dynamics rather than ignoring them. Ignoring these dynamics risks understating the problems of conflicting civilizations (or idolatries). Dropping idolatry as an analytical tool can tacitly assume that ideological commitment can be readily changed, which is far from clear. This particularly applies to Christians' relations with the world.

If idolatry indeed contains accelerating addictive tendencies, then rapprochement between Christians and the world appears remote. Rather, Jesus' warnings of a 'religious' antipathy to Christ's people are underlined (John 15:18 – 16:3, especially John 16:2).

Applications also arise over theological trends. English churches increasingly think God's justice has no retributive element in the sense of moral desert.[24] Apart from what this entails for the cross,[25] the question arises, what kind of God is it whose justice lacks any retributive element? If the worship relation involves a people conforming to its god, then the contours of our God predict in some ways our future character and contribution. Thus Christians have consistently tried to contribute to debates over penal policy and justice. In future that Christian contribution will not feature a moral desert. A Christian influenced by this view of God might feel unhappy about extenuating or exacerbating moral circumstances.

C. S. Lewis long ago pointed out the paradox in this discussion of punishment.[26] Far from leading to lighter punishments, the non-desert schools of punishment may lead to indefinite extension of punishment, or 'cure' as it is termed in Lewis's novel. Treatment continues until cure.

In dispute resolution more generally, the notion of mercy becomes problematic. Mercy characteristically has been seen as an undeserved kindness. It implies action going beyond what is normally demanded or expected in a particular relationship. God shows mercy in Jeremiah 3:12 in inviting Israel to return, when, for her faithlessness, she deserves judgment. An act of mercy thus involves recognition of wrongdoing within a relationship – hence the prayer of Luke 18:13, where the tax collector pleads not his innocence and works but God's character. Moral desert is integral here: mercy is where one does not get one's moral deserts. If there are no moral deserts, there is no such mercy.

Naturally, this goes beyond our relations with God. We are expressly told to be merciful as our heavenly Father is (Luke 6:36). Changing his mercy alters ours too. There are here profound consequences for human relations, which are marked, given the consequences of the fall, by mutual fault. It is not uncommon in counselling to find that parties need to forgive one another. However, it is extremely hard to see how to frame forgiveness without invoking a mercy which involves moral desert. On this basis the Christian contribution to, for example, marriage guidance, would not find it easy to speak of forgiveness.

Idolatry, demonolatry and the victory of Christ

Losing the concept of idolatry also affects how we see Christ's victory. One way the New Testament views salvation is as Christ's victory over idolatries that enslave men and women.[27] Here the parody is that of understatement, by denying that Christ had an enemy to fight. It is important here to see just who is conquered. Idols, be they physical or abstract, are in a sense 'nothing'. They are not the gods their worshippers imagine. But the Bible insists that behind idolatry stand demons. Idolatrous sacrifice is ultimately offered to demons (1 Cor. 10:20a) and idolatry brings the worshipper into relation with demons (1 Cor. 10:20b–21).[28] The behind-the-scenes exploiter of idolatry is the demonic, providing us as idolaters with a relationship whose true nature we do not normally suspect, either in its deceitfulness or its evil. It is, no doubt, possible to perceive that one is supernaturally enslaved.

C. Arnold suggests that the world of hostile supernatural powers was all too visible to the inhabitants of Asia Minor,[29] a view paralleled by some missionary descriptions of animist attitudes in Papua New Guinea. It is equally possible to be enslaved and be unaware of it. The question must be faced whether this better describes the modernized West, where perceptions of reality are so strongly shaped by powerful visual media, and values readily situated in a life of wealth and health, a carnival culture, to paraphrase Mikhail Bakhtin.[30] This too is an apt continuation of Genesis 3, and highlighted by Jesus' depiction of Satan as the ultimate liar (John 8:44) and the 'false' believers there as liars too (John 8:55). But in vanquishing a person's idolatry, Jesus vanquishes a covert demonolatry, a victory indeed.

Understating Christ's victory profoundly alters a believer's relationship with God. If the cross marks a minimal victory, then the effusive gratitude of Ephesians 1:3 seems exaggerated. If the cross is not a signal victory, why hope that God can deal with other problems, let alone judge? Again, this is a far cry from the beliefs of the early church. There the cross was seen as victory precisely because idolatry was vanquished, thereby also vanquishing demonolatry.[31] The cross thus gave a real hope for which men and women would die.[32]

Moreover, the character of Christ's deliverance alters. It is not simply a realization that idolatry is false and that the truth can be told of God. The link with the demonic underlines the ethical evil of idolatry and portrays false worship not simply as an intellectual error needing correction, but a sin requiring repentance and forgiveness. Understanding idolatry better deepens understanding of the forgiveness Christ won. Hence a Christian sees himself or herself as, among other things, a rescued idolater. Such a self-understanding does not necessarily breed arrogance and contempt (the third objection to the tool of idolatry noted above), but can promote humility about oneself, gratitude to one's rescuer and concern for those still needing rescue.

Epilogue

The practice of idolatry persists today. Properly understood, the analytical tool of idolatry is relevant, spiritually perceptive and breeds true compassion for others, as well as humility. The concept of idolatry helps us to see the spiritually counterfeit, for it exposes a parody of true spiritual relationship. Idolatrous practice parodies the relation of creation by reversing it, with humans making the god of their choice; it parodies true worship in true relationship by offering a lying fiction; it parodies the relation of holy marriage by offering unholy harlotry; and parodies the victory of Christ by understating it. Tertullian memorably envisaged idolatry as fraud.[33] It is doubly so, defrauding God of his glory, and humanity of true relationship. It cruelly counterfeits real spiritual currency: spiritually, it is 'funny money'.

Understanding idolatry is to understand oneself and one's world. For a Christian is a member of Idolaters Anonymous. We were idolaters, exchanging the truth of God for some lie or another, and the tug of idolatry persists. This fundamental idea was greatly used by the early church, but that was a church that tried to use the Bible's categories for analysis and did not exchange the truth of God for a lie. The price for that was an acute awareness that they were not at ease in their old world, 'with an alien people clutching their gods'.[34] We Western Christians, perhaps, do not find the people alien, because we fight shy of finding their gods alien. As we lose the concept of idolatry, we will be all too at ease.

Notes

1. *Cambridge Papers*, Volume 11, Number 1 (Cambridge: Jubilee Centre, March 2002). Reproduced with permission.

2. C. S. Lewis, *The Screwtape Letters* (London: Fount, 1942), Letter 1.

3. Whereas Article 2(1) of the 'UN Declaration on the Elimination of All Forms of Intolerance and of Discrimination Based on Religion or Belief' reads, 'No one shall be subject to discrimination by any State, institution, group of persons, or person on the grounds of religion or other belief.' G.A. res. 36/55, 36 UN GAOR Supp. (No. 51) at 171, UN Doc. A/36/684, 1981.

4. *On Idolatry* 1. Idolatry is a stock reference point in Justin Martyr (e.g. *First Apology* 9) and the Greek apologists. Athanasius devoted a monograph to it and the tradition is continued to some extent in Augustine's *The City of God*.

5. Articulated in the Nicene Creed of 325 and the Niceno-Constantinopolitan Creed of 381, but note too from this period the writings of Athanasius, Hilary of Poitiers and the Cappadocians.

6. Chalcedonian Definition 451, and note the writings of Cyril of Alexandria and Leo the Great as well as, later, Leontius of Byzantium and Maximus the Confessor.

7. Cf. Athanasius, *Contra Gentes* 28.

8. Note here Exod. 3:14.

9. *On Idolatry* 3–4.

10. Quoted by C. E. M. Joad, in *God and Evil* (London: Faber and Faber, 1942), p. 59.

11. Isa. 40:18, 25; 44:7; 46:5, 9. The cognate concept is that there is no god besides God: Isa. 43:11–12; 45:14, 21; 46:9.

12. See e.g. M. Buber, *I and Thou*, 2nd edn (Edinburgh: T. & T. Clark, 1958), p. 12.

13. Buber, *I and Thou*, p. 11.

14. M. Buber, *The Eclipse of God*, 2nd edn (Atlantic Highlands, NJ: Humanities Press International, 1988), p. 129.

15. Michael Burleigh's *The Third Reich: A New History* (London: Macmillan, 2000) examines Nazism as a religious phenomenon, even while in some respects it eschewed such a characterization.

16. Notably 1 Cor. 12:1–2.

17. Cf. 1 Cor. 12:3.

18. Truth and love are remarkably interwoven in 2 John 1–6.

19. Song 2:7; 3:5; 8:4.

20. Song 2:16; 6:3; 7:10.

21. John 17:21–22. However, the Trinity remains a pattern. Certain differences remain between the uncreated relations of the triune God and the relations of created beings.

22. Buber, *I and Thou*, pp. 15–16.

23. S. P. Huntington, *The Clash of Civilizations and the Remaking of World Order* (New York: Pocket, 1998).

24. See e.g. some of the essayists in J. Goldingay (ed.), *Atonement Today* (London: SPCK, 1995).

25. Classically it is a recipe for repudiating penal substitution.

26. *That Hideous Strength*; cf. C. S. Lewis, 'The Humanitarian Theory of Punishment', in *Twentieth Century: An Australian Quarterly Review* 3 (1949), p. 3. Also D. B. Knox, 'Punishment as Retribution', *Interchange* 1 (1967), pp. 5–8.

27. Notably 1 Thess. 1:9–10.

28. See too Deut. 32:17 and Ps. 106:37.

29. C. Arnold, *Power and Magic: The Concept of Power in Ephesians*, 2nd edn (Grand Rapids: Baker, 1997), p. 167.

30. M. Bakhtin, *Rabelais and His World* (Bloomington: Indiana University Press, 1984).

31. Again, the early writers were emphatic on the link between idolatry and demonolatry.

32. Athanasius, *De Incarnatione*.

33. *On Idolatry* 1.

34. T. S. Eliot, *The Journey of the Magi*.

21. BEYOND SCRUTINY? MINORITIES, MAJORITIES AND POSTMODERN TYRANNY[1]

When you read a detective novel, there is always a sense of unease when you meet characters who are somehow beyond scrutiny. What puts them there? How do they stay there? In modern Western life two assumptions sometimes render the decisions of majorities and groups beyond scrutiny.

Majoritarian supremacy

First, there is the assumption that majorities, whether in a legislature or a church governing body, intrinsically carry legitimacy. They can properly adjudicate on what schools should teach, what outrages public decency or what a denomination's 'official line' is. It is easy to feel 'Perhaps I must accept the voice of the majority.' We will call this 'majoritarian supremacy'.

Many Western Christians certainly see democratic institutions as biblically appropriate, putting flesh on the equality of humans alike made in God's image (Gen. 1:26ff.). Further, the dispersal of power in democratic processes mitigates the temptations fallen humans face in holding power. But does that entail majoritarian supremacy, with its implication that there is no appeal from the voice of the majority?

Amoral equivalence

The second assumption, very differently, argues that acts of power are essentially morally equal. Is democracy necessarily the antithesis of tyranny? Virginia Woolf famously commented that Great Britain and Hitler's Germany were little different. Often, of course, statements suggesting regimes are really the 'same' express strong disapproval as strikingly as possible. Sometimes, however, they express the more far-reaching view, that exercises of power are fundamentally equivalent in lying beyond ethical evaluation: they are in the zone of amorality. We will call this 'amoral equivalence'.

Such attitudes predate postmodernism and Foucault's dissection of claims to truth and right as closet exercises of power.[2] Plato's character 'Thrasymachus' claims all regimes exercise power in their own interest.[3] All are like shepherds who fatten sheep for the table, a graphic expression of amoral equivalence.

Amoral equivalence is, of course, contested. Some radical feminists argue that, since Foucault's (or Thrasymachus') analysis renders all exercises of power equivalent, actions by men against women get removed from moral evaluation.

This misgiving underlines the scope of amoral equivalence. If power in the political arena is essentially amoral, then other areas involving power are apparently also amoral. As well as male violence against women, two obvious areas of concern arise for Christians, that of the church and the family. Is a pastor who 'leads strongly' really different from one who bullies a congregation? Should we distinguish between parental authority and parental authoritarianism?

Naturally, Christians recognize some degree of equivalence: all have sinned (Rom. 3:23) and our exercises of power are alike imperfect actions by sinful people. Yet we do not normally regard all imperfect actions by sinful people as completely equivalent. The father who tries to love rather than exasperate his children, for all his imperfection, does not seem comparable with the father who finds a certain piquancy in his children's exasperation. If they really were amorally equivalent, injunctions about using authority after the fall seem pointless.

Majoritarian supremacy and amoral equivalence both tend to put certain acts of authority above scrutiny, silencing criticism. This is especially pertinent for Western biblical Christians faced with being minorities in their states and sometimes in their denominations. How should one react to entrenched minority status? What legitimates continued dissent or moral disapproval on issues such as euthanasia or abortion once the majority has decided?

One tool earlier Christians used to examine questions of authority was that of tyranny. This paper briefly re-examines that earlier framework, looks back to its biblical foundations and considers how it might be usefully extended in our current situation.

Background

We tend to hear 'tyranny' exclusively as a term of abuse rather than of clarification. It is useful, therefore, to retrace some earlier Christians' employment of the term.

'Tyrant' comes from the Greek world of the seventh century BC, and was applied to a particular kind of ruler, one dominating the state through his own abilities 'rather than by perceived conceptions of right'.[4] Where the kings of Hesiod and Homer were ideally lawgivers and upholders of justice as well as military leaders, tyrants' relationship with *dikē* (right) was more ambiguous. Some, playing on the need to protect citizens from oppression, had popular support. Equally, though, tyranny was associated with severity towards opponents and perceived rivals. Aristotle and Plato in the classical period place tyranny in a general taxonomy of schemes of government, largely maintaining its pejorative associations. Interestingly, Xenophon in the *Hiero* could by then depict the tyrant as fundamentally unhappy, fearful of the patriotic assassin, unsure whether any truly loved him. Plato, who postulates a parallel between the city state and the human individual, suggests an individual can have a tyrannical mindset and an 'internal' tyranny.

Christian adoption of tyranny ideas

Later, Christian theologians take up and modify some of this. During the Arian controversies of the fourth century Athanasius of Alexandria and Hilary of Poitiers castigated the emperor Constantius for his 'tyrannical' activities in oppressing upholders of the Nicene Creed. However, extended discussion of tyranny from a Christian perspective starts with John of Salisbury's *Policraticus* (1159). Our discussion centres on him, despite the wealth of material from Protestants in and after the Reformation.[5] For John of Salisbury, like Plato, tyranny is not confined to the state. Tyranny can occur in state, church and family.[6] Each features relations of authority, which are ultimately rooted in delegations from the source of all authority, God. Accordingly, for John, not all rulers are tyrants. Authority alone does not excite John's ire, but its corruption. John does not accept the amoral equivalence argument.

The corruption of authority into tyranny follows from John's understanding that all human authority is ultimately rooted in God, and therefore has limits set by him. Tyranny becomes associated with defiance of God's laws.[7] Within the church, such tyranny merits non-recognition; within the family, action by the state; and, on the conventional reading of *Policraticus*, tyranny within the state legitimates the tyrant's death.

Later discussion understandably focuses on political tyrannicide, which Aquinas appears implicitly to endorse,[8] although the Council of Constance forbids it.[9] Of course, this relates to the penalties tyranny deserves, not what counts as tyranny. The *Policraticus* thesis that tyranny relates to repudiation of the constraints of law is accepted. Thus the Renaissance writer Coluccio Salutati writes:

> We conclude, therefore, that a tyrant is either one who usurps a government, having no legal title for his rule, or one who governs *superbe* ['autocratically' seems the best translation] or rules unjustly or does not observe laws or equity; just as, on the other hand, he is a lawful prince upon whom the right to govern is conferred, who administers justice and maintains the laws.[10]

Salutati highlights that tyranny is not confined to the typical case of someone without title to authority seizing it. Salutati covers that case but goes further to include someone with lawful title abusing or exceeding what he has. Salutati also envisages a lawful prince being positively obliged to maintain the laws. Hence a prince's *omissions* in upholding law are also culpable, even though such a prince might look merely 'liberalizing'.

However, can tyranny be rectified, either by the usurper acquiring just title subsequently, or by the prince who has not maintained the laws having his non-maintenance subsequently ratified? In answer, Salutati distinguishes between states with and without an overlord.[11] The state *without* an overlord can, he reasons, confer legitimate title on a usurper. The rationale is clear: the state gives what it has the right to give. Equally, then, the prince with lawful title who has not maintained his state's laws can have his failures corrected, for it is the state's right to amend its laws.

Yet the state *with* an overlord has no such title to give. Since it has an overlord, it cannot sanctify the usurper, nor legitimate one who fails to maintain the laws. This means a prince may have popular endorsement both for his 'title' and for his liberal 'maintenance' of the laws, yet still be a tyrant because he has exceeded the terms of authority delegated to him. This thinking does not, then, unqualifiedly accept the majoritarian supremacy argument.

Alexis de Tocqueville's proposal that there can be a 'tyranny of the majority' becomes relevant here.[12] De Tocqueville's terms of 'tyranny of the majority' sound paradoxical – democracies are sometimes thought inherently non-tyrannical.

He observed, however, that 'democratic' majorities could significantly oppress minorities, indulging in characteristic tyrannical activities of suppression and expropriation. Moreover, this could all, in a democracy, be apparently 'legal', since a thoroughgoing democratic state would subordinate all avenues of redress and protection to the majority.[13] As de Tocqueville was writing *Democracy in America* (1835–9), native Americans were indeed suffering expropriation and ethnic cleansing by a democratic state.

British Christians, perhaps, have not always paid de Tocqueville sufficient attention. However, the Roman Catholic J. V. Schall goes beyond de Tocqueville in commenting critically on 'democratic tyranny'.[14] Schall argues we must now recognize a new variety of tyranny alongside such obvious versions as Hitler or Stalin. This new category carries, in the West at least, a distinctive form: 'The danger of democratic tyranny lies in precisely the inability to recognise what is good and what is evil.'[15] This inability Schall describes is naturally close to the view that all power is amorally equivalent.

In de Tocqueville's terms, a democratic majority that denies discrimination is possible between good and evil very plausibly seems unconstrained. John of Salisbury might comment too that cultures or majorities that deny such discrimination is possible do indeed defy law, specifically God's law, and teeter, therefore, for all their democratic credentials, on the brink of tyranny.

Tyranny within a biblical framework

God as ultimate overlord

A key feature of the foregoing argument about the applicability of tyranny concepts is that our structures of authority fall into the category Salutati describes as states with overlords. Several considerations are relevant, starting with creation.

God's creative work is strongly associated with ownership. Psalm 24:1–2 gives a classic description:

> The earth is the LORD's, and everything in it,
>   the world, and all who live in it;
> for he founded it upon the seas
>   and established it on the waters.[16]

Psalm 24 depicts God's kingship, but starts with God's ownership of the cosmos, basing that ownership (the connective 'for' starting v. 2) on his work in creation.

Such notions of ownership are foreign, indeed offensive, to our current culture. Belonging to another hardly fits with current stresses on autonomy. Yet Psalm 24 indicates that God is entitled to legislate for every human being irrespective of that human's consent. God's right to rule does not depend on consent, either of the individual or the masses, unlike our paradigm ideas of political authority deriving from popular mandates. Shatteringly, given our cultural assumptions, God's rule might be unpopular but still legitimate, his laws disliked yet still valid.

Against this backdrop of universal ownership, a pattern of delegated authority on God's terms becomes discernible. First, and most obviously, humankind is given dominion over creation. Yet this dominion is not absolute. (Thus Gen. 9:1–6 reserves the animal's blood, indicating that its life was not given by humans to be taken by humans, but given by God.)

Second, dominion between humans politically is also seen as a gift by God. Nebuchadnezzar illustrates this: his pretension to have built Babylon himself (Dan. 4:30) is starkly exposed by his reduction to powerlessness and madness (Dan. 4:33), while his recovery is interpreted as God's restoring his kingdom (Dan. 4:2, 34–37; cf. Dan. 2:21).

Certainly this raises acute questions about providence and theodicy when confronted with some of the regimes that have disfigured human life. Yet the biblical witness is that such regimes have no authority independent of God, and therefore remain accountable to him.

Third, authority in the church is also delegated and therefore limited. Paul sees limits even to apostolic authority: he himself cannot alter the gospel (Gal. 1:8), and he opposes the implicit compromises of his fellow-apostle Peter (Gal. 2:11). This must be stressed. Even if one granted 'apostolic' status to individuals or to synods and councils (a version of 'apostolic succession'), this still would not confer authority to alter the apostles' canonical teaching. For they themselves had no such authority.

Similar patterns occur with the New Testament presbyterate. A presbyter must 'hold firmly to the trustworthy message as it has been taught, so that he can encourage others by sound doctrine and refute those who oppose it' (Titus 1:9, NIV). Presbyters, then, are constrained as to their beliefs, and have duties comparable to Salutati's prince maintaining the laws: duties of teaching sound doctrine while refuting false teaching.[17]

Fourth, patterns of authority include the family. Ephesians 6:1–3 sets out children's duties of obedience, while Ephesians 6:4 clarifies that paternal authority (judging from Proverbs, this duty also applies to mothers) has constraints; notably the parent's right is not to bring a child up simply as he sees fit, but rather in the teaching of God. Obviously within this family sphere, many

Christians see duties of authority and responsibility placed on husbands (Eph. 5:22–33;[18] Col. 3:18–19; Titus 2:4–5; 1 Peter 3:1–7). This, too, is a constrained authority since a husband must mirror and emulate Christ.

Fifth, all human authority must be placed within the framework of God's final plan for the cosmos, to bring all things under the headship of Christ (Eph. 1:10). Any human exercise of authority must then be seen within Christ's over-lordship. There are no free-standing areas of authority where humans somehow remain unaccountable.

Clearly, then, the biblical material countenances neither amoral equivalence, nor majoritarian supremacy. It is worth, though, pausing on the striking extension of earlier reflections on tyranny, that failures to exercise authority can be criticized as tyrannical.

Extended concepts of tyranny

Abuse of power is trenchantly criticized in Israel's history – warned about in Samuel's descriptions of kingship (1 Sam. 8:10–18) and instantiated in the actions of Saul, Solomon, the Assyrians, and so on. Worldwide, such abuses continue. They exceed the biblical mandates for state authority, so that on occasion particular pieces of legislation should not be obeyed (Dan. 6) and considerable Christian thought (see Thomas Aquinas[19]) regards armed response in such situations as not necessarily sinfully seditious but as up-holding law.

Nevertheless, refusing to fulfil God-given responsibilities is also criticized. Eli's failure as priest and father to discipline his sons results in judgment (notably 1 Sam. 3:13). David's failure as king and father to discipline and judge Amnon for the rape of Tamar (2 Sam. 13), and Absalom for the murder of Amnon (2 Sam. 14) alike receive implicit criticism, as David's function as law-maintaining king is first parodied by Absalom's vendetta and then nearly displaced in Absalom's rebellion. In the New Testament Revelation 2:18–29 warns the church of Thyatira against tolerating the teaching of 'Jezebel'. No doubt the failures of responsibility were popular in one sense. Yet the holders of responsibility do not have discretion to refuse to exercise their authority. Their refusal defies God's law, as firmly as the more obvious abusers of power.

Thus John of Salisbury's root contention that authority properly derives from God is well taken biblically, as is his point that delegated authority can be abused. The gift of authority is no carte blanche. Unilateral alteration of the contours of God-given authority is not possible, even by popular demand. 'Tyranny' can usefully be extended beyond its more obvious applications.

Applications of extended concepts of tyranny

John of Salisbury envisaged tyranny in three spheres: political, ecclesiastical and familial. It is worth examining these spheres in the light of extended ideas of tyranny.

Politically, a particularly acute example of the state's benevolently meant but tyrannical activity is in education. In the UK, the state's assumptions of responsibility in areas of sex education and 'good citizenship', even if well intentioned, risk being tyrannical both as it 'relieves' parents of responsibilities that properly lie with them and as it introduces its own agenda of good citizenship. In France, the prohibition of certain styles of dress in schools again introduces a principle by which the state can displace the parent in a child's upbringing.

Here, education can manifest a double 'tyranny': that of parents refusing responsibilities of instruction on the grounds the state will discharge them, and that of the state inculcating values of liberal secular pluralism.

Again, the UK is seeing significant erosion of Christian freedoms: Christian freedom of association is potentially impacted by recent legislation, making employment of specifically Christian staff more difficult. Christian freedom of speech is pressured by categorizing the public statement of some Christian moral positions as hate crimes (witness the way the Chief Constable of Cheshire 'publicly rebuked' the Bishop of Chester over his statements that counselling was available for those facing homosexual temptation[20]).

These cases highlight that Christians cannot give unqualified commitments to obey majorities. If they did, that would amount to saying the majority has no 'overlord' and either derives its power legitimacy from something other than God or simply from itself. Such absolute commitments amount to complicity in the tyranny – to use the word in an extended sense – of majoritarian supremacy.

Ecclesiastically, the recent agonies of the Church of England reveal two proposals relying on majoritarian supremacy. One is that denominations should mirror the values of the surrounding culture. Another is that Christians today may reach new understandings from their own general experience despite conflicts with expressed biblical truth. Appeals are often made here to 'seeking the mind of Christ' and 'being guided by the Spirit' (appealing to John 16:13).

Both proposals employ popular consent for legitimation and, characteristically today, feature liberalizing effects. Sexual ethics are perhaps most obvious, but equally important are the pressures to drop teaching perceived as obnoxious, such as the uniqueness of Christ's saving work. The mood, then, is to depict these changes as liberal in intent and popularly warranted.

However, authority within the church derives from God and is given on his terms. The British public does not satisfy the criteria of teaching given in Titus 1:9, nor do media commentators. Clearly then, they should not have teaching authority within God's church, which is what the first proposal amounts to.

Similar considerations apply to the contention that current church members can formulate what they think is the mind of Christ. This ostensibly submits to Christ's guidance, but such 'guidance' seems empty since Christ is allowed no voice but theirs. This sits poorly with Paul's understanding of his apostleship, since he does envisage external constraints on what he can teach. The appeal to John 16:13 decontextualizes the verse from John's general teaching about the Spirit, which is that he witnesses to Christ and does so consistently with the teaching of the incarnate Christ: John 14:26; 15:26. It does not justify claiming the Spirit himself contradicts what he says elsewhere in Scripture. Calvin was surely right to see such arguments as ecclesiastical tyranny, for all the consensualist, liberalizing stances.[21]

Turning to the family, here too an extended tyranny is discernible. English educational philosophy currently tends strongly to refuse to let children be children. Thus, argues Melanie Phillips, so-called child-led educational strategies impose responsibilities on children which they cannot meet, while allowing adults to refuse responsibility.[22] Clearly, child-led ideology appears to maximize individual choice and freedom and seems liberal. However, it is tyrannical in its inconsistency with biblical expectations of parental responsibility for instruction.

The analysis of John of Salisbury can profitably be extended in one further way, though. John analysed tyranny in political, ecclesiastical and familial spheres. His logic suggests a fourth sphere, that of the individual. For here too the concept of overlord applies. If we are owned by God (for he made us), then those rights of ownership that underpin discussion of delegated authority socially must also entitle him to delegate the terms on which the individual may dispose of herself. This opens up, as Plato saw so long before, the prospect of internal tyranny, again a tyranny marked by 'liberalism' as laws of self-control we should maintain are dispensed with. Similar understandings lurk within Bunyan's *Holy War*, where the city of Mansoul is alienated from its true overlord.

Contemporary notions of individual autonomy make this highly relevant. In the Byzantine Empire, the emperor alone was said to be *autokratōr*, self-ruler. The individualism of the postmodern West implies a society of *autokratōres*. For this is the spirit articulated by J. S. Mill's essay *On Liberty* and its claim that the individual is the sovereign of himself or herself.[23]

Such self-tyranny is obviously attractive – one can legitimate a more liberal moral regime for oneself. Moreover, the temptation to collusion and complicity, to acknowledge the legitimacy of another's self-tyranny, is also obvious. For in acknowledging the legitimacy of self-tyranny, one has a claim on support for one's own.

Conclusion

We have examined the tyrannical implications of majoritarian supremacy and amoral equivalence in that both imply rejection of an overlord. Yet humanity's inclination is to repudiate its divine overlord, and the moral authority of majoritarian supremacy offers powerful justifications for this. Thus Philip Pullman's trilogy *His Dark Materials* opens up the prospect of a 'Republic of Heaven'. It sounds grand, seemingly egalitarian, democratic and liberal, and articulates, judging by its popularity with the intelligentsia, a common hope. Such rationalizations are hard to resist in our culture, but the material we have examined enables us to see Pullman's vision for what it is – a defence of tyranny. That defence of tyranny is marked in the trilogy by the death of the celestial overlord, a very graphic way of abolishing human accountability. But there Pullman's work (unconsciously?) approaches reality, for humans actually did put our celestial overlord to death in our murder of God the Son. The mistake is to forget that the Son was raised, and to accept the illusion of a 'Republic of Heaven' rather than the reality of the kingdom of the Son.

Notes

1. *Cambridge Papers*, Volume 13, Number 2 (Cambridge: Jubilee Centre, June 2000). Reproduced with permission.
2. See e.g. 'Truth and Power', in C. Gordon (ed.), *Power/Knowledge* (New York: Pantheon, 1980), pp. 109–133.
3. *Republic*, Book 1.
4. J. F. McGlew, *Tyranny and Political Culture in Ancient Greece* (Ithaca and London: Cornell University Press, 1993), p. 52.
5. E.g. Samuel Rutherford's *Lex Rex*, 1644, and the *Vindiciae, contra Tyrannos*, 'Stephanus Junius Brutus' (a pseudonym), 1579.
6. *Policraticus* VIII.17.
7. *Policraticus* IV.1; VIII.17.
8. In *Summa Theologiae* 2a2ae.42.2 resisting the tyrant is not sedition, but a defence of justice.
9. In 1415, Session XV.

10. *De Tyranno* 1.

11. *De Tyranno* 2.

12. *Democracy in America*, trans. Henry Reeve, 2 vols. (repr., New York: Langley, 1841), I.xv.

13. *Democracy in America* I.xv.

14. J. V. Schall, 'A Reflection on the Classical Tractate on Tyranny: The Problem of Democratic Tyranny', *American Journal of Jurisprudence* 41 (1996), pp. 1–19.

15. Schall, 'Reflection', sect. XI.

16. NIV; cf. Pss 89:11; 95:3–5; 100:2–3.

17. Cf. Eph. 4:7–16: the church belongs to Christ, and he gives gifts to preserve its life, ministry and faithfulness in the truth.

18. The argument that Eph. 5:22 deals with 'mutual submission' fits the immediate context poorly, produces inconsistency with the other passages cited, produces eccentric results for Christ's relation with the church and unduly restricts the semantic range of *allēlois* in 5:21. It is accordingly rejected.

19. *Summa Theologiae* 2a2ae.42.2.

20. *The Times*, 11 November 2003.

21. *Institutes* IV.

22. *All Must Have Prizes* (London: Little, Brown, 1996).

23. J. S. Mill, *On Liberty* (London: Penguin, 1974), pp. 68–69.

22. VICTIM CHIC? THE RHETORIC OF VICTIMHOOD[1]

In 2004 Rocco Buttiglione's nomination as a European Commissioner was successfully opposed because of, among other things, his view that homosexual practice was sinful. His 'homophobia' was intolerable to the gay community in particular, which envisaged itself as a victim of his views, even though Buttiglione advocated no public policy based on his opinions.

The rewards of the role of victim emerge from such examples. Successfully projecting oneself or one's group as victim can result in legislative protection, or the barring from certain offices of one's opponents. Such successful projection can deflect criticism and minimize accountability. This role should concern Christians for two reasons: one relating to justice; one relating to temptation.

Concerning justice, such successful posturing as victims risks encouraging a double injustice: the injustice that real victims have not received justice, and the injustice that those who do not deserve compassion as victims have received it. Such inversion of justice naturally concerns Christians. Proverbs 24:11–12 tells us that refusing to act for the oppressed risks God's anger, while Proverbs 24:24 describes the curse on those who state the wicked are innocent.

As for temptation, of course fallen people find not being held accountable tempting. The role, if not the reality, of victim can be richly rewarding.

For these reasons, the strategies by which I might clothe myself with victimhood deserve attention. We start with Stephen Karpman's analysis of some personal relationships as a 'Victim Triangle'.[2]

The Victim Triangle / 'Drama Triangle'

Karpman drew on the framework of Transactional Analysis to describe the Victim Triangle, a triad of relationships. This triangle has three roles – Persecutor, Victim and Rescuer – which Karpman explained using fairy tales. Thus Little Red Riding Hood is a Victim of the wolf, who is her Persecutor, and she needs a Rescuer.

Karpman's Victim Triangle proves an enormously fruitful analytical tool.[3] First, we note that the three roles can be a continuum.[4] Someone may move from Victim to the roles of Persecutor, then Rescuer, before reverting to Victim. A Victim may react to a Rescuer by turning on her, and becoming Persecutor to the erstwhile (perhaps bewildered) Rescuer.[5] The original Victim may be unaware of this role change, but still see himself or herself as Victim. Victims, though, do not always stay Victims.

Second, Rescuers may not be disinterested. They may assume the role for their own reasons, not solely to help Victims.

Third, the roles of the Victim Triangle are unregulated or unlimited. Demands made on Rescuers can be unending, while the Victim role can produce helplessness and dependence. This unlimited aspect of the triangle's roles can make one feel one is 'nothing but a victim', or, of course, that a Persecutor is purely demonic, or can result in someone being so identified as a Rescuer that this consumes the person. The roles can become 'blanket' characterizations of those inhabiting them, totalizing descriptions and exhaust-ive labels. We will see later how significant this totalizing aspect is, especially for those designated Persecutors.

Fourth, while the roles in Karpman's original schema are not necessarily morally loaded,[6] more colloquial uses of victimhood ideas do carry moral judgments.

Who is a victim?

However, this use of the word 'role' suggests one may not genuinely be a victim, but only playing a part.[7] What makes a real victim? First, a victim is someone's target. P. Utgaard discusses real victimhood when dealing with Austria's self-image as a victim of Nazi aggression.[8] He notes that a real victim is the target of another's actions with the intention of harm, and that Austria was not inten-tionally targeted by Nazis for harm as other groups were. Real victimhood presupposes hostile intention by another, and is not something one appropriates for oneself without that intention. This differs from Karpman's Victim Triangle, because there one has (or plays?) the role of Victim without necessarily being the target of someone's hostile intention.

Second, victimhood readily suggests being the undeserved target of another's actions. Utgaard needs supplementing: an armed gunman with hostages is legitimately targeted by police. An important part of current victim discussion is undeservedness or innocence. Thus key works in post-war Japan endorsing Japan as victim stress the purity of their protagonists.[9]

The corollary of these elements of real victimhood is that the victimizer becomes an intentional inflictor of harm on the innocent. Naturally, such a person can readily be pictured as a 'demon', as D. B. MacDonald indicates happened in the characterization of opponents in recent Balkan conflicts.[10] This makes the mantle of victim still more attractive: it proclaims not merely our own innocence but our opponent's guilt. Yet if one may be a Victim within Karpman's Triangle without being a true victim, one may also be a Persecutor without being a true persecutor or victimizer. How roles are claimed or imposed therefore assumes acute significance.

The rightness of retaining victim terms

Obviously some do not deserve the targeting they receive, and not only are they Victims in the limited Karpman role sense, but also in the sense of genuine victim. Self-perception as a victim is clearly not necessarily wrong, and the appropriate biblical expectations when faced with wrongs are, where possible, to right them. Nor is self-perception as victim necessarily simply harmful to oneself or others. Certainly P. C. Vitz notes that perceiving oneself as a victim can encourage passivity,[11] but post-war Austria suggests more positive outcomes remain possible. Austria's self-perception for some while after the Second World War was as a victim of Nazism, but this helped build social consensus about Austrian identity which arguably assisted in nurturing a democratic ethos. This benefited Austria, and its neighbours during the Cold War. Orr likewise notes that some Japanese pacifists saw victim status as generating more energy for pacifism than awareness of having been a victimizer would have done.[12]

The dangers of thinking in victim terms

Nevertheless, victim-thinking brings real dangers. In particular, some current victim-thinking goes hand in hand with ideas of collective innocence or guilt. Controversially, post-war Japan has sometimes been pictured (and perhaps pictured herself) as a victim nation following the A-bomb attacks on Hiroshima and Nagasaki. Several striking tendencies result: first, a tendency to exonerate members of the Japanese armed forces as nationals of a victim nation (notwithstanding war criminal trials: given the scale of Japanese imperial army activity in China and south-east Asia, the trials could be described as token). Second, victim status tends to be extended to subsequent generations and those from areas physically unaffected by the attacks. Third, there is a tendency to seek a preferential voice in disarmament discussions, especially when linked to the idea that Japan's victimhood is unique.

The problem here is how wide the collective innocence has gone. The scant recompense for *real* victims of the Japanese army is less surprising given the nation's *status* as victim. Similarly, argues Utgaard, Austria minimized war indemnities by her successful self-casting as collective victim.

Moreover, as noted above, the corollary of victim status is that the victimizer is evil. Again, the Balkans afford painful recent examples. Even granting certain claims about Kosovar activity before the wars, Serb reaction in propaganda was to impute collective guilt (Serbs were not unique in this) and, with the 'other' safely categorized as demonic and guilty, act without restraint. One's opponents 'deserve' such treatment. Thus MacDonald speaks of the 'construction' by Serbian writers of the myth of 'Serbophobia', 'an anti-Semitism for Serbs, making them victims throughout history'.[13]

This is striking. First, Serb propaganda turned on being a victim as an act of self-definition, not because of concrete actions by others. Second, someone else's perfectly genuine status as victim is assumed (Serbs and Croats courted Israel as a fellow-victim). Third, being victim is not morally neutral, as in Karpman's original models, but in itself indicates moral innocence. Fourth, action against 'Serbophobes' becomes legitimated self-defence, an act of justice. Fifth, refuting the charge of Serbophobia becomes increasingly difficult, since denial is readily construed as a cunning Serbophobe ploy. Sixth, tragically, the myth of Serbophobia can become reality.

Hence the power associated with victim status should not be underestimated. A victim claims to speak with unique authority because he or she has been wronged.

However, this power associated with victim status can be shared. I may cast myself as a 'white knight', succouring the victim against the victimizer. Analysts rightly comment about the Karpman Triangle, that a Rescuer may have mixed motives in assuming that role. For a white knight's actions are also cloaked with innocence and righteousness as he battles the victimizer, and, like the victim, he can enjoy the benefits of non-accountability. The interests of white knight and victim may not be identical, but can coincide, both benefiting from depicting a third party as victimizer deserving punishment. Thus the American Democratic Party has been criticized with elevating victim groups so as to cast itself as a hero in this way.

How does one claim victim status?

However, since such enormous rewards come from victim status, how does one achieve it? MacDonald is disturbing and illuminating on this point. He suggests both Serb and Croat propagandists made highly selective readings of history, suppressing material that qualified understanding the other side as irrevocably seeking one's own destruction. The relationship with a putative victimizer is read in unqualified, simplistic terms: all there is to Croat treatment of Serbs is Serbophobia (and vice versa).

This suggests that, to cast myself as a victim, I characterize another as victimizer. To be best seen as victim, I need another to be seen as victimizer. I am the casting director, awarding myself victim status, the innocent target, and casting my opponent as demonic, evil victimizer. My actions against him are righteous; his against me, wicked. Such self-adjudication is closer to Western thought, and therefore easier, than we might imagine. J.-J. Rousseau, a notable influence on Romanticism, models this process. In answering charges of immorality against him (notably over placing his children in orphanages), Rousseau suggests first, a man's goodness is not weighed by his outward actions: his actions may appear one thing, but in fact are not. Thus in *The Confessions* Rousseau acknowledges acts of theft but insists he is not 'a thief'.

Second, a man is weighed by his intentions and motives. Rousseau knows his intentions were pure, so he acquits himself of wrongdoing.[14] *He* acquits *himself.* No wonder one apologetic work is titled *Rousseau the Judge of Jean-Jacques*: no one else could be the judge. Rousseau has unique access to his inner state, and Rousseau has already ruled out evaluating someone's true character by external actions.

We have already noted that adjudicating oneself a victim carries the corollary that the other is a victimizer. Hence in Rousseau's case: the result of his self-award of innocence was that those who targeted him were therefore, he felt, malicious – he was the victim par excellence of his enemies.

The obvious question is why others should accept such a self-award? Several observations are appropriate. First, modern Western cultures feature very limited agreement over universal norms. Instead, moral evaluations are frequently treated as irretrievably perspectival and relative. This makes objective judgments of innocence difficult but renders a Rousseauvian subjective framework more plausible. Second, collusion becomes tempting: both of us stand to gain by accepting the other's self-acquittal. Third, collusion becomes still more tempting because white-knight status is so advantageous: by accepting your self-award of victimhood, I can be your white knight, thereby legitimating my actions against your victimizer.

Is this theologically or otherwise significant?

Self-righteousness

The victim pattern therefore represents a very significant temptation for human beings. Humans very frequently are genuine victims who do not deserve particular actions aimed at them. However, victim status can be treated as an exhaustive, totalizing account of who someone is. Defining oneself as a victim can involve seeing oneself as innocent and right, not just in relation to a particular relationship or action, but more globally. Seeing oneself globally as a victim lies very close to self-righteousness.

This link with self-righteousness is deeply troubling because the Gospels criticize self-righteousness so heavily. Spiritually, we frequently experience strong temptations to self-acquittal and self-righteousness. The problems with self-righteousness perhaps deserve development. First, self-righteousness tends to stop us realizing we need mercy. The parable of the Pharisee and the tax collector (Luke 18:9–14) illustrates this danger (although neither character portrays himself as a victim). The parable is told to those who trust in their own righteousness while despising others (v. 9). Self-adjudicating oneself as victim and others simply as victimizers can risk this. Self-righteousness accounts for the two different prayers. The tax collector's lack of self-righteousness, his refusal to categorize himself as innocent, means, unlike the Pharisee, he prays for mercy (v. 13). Yet the Pharisee actually does need God's mercy, for all fall short of the glory of God (Rom. 3:23). The Pharisee, like the rest of us, may not deserve a hostile human action directed against him, yet is still not innocent in an absolute sense. Designating myself as victim may hide this from me.

Hence a blanket verdict on myself that I am 'victim' and fundamentally innocent starts to resemble a denial of the helpless bondage of humans in sin. Such a denial implicitly denies Christ's atoning sacrifice for sin was a necessity.[15]

Second, human self-righteousness is associated with hostility to Jesus. Jesus is certainly opposed because of who he says he is, but also because of who he says we are. The persistent opposition described by the Synoptics to Jesus from the self-righteous, the hypocrites, indicates this. In John, Jesus is explicit, pointing out that the 'world' (John's term for humanity in its opposition to God) hates him because he testifies that its deeds are evil (7:7). Jesus does not allow the world to depict itself simply as innocent victim, and the world hates him for it.

Third, our self-righteousness is associated with our self-construction. Conferring self-righteousness on myself is a sovereign judicial act. I define myself. This readily looks like establishing my own identity and nature independently of God. But, of course, to be a victim, I need another to be seen as victimizer. My act of self-acquittal has its corollary in my act of sovereign condemnation of the other as victimizer. Both acts resemble infringements on God's role as creator. For when I define myself so fundamentally, I risk ignoring that I am God's creature and that, as my creator, he directs my purposes and weighs them. Moreover, when I weigh one of his creatures as if judgment belonged to me, I risk usurping God's place as creator-judge of his creation. Similarly, Proverbs counsels restraint on seeking vengeance: it too readily displaces God. Moreover, to maintain my victim role I may acquire an unhealthy interest in maintaining others as victimizers, while the Bible teaches I should seek their salvation and sanctification. My vested interest may be in their guilt, not their justification.

Fourth, self-righteousness can mask the true nature of my actions, lessening suspicion of my motives or any inclination to think I may deceive myself, which Romans 1:18ff. indicates cannot be ignored after the fall. Importantly, my lack of self-criticism, born of self-righteousness, may mask from me that my actions allegedly undertaken in legitimately repelling oppression, are themselves oppressive.

Subversion of justice

The pattern of self-award also risks subverting two very basic principles of justice. One is that no one should be his or her own judge (*nemo iudex in sua causa*). Vitz develops this trenchantly as he describes encounter and recovery groups dealing with recovery from dysfunctional families.[16] There, a child may indeed blame and condemn her parents, thus acting as a judge deciding that she is an innocent victim and the parents guilty victimizers.

The second principle is that both sides of an issue must be heard (*audi alteram partem*). Vitz points out that in the circumstances he describes, the supposed victimizers have no chance to answer their accusers, so that such groups risk resembling a 'typical lynch mob'.[17] To revert to the Balkan case, humans have strong incentives not to abide by this rule of justice. Listening to, say, Croat responses to charges of 'Serbophobia' would mean that Croats were perhaps not victimizers and hence Serbs could not properly be seen solely as victims. This in turn would undercut the legitimation of creating a greater Serbia by force. To be a victim most effectively, I need there to be a victimizer: I have no incentive to listen to their pleas of innocence.

Real difficulties exist here. Doubtless the groups Vitz describes contained children who were real victims. The problem such groups create 'procedurally' is that inequitable processes may make genuine cases of victimhood *more* implausible. Unreal victims cheapen the concept.

An obvious question arises here for UK society. Our culture features two chic victim categories in homophobia and Islamophobia, among others. The difficulty is twofold: first, the relative imprecision of the charge (both 'phobias' are variously defined), and, second, the difficulty of acquitting oneself. These two points are, naturally, related. Thus when Polly Toynbee was nominated 'Most Islamophobic Media Personality of the Year' at the Annual Islamophobia Awards overseen by the Islamic Human Rights Commission in May 2003, one problem was knowing what constituted the 'offence', for the offence itself is unclear.[18] Certainly Toynbee's defence that she wrote the truth seems not to have moderated the Islamic Human Rights Commission's view of her.

Both factors, imprecision of the offence, and the difficulty of answering the charge, are significant. The first relates to the concept of rule of law, the idea that offences and rules should be defined with sufficient clarity for people to be able to guide their conduct. The second, of course, relates to the biblical obligation not to condemn someone unheard (John 7:51).

These justice problems are compounded by collective victim or collective victimizer categories. For one may identify oneself with a victim group, which has awarded itself victim status, and indeed identify another as a member of a victimizer group which has been awarded that status by its putative victims. Yet in this latter case the other might resist both the identification of collective membership and the guilt of the group.

'Victimhood' in practice

Where do we see victim claims at work? Such claims can be seen both in the individual and collective sphere. Vitz and others see some psychological practices as encouraging a victim-mentality culture in the United States, particularly in parent–child relations, to which one might add marriage and work. Yet perhaps greater dangers lie at group or collective levels, because of the ready association with collective guilt and innocence. Perhaps the outstanding 'collective' questions here are whether all current Israelis are victims by virtue of the Shoah (Holocaust), or whether all Palestinians are victims by virtue of Israel's occupation of various territories.

Others see victim rhetoric in domestic politics, on issues of race, gender, class, religion, sexual orientation, and so on, observing how classifying groups as victims enables governments to be white knights, whose interventions to modify social behaviour are ethically justified.[19] Still others observe the corollary, that opponents of such white-knight governments must obviously be in bad faith, bad people.[20] Anthony O'Hear observes that a precursor to such attitudes is found in Oswald Mosley's New Party, scarcely an encouraging parallel.[21]

An alternative

Naturally, with victim games played so rewardingly, one wonders whether such games are inevitable. However, Jesus' example shows they are not. Jesus was the real victim par excellence, innocent (John 19:6), and the target of malice (Mark 15:10). Yet strikingly the lesson we must imitate from the passion is not to revile in return, nor resort to strategies of intimidation, but to trust in the God who judges justly (1 Peter 2:23). If this is so in cases of real victimhood, and where there is such stress on the justice of God, then adjudging ourselves as victims is precluded.

But Christ's example is relevant in another way. As the parable of the Pharisee and the tax collector indicates, Christ did not collude with people who designated themselves as righteous. Nor should we collude with self-dramatizations of 'victim' or a white knight where those roles are delusions, particularly since such self-dramatization needs another to be victimizer. Encouraging people to think they, as victims, do not need mercy can encourage, as the Balkans situation indicates, the thought that they need not show mercy.

Conclusion

We have seen how tempting it is for humans, both as individuals and groups, to use victimhood rhetoric, and its totalizing dangers of inducing us to see ourselves as not needing mercy, and our victimizers as beyond mercy. No doubt part of the remedy is to remember ourselves in relation to God as his creatures, not to concentrate exclusively on interhuman relations. If we did, we might remember that victim and victimizer alike need God's mercy and stand under God's scrutiny.

Yet also if the lessons of Karpman's Triangle are right, we must beware entering the Triangle in any role, Persecutor and Rescuer as well as Victim. This would be true of our individual relations, spouses, family members, friends, fellow-believers, and so forth, and our collective relations. It is enticing to be a Rescuer, yet fraught with temptation to collude with *soi-disant* Victims to create real but unacknowledged victims. Perhaps we should analyse the chic Victims of the day with more care, rather than rushing in self-congratulation to be their Rescuers. Perhaps, too, evangelicals should be a little more suspicious of attempts to enlist us within the Triangle, as Persecutors, as the proponents of homophobia and Islamophobia, among others, have so successfully done. For such depictions of evangelicals as Persecutors tend ultimately to silence them, thereby silencing the gospel they preach. And the real losers there would be the very groups claiming to be Victims.

Notes

1. *Cambridge Papers*, Volume 15, Number 1 (Cambridge: Jubilee Centre, March 2006). Reproduced with permission.
2. The writer is indebted to Mrs Auriel Schluter for pointing out the contribution of Karpman's work. The Victim Triangle is described in Karpman's influential article 'Fairy Tales and Script Drama Analysis', *Transactional Analysis Bulletin* 7.26 (1968), pp. 39–43.
3. '[T]his simple but powerfully accurate instrument': Lynne Forrest, 'The Three Faces of Victim', online at <http://lynneforrest.com/html/the_faces_of_victim.html>.
4. Forrest, 'Three Faces'.
5. Forrest, 'Three Faces'.
6. Thus Little Red Riding Hood and the wolf can each be classified as both Persecutors and Victims.
7. In what follows, terms about victimhood are not used in Karpman's technical sense.
8. P. Utgaard, *Remembering and Forgetting Nazism* (New York and London: Berghahn, 2003).
9. J. J. Orr, *The Victim as Hero* (Honolulu: University of Hawai'i Press, 2001), p. 135. Thus Tsuboi Sakae's book *Twenty-Four Eyes* (Tokyo: Kenkyusha, 1963) follows the lives of several children and their teacher into the Second World War. We meet the protagonists as children, continue to see them as such, while, very largely, men of soldiering age are absent from the book. Yet the innocence or guilt of just such men goes to the heart of whether Japan was primarily a 'victim' in the war.
10. D. B. MacDonald, *Balkan Holocausts?* (Manchester and New York: Manchester University Press, 2002).
11. P. C. Vitz, *Psychology as Religion: The Cult of Self-Worship* (Grand Rapids: Eerdmans, 1988), p. 64.
12. Orr, *Victim*, p. 116.

13. MacDonald, *Balkan*, p. 83.

14. C. Blum, *Rousseau and the Republic of Virtue* (Ithaca and London: Cornell University Press, 1986).

15. The tendency of such attitudes is towards Pelagianism.

16. Vitz, *Psychology*, p. 64.

17. Vitz, *Psychology*, p. 64.

18. Thus it is not agreed whether the 'phobia' is simply fear of Islam or irrational fear of Islam. The Runnymede Trust issued a widely cited definition of Islamophobia in 1997, but it consists of a congeries of factors, several of which are open to the objection that they refer to judgments which might legitimately be formed.

19. See P. E. Gottfried, *Multiculturalism and the Politics of Guilt* (Columbia and London: University of Missouri Press, 2002), pp. 1–2.

20. A. O'Hear draws this out, in *Plato's Children: The State We Are In* (London: Gibson Square, 2005), p. 100.

21. O'Hear, *Plato's Children*, p. 99.

PART 3:

GOSPEL AND ATONEMENT

Mike Ovey did not enjoy controversy, and he did not court it. His reactions were never knee-jerk, nor did written words flow swiftly. But the controversy about penal substitution touched him deeply, because he saw denying it as an assault on God's holiness, justice and love, and that it penetrated to the heart of the doctrine of the Trinity. Hence his thorough clarity on the subject.

[T]he virtues do more terrible damage ...

(G. K. Chesterton)[2]

We sometimes hear the charge that modern Britain, like other modern Western countries, is a somewhat immoral place. Old-style Marxists used to speak of the decadent capitalist West. Current Middle Eastern mullahs speak of its satanic character. Classic evangelicals likewise have decried how unethical many aspects of our national life have become, on areas ranging from embryo experimentation, to sexual faithfulness, to financial probity. It seems obvious to us. So it is perhaps worth remembering how modern Britain outside the churches can think of itself very much as a moral country, with strong ethical standards, not least because of its self-image as increasingly a model of pluralistic virtue, a country in which all kinds of diversity thrive. Possessing such pluralistic virtue can seem to be a, perhaps the, ground of moral self-congratulation, and acquiring greater degrees of pluralistic virtue an appropriate national aspiration.

Some snapshots

However, let us now look at some snapshots on how virtuously pluralist Britain can work. First of all, is the 'gospel on a plate'. This requires some explanation. There was a training course in one of our major denominations that made extensive use of paper plates. This was not for practice in how to run a vicarage tea party with copious thin-sliced cucumber sandwiches; the point rather was that participants would all sit in a circle and pass the paper plate round to each other. Each person would be asked to write on the plate what the gospel was for them, and pass it on for the next person to do the same. The plate would then be taken by the person running the exercise who would read out the inscriptions and say, 'This is the gospel for us.' Of course, by the time the plate had circulated round a relatively large and diverse group, the various accounts of the gospel were not just differently nuanced but actually downright contradictory. But all were allowed to stand side by side.

Our second snapshot stays within the major denominations. One theological college instituted the practice on day one for its new students of taking them through Mark's account of the feeding of the five thousand. So far, so good. However, each student is asked what the incident means. Characteristically, one would say it is a miracle demonstrating Jesus is the Son of God. Another would refer it to the Lord's Supper. Another would say it is not miraculous but an acted parable on the redistribution of wealth. And so on. No interpretation is criticized by the tutor, none preferred above others: all are allowed to stand. All the meanings, at any rate those currently in play, the conduct implies, are valid.

Next, imagine the scene at a British seaside town. An elderly man is surrounded, being harassed and jostled by a crowd of much younger and fitter men. Fortunately, the police are shortly on the scene and make an arrest. Of the elderly man. The elderly man has a placard saying that homosexuality is sinful and incurs God's wrath. So, naturally, the group of homosexuals and their sympathizers feel obliged to vent their disgust by physical assault. Mercifully, or not, the elderly victim of the assault, Harry Hammond, was successfully prosecuted under Britain's law and order legislation. If you like, the homosexuals' right to be outraged could not be compared or evaluated against other considerations.

Our last snapshot remains with so-called fundamental freedoms, but features the EU and the strange case of Rocco Buttiglione, a distinguished Roman Catholic intellectual. He was, we may remember, the man who considered practising homosexuality sinful but also that it should not be criminalized, a conventional enough distinction between moral evaluation and what should be illegal. We may also recall that various European lobby groups successfully opposed his installation as an EU Commissioner. The grounds of opposition repay attention. It was not because of any action of his in public office nor any proposal of his concerning public policy, but rather because of his personal opinions and religious beliefs. Remarkably, perhaps, little mention was made, certainly in the media in this country, about European commitment to freedom of belief, or, come to that, to UN commitments against religious discrimination. Rather, in the name of plural Europe, an entire raft of people with particular beliefs, including, it may well be, many evangelicals in the United Kingdom, had in principle been excluded from public office at that level of the EU, because of their personal beliefs, even when those beliefs did not result in any different conduct of public office. One naturally wonders what other jobs such lobby groups may deem one unfit to fill.

What's at stake? The question of plurality

Each of these snapshots features in some sense the question of plurality, plural accounts of the gospel, plural interpretations of the Bible, plural beliefs about sexuality, often with the sense 'there's no wrong answer'. With the proviso, of course, that we must all accept there is no wrong answer. What would be wrong would be the suggestion that some answers are wrong. These are attitudes many Christians no doubt meet from time to time in our evangelistic or apologetic ministries.

It is perhaps, though, worth briefly recalling how that proposition 'There's no wrong answer' comes to be asserted. We sometimes hear a false dichotomy that goes like this:

- *Either* we have exhaustive, 'monolithic' understandings. (We might paraphrase these understandings as asserting, 'This is all there is to it' or 'I've got it completely taped.')
- *Or* we have unrestrictedly plural understandings. (We might paraphrase this as asserting, 'It could mean this, could mean that, but I have no ultimate vantage point from which to rule any idea in or out.')

The argument then runs that, if we cannot claim *exhaustive* understanding (the first part of the dichotomy), we can be left only with the alternative 'there's no wrong answer'. That is, after all, the only remaining possibility on this argument.

It has frequently been pointed out over the last forty years (at least) that this is a false dilemma.[3] Why? The reality is far less crude than this dilemma allows. For evangelicals (like others) do accept levels of meaning; for example, over Old Testament prefigurings of Christ, and the fact that God brings forth fresh light from his Word. One reason why evangelicals delight to preach and study the same passages many times is precisely because we think God does bring us to further and deeper understandings of his infallible and inerrant Word. However, the point is this: God does not bring forth *inconsistent* light. He does not one minute bring forth the truth that Jesus is fully man and fully God and then at a later stage bring forth the truth that Jesus is not. We believe in a God who is eternally truthful and that implies a consistency to what he says.

We should not here confuse 'exhaustive' with 'excluding'. We may well say we do not have an *exhaustive* understanding of the statement 'God is holy', for instance, but we would say even our non-exhaustive understanding *excludes* certain things, like, obviously, 'God is not holy.' For when we make any positive predication about God and say that God is something or some quality (such as 'God is just'), then that positive predication carries an excluding sense, for it necessarily implies that God is not the contradiction of that quality (in our example, 'God is just' rules out 'God is not just'). If we deny this and say that 'God is just' does not exclude 'God is not just', then naturally people would ask us whether the first statement 'God is just' actually meant anything.[4]

Plurality with or without coherence
This takes us to a truer dichotomy within which to consider pluralism. The dichotomy is between two kinds of plurality. On the one hand, there is a plurality which envisages that, although there is plurality and diversity of authentic values and virtues that bind humans, there is still coherence between the various elements. On the other hand, there is a plurality of authentic values and virtues that bind humans where there is no coherence between all of the elements. We could illustrate this diagrammatically thus:

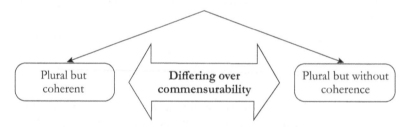

A key notion lying between these two different ways of seeing plurality is commensurability. This somewhat cumbersome word is chosen because one kind of pluralism uses this notion. Commensurability, of course, relates to the idea that two things can be properly measured against each other, so that there is some legitimate standard of comparison. Thus in arithmetic, two fractions (say three-quarters and two-thirds) can be properly measured against each other when put in terms of a common denominator (in the example, they would be nine-twelfths and eight-twelfths). With a common denominator we can work out which is greater, how they can be added, and so on.

To return to our different kinds of pluralism, in the 'plural but coherent' category, one can ultimately measure one element against another. They can be related in some way. We might say that a common denominator exists and therefore they are commensurable. In the plural but without coherence category, one cannot measure or compare one element against another. We can illustrate this with a commonplace example. We use the maxim 'You can't compare apples and oranges.' The maxim reminds us that some things are simply different and comparisons are inappropriate. They taste different and most aptly fulfil different types of physical appetite, hunger and thirst. On that basis, how can one compare? An apple is not meant to taste like an orange, and we choose first one, now the other, depending on what appetite we wish to satisfy or what sensation we wish to enjoy. Such thinking emphasizes plurality without coherence.

Yet we can run the apples and oranges question another way. In another sense, we do sometimes compare apples and oranges. One might see apples at £5 an apple and compare it unfavourably to oranges at 30p each. Here there is a medium through which we can compare: money is the common denominator. It emphasizes plurality with coherence.

Thus, on, say, Old Testament prefigurings of Christ, we may well admit plurality of meaning, but contend that the meanings are related and coherent – they are not incommensurable. The Passover lambs of Exodus and the Passover Lamb who is the Lord Jesus bear related meanings. This is not to claim they are at all points the same, nor that we necessarily exhaustively understand each. Yet if we interpret the Exodus lambs and the New Testament Passover Lamb in contradictory ways, then we would in principle be committed to a plurality without coherence. We would also have enormous difficulty in specifying how the Exodus lambs actually do prefigure Christ.

Let us apply this framework of plurality with and without commensurability to the snapshots we first looked at. In those examples there are strong patterns of incommensurability. In the first example, of many differing accounts of the gospel written on the plate, the acceptance of high degrees of inconsistency between the different elements suggests plurality without coherence or commensurability: different accounts of the gospel seem incommensurable. Similarly with the various interpretations of the feeding of the five thousand. Concerning Harry Hammond and Rocco Buttiglione, the value of their freedom of expression or freedom of religion does not seem to be compared, at least in the public mind, with the alternative rights, the right not to be offended, and the right to have public figures personally approve of one's sexual choices. In the Buttiglione case there appeared to be no weighing of competing rights. Incommensurability seems indicated in these cases by the way that the right not to be offended, and the right to have public figures personally approve of one's sexual choices apparently function unchecked, and are, so to speak, 'trump cards'.

The aim in what follows is not to provide a global explanation of 'pluralism'. There are arguments for different kinds of pluralism, and space precludes dealing with all of them. Instead, this paper aims to draw out one theme in pluralist thinking – the question of incommensurability. There is more to contemporary pluralism, and there may be better pluralisms, than this, but incommensurability is a highly significant theme. Let me explain why.

Why does incommensurable pluralism matter?

Obviously one wonders why incommensurable pluralism should matter to Christians. Two areas immediately spring to mind: first, that of our biblical duties, and second, that of our place in the public square.

Biblical duties

In terms of our biblical duties, Titus 1:9 and Acts 20 (where Paul addresses the Ephesian elders at Miletus) lay some clear and significant duties on all ministers. Titus 1:9 tells us to encourage the flock by sound teaching and to refute those who oppose it. It is worth noting that Paul's word is 'refute' (*elenchein*). 'Refute' is a strong term,[5] which implies specifying where and why that false teaching is wrong.[6] In a similar vein Acts 20:28–31 warns us to protect the flock, notably against those even arising from within the presbyterate who will bring forth false teaching.

Yet if claims to truth are incommensurable, we cannot say 'this biblical truth precludes that view'. Evangelistically we could not say as Paul and Barnabas did in Acts 14:15 that the Lystrans should turn from these worthless things. For, if claims to truth are incommensurable, one could not simply call the Lystran idols 'worthless things'. Such judgments could only be made from within our own system, and do not have a universal binding nature. One therefore should not insist the Lystrans are obliged to 'turn' from these 'worthless things'. Paul and Barnabas unmistakeably think the Lystrans are doing wrong as they seek to offer sacrifice.[7] If claims to truth really are incommensurable, the gospel loses its character of proclamation and evangelism is inhibited. For the same reasons, within a local church or denomination we cannot effectively pastor our flocks against false teaching. Similar considerations arise in applying Galatians 1:8. There Paul enjoins an anathema on those who preach another gospel (literally 'alongside' [*para*], with the sense of something different).[8] For this to have meaning one must be able to see that something is not the same gospel as the one Paul taught. This requires some comparison of concepts.

This means that real care must be exercised over the claim to find 'different proclamations' within the biblical material. Recent years have seen claims not merely to provide different presentations of essentially the same gospel (as in the choice between using presentations of, say, *Two Ways to Live* rather than *Christianity Explored*), but also the idea that the New Testament material contains diverse gospels with different orientations; for example, in the idea that the gospel of Jesus is not the same as the gospel of Paul. There is a point where plurality becomes incoherent and comprises contradictory accounts.

The issue, though, is not whether the gospel must be taught and proclaimed in essentially the same words on all occasions. Misgivings about 'different gospels' are not necessarily insisting on that. For there are differences between Paul's proclamation in the synagogues at Berea and Thessalonica (Acts 17:2ff. and 17:10ff.), on the one hand, and his proclamation at the Areopagus, on the other (Acts 17:22–34). In the first case he reasons about the fulfilment of the Old Testament scriptures, and in the second he utilizes ideas from creation theology to convict the Athenians' idolatry. This framework admits plurality and diversity, but a coherent plurality.

The issue is, though, whether different proclamations, different *kerygmata*, are in a framework that entails that they are not commensurable. In such a case the framework is one of pluralism without coherence, and this generates enormous difficulty in giving due weight to the warnings of Galatians 1:9. As it happens, in the case of Paul's various proclamations in Acts 17, his work in the synagogues and on the Areopagus does represent a coherent diversity, because, of course, the same Old Testament that provides the framework of promise and fulfilment in Jesus also provides the creation theology he uses on the Areopagus. The God who gave the promises to Israel is also the creator of heaven and earth.

More generally, outside the sphere of presbyteral responsibility, believers have a duty to give an account for the hope they have (1 Peter 3:15) – this becomes far harder when common ground between believer and non-believer disappears, as incommensurable pluralism suggests. We will return to the point that incommensurable pluralism destroys common ground.

Public square

Some developments of incommensurable pluralism can mean we lose the civic liberty to proclaim the gospel. This is an important claim and a surprising one, perhaps, for, as we will see shortly, one of the claims often made for incommensurable pluralism is just that it preserves liberty. In that sense the case of Harry Hammond is indicative. And, of course, it is the nature of the gospel to cause offence. Paul himself notes that apostles bringing the gospel can be the smell of death to some (2 Cor. 2:16).

Given, then, that incommensurable pluralism is a matter of Christian concern, we must examine how this idea is generated and what supports it.

Incommensurable truths and values

Outline of Isaiah Berlin's idea

First, we must go to the highly influential Oxford historian of ideas, Isaiah Berlin (1909–97).[9] In his essay 'The Pursuit of the Ideal' Berlin outlines the germination and development of what some would see as his central idea, the incommensurability of values.[10] Berlin suggests he arrived at this principle via consideration of, notably, Niccolò Machiavelli (1469–1527),[11] Giambattista Vico (1668–1744)[12] and Johann Gottfried von Herder (1744–1803),[13] all of whom undermined the idea of unique, single answers to human problems.[14] This idea of incommensurability of values forms the linchpin of a particularly famous and important essay of his called 'Two Concepts of Liberty'.[15]

Now, in discussing incommensurable values, Berlin is not just making a point about interpretation, the idea that we see different things in a text, whatever that text may be, whether *Beowulf*, the Bible or *Black Beauty*. Rather, Berlin's point is that there are genuine values and they are genuinely disparate and compete with each other. As it happens, Berlin is not the originator of this idea. We can trace it much earlier, as he himself points out, but he is a highly influential and clear advocate. It is just his conspicuous ability that suggests we should spend time considering him.[16]

Berlin speaks of 'the fact that human goals are many, not all of them commensurable, and in perpetual rivalry with one another'.[17] Similarly, G. K. Chesterton had much earlier observed:

> The modern world is full of the old Christian virtues gone mad. The virtues have gone mad because they have been isolated from each other and are wandering alone. Thus some scientists care for truth; and their truth is pitiless. Thus some humanitarians care only for pity and their pity (I am sorry to say) is often untruthful.[18]

In support of his thesis, Berlin relied particularly on two points: first, that the idea of commensurable human goals was incoherent; and, second, that the idea of a single harmonious system of values and goals was dangerous.[19]

However, this argument is not simply saying, 'There are several genuine goods and we want to get a good balance between them; we must trade-off between them to get the right answer.' On that view one can get better trade-offs or worse trade-offs and one has a way of comparing trade-offs. In other words, there is a measure of commensurability, in the same way that we might compare 20 apples bought for £5 to 40 oranges bought for £5. The Berlin point goes further. It is rather this: 'We have lots of goals and since there is no real basis of comparison between them, trade-offs are arbitrary.'

The result is a proposition that goes like this: *humans have values but they are set at war with each other.*

Comments on Berlin's idea

This proposition requires some comments. First, it is not always clear whether Berlin thinks that all values or only some of them are at war in this way.[20] Thus one might think that some values, such as truthfulness, faithfulness and right-eousness, are closely related, such that a denial of one would involve denial of the others. Yet clearly even if some values could be grouped into families in this kind of way, Berlin's arguments about incommensurability might still apply between families of values.

Second, in Berlin's view there is *inevitable* war between different values. He writes, 'These collisions of values are of the essence of what they are and what we are.'[21] The example often cited in support by Berlin and others agreeing with him is the conflict between liberty and equality. The perfect liberty of all may interfere with the equality of all. There is no way perfect liberty and perfect equality can coexist in the same society. It is for this reason that he thinks the idea of harmony among human values is simply incoherent.

However, there is some ambiguity and vagueness in the proposal that *humans have values but they are set at war with each other.* To begin with, the statement that humans 'have values' is ambiguous. On the one hand, this might mean that humans think and act in terms of values but we must always be agnostic about the real status of these values, as to whether they are ultimately purely human construc-tions or not. On the other hand, this might mean that humans think and act in terms of values, some of which at least are not simply human constructions.

At this point, Berlin's own citation of Vico is highly illuminating. Among other things, Berlin reads Vico as suggesting that humans create and work in the context of particular cultures, so that what is possible in one culture is not so in another. The human framework which made possible the creation of the *Iliad* or the *Odyssey* is simply not there in other times and places.[22] It is, it seems, this incommensurability of cultures that Berlin reads in Vico, and from this he envisages an incommensurability of values. 'Values' here seems to refer primarily to values as human constructions, albeit possibly unintentional ones.

If this reading of Berlin is right, then there would be clear dangers in adopting him for Christian theologians committed to the idea that values are not simply human constructions but reflect the mind and will of God.

One also wonders quite how Berlin can be so sure that the claims of those who do believe in values revealed by God are wrong – the criticisms about incoherence seem to imply this very strongly. He clearly does think values are not revealed by God, yet such global adjudications of wrongness are precisely the things that his theory of incommensurable pluralism rules out in other cases. It is difficult not to sense some incoherence here.

Further, the part of the proposition that suggests values are 'at war with each other' also needs some further probing. If there are such things as divinely revealed values and such things as values which are purely human constructions, then the conflict can be one between what God wills and what humans will. Even the possibility of such conflict does not seem to be contemplated by Berlin's scheme. On this view, his account of the kinds of conflicts that occur between values is too simplistic. Instead of the simple idea that values are at war, we should recognize two distinct wars of values. There may well be war between two sets of values which are both purely human constructions. Christians might well expect just this, given our finitude and our fallenness. But there may well be (and Christians would insist there are) conflicts between values willed by God and values willed by finite and fallen men and women. However, Berlin's argument in effect means that we could not call the willing by humans of values which contradict God's, 'sin'. Orthodox Christians would add that this is both an attraction and a danger in the idea of incommensurable pluralism.

We should add finally under this question of vagueness and ambiguity, the question of what Berlin means by a 'value'. Berlin suggests that liberty and equality inevitably conflict. So they do – on his definitions. Yet it is not absurd to envisage different definitions which avoid conflict, for example that 'real' liberty does not extend to harming others, and that such harm is an abuse of liberty and a distortion of it. Nor is it absurd to envisage definitions of liberty and equality which are in some way given a common denominator and made commensurable, for example by rooting both in ideas of what is due to a human individual.[23] Berlin (understandably given his commitment to particular forms of plural civic life) has rather different ideas of liberty and equality in mind. It is not obvious, though, why his definitions should be accepted, and if we do not accept his definitions, then his insistence on the *inevitability* of conflict of values is far weaker.

Third, Berlin insists that the field of possible human values is not unending: 'Ends, moral principles, are many. But not infinitely many: they must be within the human horizon. If they are not, then they are outside the human sphere.'[24]

The result of this is that for Berlin and the more sophisticated derivatives of his theory, we cannot accept each and every value as privileged by incommensurable pluralism as legitimate goals of human endeavour. Within the sphere of 'the human horizon', particular goals are to be allowed to flourish, because the principle of incommensurable pluralism protects them from falsification. Outside that sphere, goals are not necessarily to be so allowed.

When applying this principle, Berlin uses the example of those who worship wood. Some reasons for worshipping wood he finds himself able to understand, if not to accept. One reason, though, he does not understand, and he says of those who hold it, 'They are not human for me. I cannot even call their values subjective if I cannot conceive what it would be like to pursue such a life.'[25]

These are disturbing words. The litmus test, it seems, for accepting a particular idea within the scope of allowable incommensurable pluralism is whether or not an onlooker finds this idea conceivable and one with which he can sympathize. Of course, it may be difficult to conceive following a set of ideas because of some fault in the ideas: they are so repugnant, perhaps. One may find it inconceivable, for instance, to think of being a slave trader. There the inconceivability arises because of the idea, and the fault is located there, so to speak. This is the case Berlin envisages.

However, it is also possible to envisage inconceivability arising because of the onlooker and some fault there. For example, a devout Nazi might indeed have found it inconceivable that Gentiles should pursue full equal civic rights for Jews as a goal in life. Such a person might well say, 'I cannot conceive what it would be like to pursue such a life.' At this stage in the argument, it is very far from clear that Berlin has given due weight to the point that his onlooker has a world view and a nature, too, and that what is conceivable for someone is wedded to this nature and world view.

The dangers of this are increased by the dramatic nature of Berlin's account. Once the point of inconceivability is reached, those holding the opinion or goal seem on this line of argument less than human: 'They are not human for me.' Yet twentieth-century history is tragically replete with examples of what human beings are capable of when they feel that another group, for reasons of race, religion or politics, can be classified as 'non-human'.

Fourth, the *former* part of the proposition, that humans have values, we fully affirm – in fact, some of the values Berlin and others endorse we endorse too, and happily. However, we distinguish between values which are purely human constructions and those which are divinely revealed in the Bible. This distinction means that in terms of the *latter* part of the proposition, that these values are at war, we concede that humanly constructed values may be at war both with each other and also with divinely revealed values. What we will deny is that divinely revealed values are intrinsically at war with each other.

So the point at issue is *the relation divinely revealed values bear to one another.*

The moral passion of Berlin's thesis
Two kinds of moral passion
There is no denying the moral passion with which Berlin pursues this idea of incommensurable pluralism. This passion arises from two considerations. First, Berlin sees this acceptance of incommensurable pluralism as undermining the

impulse to various types of totalitarian or dictatorial action. It is precisely the idea of uniquely right answers that encourages the attitude that the ends justify the means. Berlin writes of the person who thinks that he or she has this unique answer:

> to make mankind just and happy and creative and harmonious for ever – what could be too high a price to pay for that? To make such an omelette, there is surely no limit to the number of eggs that should be broken – that was the faith of Lenin, of Trotsky, of Mao, for all I know of Pol Pot.[26]

But if one has lost the idea that one has the uniquely right answer to the human predicament, one loses the motivation for this kind of conduct. Berlin's impulse here is to support a humane liberalism.

The second way in which Berlin's moral passion emerges is over how one should hold one's values in this framework of incommensurable pluralism. Berlin's suggestion is not, he insists, an amoralism, where nothing is either right or wrong. It is a mistake to think this kind of pluralist thought sees itself as endorsing no values. For Berlin, this is one of the crucial differences between incommensurable pluralism and 'relativism'.[27] 'Relativism' is identified by Berlin more with statements which are thought of essentially as only statements of personal preference, as in 'I like coffee, but you like tea.' These preferences do not have a moral flavour. Instead, Berlin envisages precisely high degrees of morally based action. For the point is to live *as if* whatever ultimate value has been selected really is ultimate: 'Principles are not less sacred because their duration cannot be guaranteed,' writes Berlin – we should still stand for them 'unflinchingly'.[28]

Let us pursue the moral ardour with which one stands for one's values in this system. In fact, we may stand for any given value *all the more unflinchingly*, because it is not commensurable with other values/virtues – it is 'free'; it is not necessarily regulated or mitigated by other values, for they are incommensurable. Take fox hunting, for example. This really is worth going to the stake for, either to ban it, or to protect it, because its value is not, indeed, cannot, be set in any relation to other values. W. B. Yeats catches some of the consequences well when he speaks of a centreless world.[29]

Let loose from the centre: with no coordinated frame of reference, the problem is not that there are no values for us, but that virtues, in Chesterton's words, 'are isolated' from each other.[30] Yeats here envisages two opposite consequences of this isolation. The first is a lack of conviction: for in incommensurable pluralism who is to say that a particular value should prevail over others? Incommensurable pluralism may rob us of the ability to say one value or virtue should moderate or even overrule another. In some cases it can rob us of a sense of priority, even when there really is such a priority. The second is the passionate intensity with which some values are held. Perhaps it is not surprising that this is an age of many impassioned single-issue lobby groups, whether it is anti-vivisection, Fathers for Justice, or whatever. This is not to say these groups do not reflect or protect a virtue, but rather it is a question of what relation these virtues bear to other virtues, whether a virtue is pursued with rightly proportioned passion.

Relating the two strands of Berlin's moral passion – a dilemma

There is, it seems to me, no doubting Berlin's moral seriousness on either of these two heads mentioned above. What is troubling is how the two interrelate. There seems to be a dilemma here.

For, on the one hand, let us suppose that I still hold my convictions and values with ultimate seriousness, standing for them 'unflinchingly' and treating them as still 'sacred'. If so, then what difference is there between that way of holding to those values, which Berlin commends, and the way of holding which says, as in the model Berlin criticizes, that these are the uniquely right answers to the human problem? It appears that under both schemes values are held with equivalent passion, for that equivalence is Berlin's point. And if they are, then why should my holding my values as 'sacred' within incommensurable pluralism not produce the same results that Berlin fears in the 'monistic', one-right-answer systems he castigates? But if one can 'unflinchingly' hold a value as 'sacred' without resorting to the most repellent kinds of coercion within the framework of incommensurable pluralism, then it does not seem necessarily impossible for those outside the framework of incommensurable pluralism likewise to be both morally passionate and unwilling to resort to coercion.

Yet if, on the other hand, Berlin were to concede that within incommensurable pluralism values are held as less sacred and not as unflinchingly, then his attempt to differentiate incommensurable pluralism from relativism looks correspondingly less successful, for the thrust of his distinction is that values are still held as more than purely personal preferences within incommensurable pluralism.

The application of incommensurable pluralism: the case of Machiavelli

It is also intriguing to see how Berlin develops this idea of incommensurable goods. As we have seen, he draws upon it in dealing with Machiavelli,[31] the

famous, or notorious, writer of Renaissance Florence. There are many interpretations of Machiavelli.[32] Berlin adds his own.

In Berlin's view the thing is this: it is *not* that Machiavelli simply separates
politics from ethics, rendering politics an 'ethics-free zone'. Machiavelli is not
just an amoralist in politics. *Rather*, it is that Machiavelli recognizes two different
moral systems. There is a Christian one ('not indeed . . . defective in itself')[33] and
a 'pagan' one. For Berlin, Machiavelli endorses both and applies, in politics,
the 'pagan' one. Machiavelli is therefore a profoundly moral political writer,
attempting to apply morality, not abolish it.

This is rather chilling: on the adoption of these 'pagan' virtues, which can
necessitate deceit and political purges, Berlin notes that '[Machiavelli] calls for
great sacrifices in their name.'[34] Indeed. However, on this take of Machiavelli,
which is just where Berlin thinks Machiavelli is so good, those actions are morally
justified. This must be stressed: the 'pagan' values cannot be criticized from
within the Christian system because of the principle of incommensurability.

At this point, the comparative lack of a full account of human nature within
this idea of incommensurable pluralism seems deeply disturbing. If humans
are prone to producing moral rationalizations of their actions, finding ways in
which they can describe any actions of theirs as morally justified, then the Berlin
thesis provides a way of reinforcing this still further, for my rationalizations are
still more immune to criticism. This, again, is not a recipe for less repressive
actions in human life, but more. A Stalin will have further grounds for saying
his purges are beyond reproach.[35] Berlin's thesis risks frustrating one of its
primary goals: the restraint of tyranny.

Machiavelli's preferences

The Machiavelli example, however, reveals another problematic feature about
the actual application of incommensurable pluralism. Let us suppose that Berlin
is right and that Machiavelli does envisage two moral universes. The point is,
he prefers one. What is more, his preference is not arbitrary, but reasoned: if
one wishes to retain power, then this is what one must do. Yet here, of course,
we find Machiavelli using a basis of comparison. Christian ethics and 'pagan'
ones are compared on the basis of effective retention of power. But there is a
basis of comparison. As such the two systems are clearly not incommensurable. Machiavelli himself does not seem to be, then, a simple incommensurable
pluralist.

It is true that the two systems (in the way Machiavelli describes them) are
not compatible, by which we mean that in certain given situations, say, over lying
to the populace, the two different systems tell us to do different things and so
produce two different results. But this does not mean they are necessarily

incommensurable. The mere existence of incompatibility between moral values does not, by itself, tell us the systems are incommensurable.

This difference between incommensurability and incompatibility needs some explanation. Some things may indeed be incompatible because they are incommensurable. However, incompatibility may arise for other reasons: one value may have no objective justification, and exists purely as a product of human imagination, while the other may be rooted in the will of God for his creatures. Incompatibility there may arise because of the sinful defiance by humans of their creator. Incompatibility may also arise when two values, rooted in the will of God for his creatures, are imperfectly understood by those creatures. Thus a promise to give to charity may conflict with a duty to support one's family.[36] Here the duties of truthfulness and love of family apparently conflict. But this may be because we do not fully understand the scope of either duty. To adopt the terminology of jurisprudence for a moment, the norms are imperfectly individuated, that is to say the content of the rules is not set out with perfect precision. For instance, our competence to make promises to bind ourselves may be limited. English law recognizes this, of course, with its idea that one cannot make a contract by which one sells oneself into slavery.

Yet Berlin's thesis tends to obscure the fact that we do have preferences between goals, and we think these preferences are rational. Such preferences imply commensurability of some sort. At this point we perhaps should recognize more strongly the role of these preferences and why they should be laid open to scrutiny. After all, Berlin himself prefers his system of incommensurable pluralism to earlier ideas of a unified moral universe, and it would be a great disservice to him to say this preference was arbitrary. His choice is a reasoned one based on what he sees as incoherence and a tendency to justify tyranny. But if Berlin is right and incommensurable pluralism is true, so that one cannot properly, rationally, compare one moral universe with another, why should I anyway prefer incommensurable pluralism to any other moral universe?

We must, then, note some key points. First, Berlin gives us a strongly moral framework in this kind of pluralism. Second, the cardinal values that we have adopted in Berlin's system enjoy a freedom from criticism. Why? Because alternative values have been weeded out, and put in another 'incommensurable' system. One does not have to listen to the criticism implied by an alternative value, because – the apples and oranges principle – one cannot compare the two. Hence one's first principle operates intact and unrestrained. Third, there is a real question of selectivity. Berlin tells us about several incommensurable systems: Which system applies when? And who says? Fourth, Berlin's system can be as readily appropriated by tyrants as the ones he criticizes, possibly even more so.

Theological evaluation

After this description of, and brief comment on, incommensurable pluralism
we must proceed to more specifically theological evaluation. We will do this
under two main headings, evaluation in relation to God, and in relation to
humanity.

In relation to God . . .

Incommensurable pluralism implicitly denies things about God. It is worth
here distinguishing two different ways that discussion of values can affect our
understanding of God. We might mean by 'values' what God wills for human
beings: how he has decreed we should live our lives. We might also mean by
'values' qualities or aspects of God's own nature. Incommensurable
pluralism,

- first, is polytheist, so it denies biblical monotheism; and
- second, deals in incommensurable plurality so that it denies God's
  simplicity.

Let us develop these in turn.

Denial of monotheism

As we consider the constellations of incommensurable values, we should realize
this bears many of the hallmarks of polytheism. After all, those values are in
practice treated as ultimate and are discrete and incommensurable. There is no
overall order; that is, one might say, the whole point. One goes from one to
another. But it is just there that there are echoes of the fractured, localized
polytheism of 1 Kings 20:23 and 2 Kings 17:26, where gods compete with each
other in no particular order, and there is no genuinely overarching value or god.
In contrast, passages like Isaiah 40:18–31 show God alone is incomparable as
sovereign and creator of all.

The regime that Berlin describes is polycratic – polycratic in that there are
many competing centres of power and authority. For Berlin this stands in opposition to 'monism',[37] where things can be reduced to an integrated single moral
universe.

In fact, it is enormously difficult to integrate this incommensurable pluralism into a truly monotheistic framework. It is worth here recalling some earlier
ideas about monotheism. It was common patristic and Reformation ground
that monotheism goes hand in hand with cosmic monarchy. It is especially
an Athanasian idea.[38] On this view, monotheism indicates a supreme being

with cosmic monarchy and order. There is an interrelation of parts, both physically and ethically. They fit together, and this causes no surprise since they are products from nothing of the Creator, and are sustained by his single will and mind. There is one unified cosmos because there is one single creator.

So the pattern tends to be *monotheism implies cosmic monarchy, which in its turn implies ordered relations within the cosmos.* All very well, someone might reply, but could there be a biblical monotheism where God willed mutually contradictory and incommensurable virtues? We need to be clear about what this would involve. First, this would not be a case of so-called conflict between God's permissive and decretive wills, because in that way of putting things there is ultimate resolution. Second, this is not a case of bringing good out of an evil action, because again there is a single integrated end in mind. Rather, the issue is this, that at the same level of willing there are two ends equally willed. At this point God's relation to the world is very definitely not that of a monarch whose plan ultimately comes to fruition (Eph. 1:11); it cannot be, because there are several plans or purposes for him at the same level of willing. Even if only one thing happens, other equally willed things do not. To that extent, the idea that God wills two contradictory values or virtues for us and for us to act upon eliminates the idea of biblical monarchy. It also eliminates the idea of sin, although this is another point.

I should add that texts about double-mindedness on God's part do not in fact constitute exceptions to this, given that they are accommodated to us and our place within time.[39]

This question of plural, contradictory wills in God affects our consideration of plural gospels. For the gospel is not just a communication of information, a news flash to an otherwise uninformed world. It is a command by God to his human creatures and requires their obedience. Thus in 2 Thessalonians 1:8 disobeying the gospel is a ground for punishment (see also 1 Peter 4:17). The gospel is something that God wills men and women to believe. This means that plural, in the sense of incommensurably different and incompatible, gospels involve God's willing different and incompatible things. As we have seen, this kind of incompatible willing by God cannot be reconciled with his divine monarchy. Hence incommensurably different and incompatible gospels cannot be reconciled with God's monarchy.

Denial of simplicity

Let us move to our second denial, the denial of simplicity. Simplicity is a term that is perhaps less familiar to us as evangelicals these days than was once the case. To say that God is simple is not saying that God is somehow simple-minded, or that he is a primitive prototype as against later and more advanced models. To say that God is simple is to say, first, that in God, all his attributes are essential. There are no optional extras in God, something added on to the basic product. So, a car might have air conditioning. Now that air conditioning is a secondary characteristic; that car, that model, that colour, is available without the air conditioning. But with God, it is not the case that there are add-on extras, as if his justice were an optional extra with him, which could be taken away and he would still be the same essential being. Rather, take away the justice and he is no longer the God of the Bible. It is not the case with God that some attributes are primary, some secondary.

The reason why this matters is that if we did have a God with primary and secondary attributes, we would always be tempted to downplay the attributes we felt less comfortable with as secondary attributes. So, it is wonderful to say God is love, but it would be wrong to say that other things such as holiness are somehow less important to him. Simplicity minimizes the designer-deity tendency humans have, the urge to pick'n'mix the attributes we personally like best.

Second, simplicity means that all God's attributes are integrated. God is not a mixture or composition of more basic principles, into which he can be divided. As all the attributes are equally essential, so all the attributes are inseparable. So, going back to Chesterton's remarks, with God, because he is simple, his truth is pitying, and his pity is truthful.

The great, the fantastic, thing that earlier generations emphasized about God's simplicity was that it supports, perhaps even entails, his faithfulness to his promises. There is no other conflicting attribute in God that will prevent him from fulfilling his promise to have mercy on those who believe in the Lord Jesus, for instance.

We see this biblically in Psalm 85:10–13. Consider verse 10, for instance. *Righteousness and peace kiss.* The image is of justice (righteousness) and salvation attributes (peace) meeting and being reconciled. Please note, they are not set in conflict: one does not trump the other; they are not traded off so one gets a little bit of righteousness and a little bit of peace. The language is of both being fully present and realized, and in harmony, not as incommensurables or irreconcilables. Perhaps even more strikingly in the New Testament, we could cite Romans 3:25–26, where the point is that God's forbearance is not at odds with his own righteousness.

So simplicity means we cannot set God's attributes in opposition to each other: his is a pitying truth and a truthful pity. William Ames (1576–1633) catches it well: 'the divine attributes are not contrary to one another, but agree emphatically'.[40] This also means we cannot prioritize one of God's attributes as '*the* essential' attribute of God.

The instability of incommensurable pluralism

However, we also need to see how the church fathers in particular see polytheism developing. For they did not envisage polytheism with its polycratic emphases as a stable system.

Remember, Athanasius argues that

$$\boxed{\text{No monarchy} \rightarrow \text{no God}}$$ [41]

God's cosmic sovereignty is not something that is an optional extra for God. Rather, if we deny God's cosmic sovereignty, this entails 'atheism', in the sense that there is no god who answers the biblical description of the word.

Gregory of Nazianzen, one of the Cappadocian fathers who succeeded Athanasius, continues and develops this. He sees three basic alternatives: monarchy, polyarchy and anarchy.[42] But he adds this twist. He thinks ultimately polyarchy becomes anarchy, so that finally there are two alternatives: monarchy or anarchy. That alternative of monarchy or anarchy is ultimately related to the alternative: monotheism or 'atheism'. After all, as we've seen in this line of thought, monotheism goes hand in hand with monarchy, and atheism is the denial of monotheism, and therefore of monarchy.

This sounds merely theoretical, but we should think it through more concretely. What happens in anarchy? Why do we fear it so much in some respects? Well, because things are decided on the basis of might is right. Might acts unrestrained by principle or law. In anarchy, by definition, you do not get the rule of law. This absence of law and principle does not just arise in so-called primitive societies. We might well in a Western context speak of the 'tyranny of the majority' as anarchistic. 'Tyranny of the majority' is Alexis de Tocqueville's pungent phrase for describing how in a democratic society the majority can behave tyrannically, because the majority reserve the prerogative to redefine right to suit themselves.[43] The example de Tocqueville cites for this is the expropriation of native American lands by 'due' legislative and judicial process. Is not tyranny of the majority an apt phrase for what happened in Rocco's case? That his rights, theoretically guaranteed by the European Convention, scarcely even rated a mention, while the media was full of the rights of those who wanted to deny him his?

And in this anarchistic world, an unbelieving majority will feel itself entitled to disenfranchise messages and beliefs of which it strongly disapproves. However, in the case of the gospel, this feeling of entitlement will be married to a basic antipathy to the gospel message. This could well create a profound temptation, even an inevitable tendency, to disenfranchise proclamation of the gospel itself. In the light of that, it is important to see how the feeling of entitlement arises, as I have shown here.

Lastly, in this anarchistic world, one of the regularities that disappears is God's faithfulness. After all, if a promise made with one thing in view is subject to competing values which may master or frustrate it, how can promises be sure?

The gospel of Christ

What does this mean, then, for the proclamation of the gospel? First, it highlights the centrality of proclaiming a kingdom, a monarchy; in particular the monarchy or kingdom of Jesus, for it is on him that the Father has bestowed the kingdoms of the world: Psalm 2:8. We should add that this is how Jesus himself understands matters. He states that the Father has given him all authority (John 17:2, before the passion, and Matt. 28:18 after the passion). We have already seen how kingdom or monarchy is inseparable from the biblical God who is creator of all, seen and unseen. If we have a gospel that sacrifices the idea of God's monarchy, vested in his Son, then this is not the monotheistic biblical God of the Bible. It is, of course, for just this reason that the papers in *God's Power to Save* inevitably deal with the idea of kingdom in one way or another. A gospel featuring the biblical God inevitably deals, expressly or by necessary implication, with his kingdom or his monarchy.

Followers of Berlin may feel some misgivings at this point. Berlin understandably voices suspicion of those who go to extreme lengths to fulfil their monolithic utopian vision, whatever it may be. Recall the sentiment noted earlier: 'To make such an omelette [a perfect society], there is surely no limit to the number of eggs that should be broken – that was the faith of Lenin, of Trotsky, of Mao, for all I know of Pol Pot.'[44] However, followers of Jesus Christ note this difference in the kingdom of Christ. Where Lenin made his omelette by breaking others, Jesus gives his own body to be broken. Characteristic evangelical presentations of the gospel stress precisely the finished nature of Christ's work and its sufficiency, focused in the idea that salvation is by grace alone and not by human works. In this sense the content of the gospel itself, as the message that the king has died for his people, is at odds with the fears that Berlin has, for those fears relate to what humans must do to construct their heaven on earth. Put another way, Berlin's argument has not grasped that the kingdom of Christ is constructed by his work and sacrifice, not ours.

Second, our gospel involves proclaiming a simple God, in the way that I have explained simplicity. We deal with the Jesus in whom God's one plan for salvation is fulfilled in human history – we do not meet God pursuing incommensurable goals, and to that extent we have to recognize how 'un-gospel' the sentiments of incommensurable pluralism are, even when some of the values one finds (such as the importance of the individual, the antipathy to tyranny) are ones with which we agree.

This is undoubtedly complex, because it leaves us needing to distinguish between our agreement on the point that individuals matter and our disagreement about the context in which that point is set. However, this offers an opportunity, too, for we may rightly argue that these legitimate values can be properly supported only from within a biblical framework. For example, respect for other humans finds its best basis in biblical understandings of human beings as creatures made in the image of God. This is, of course, strongly present in the presuppositional apologetics of Cornelius Van Til and others.

Third, we must turn to the cross, so frequently the focus of evangelical presentations of the gospel. The cross is naturally at the heart of gospel proclamations, because it is about the kingdom of God, as judgment executed on sin, vindicating God's sovereignty. We must recall that the cross does not take place because of miscalculation or accident, but by God's set plan and foreknowledge (Acts 2:23). Note too the Johannine stress on the fulfilment of prophecy in the crucifixion, and Jesus' explanation of the prophets on the road to Emmaus (Luke 24:26–27). In that way the cross is a testimony to God's sovereignty, but it is also a testimony to God's simplicity. This must be stressed. The cross is a case, perhaps the case par excellence, where several attributes are simultaneously perfectly satisfied, notably justice and mercy meet.

This reconciling of justice and mercy is especially striking in the context of this discussion, since the irreconcilable conflict of justice and mercy is an example of incommensurability cited by those persuaded by Berlin's thesis: their point is that justice and mercy do not meet.[45] Instead, so the reasoning runs, there are two choices before us in situations where justice and mercy both apply. We can opt for one or the other and have it perfectly, in which case the other may not be realized even imperfectly. Alternatively, we can choose to have imperfect justice and imperfect mercy, but, stresses the Berlin line of thought, we should acknowledge the imperfection.

However, the Bible presents us with a God who is both just and merciful. This is evident from the key theophany of Exodus 34:5ff., where God reveals his character in terms of both his mercy (Exod. 34:6) and his justice (necessarily implicit in the phrasing about not clearing the guilty, Exod. 34:7). God's commitment to justice emerges in the history of Israel and Judah. Thus in Amos chapters 1 and 2, God decrees merited punishment on the Gentile nations surrounding the kingdoms of Israel and Judah. These decrees are, of course, expressed in a repeated formula: 'for three transgressions of [whichever city or kingdom] and for four, I will not turn away the punishment . . . because . . . [and then a clause specifying the crimes committed]'. The formulaic expressions Amos employs here stress that the actions about which God complains are sinful or criminal, and that his reactions are morally merited responses to what has been done. However, an obvious feature of justice is that similar crimes deserve similar treatment. As such, given the commitment to justice shown in the condemnation on Gentiles by Amos 1:3 – 2:3, it is no surprise to find a just God likewise stipulating judgment on Judah (Amos 2:4–5) and Israel (Amos 2:6ff.).

Other pre-exilic prophets like Isaiah and Jeremiah provide further examples of God's commitment to justice, even when that involves the execution of justice on his covenant people. In addition we should note the way that the post-exilic penitential prayers of Nehemiah 9 (e.g. v. 33) and Daniel 9 (e.g. vv. 7 and 14) alike feature confessions of God's justice, covenant faithfulness and consistency in bringing the exile on Israel and Judah. At this point it is evident that the justice of God is a perilous thing for men and women who have failed to live by his word. Justice becomes simultaneously something to be desired and to be avoided.

Yet the same material also contains promises by this promise-keeping God that he will show mercy. Thus Amos 9:11–15 closes with predictions of mercy and favour to the people who have deserved judgment. Likewise, the prayers of Ezra 9 and Daniel 9 (especially at v. 18) appeal to God's mercy. These prayers are perhaps particularly striking: there seems no sense of appealing to an inconsistent attribute of God in appealing to his mercy. Rather, there is a consciousness that God is faithful to his word and that the exile shows precisely this (Neh. 9:29–30, 33–35 and Dan. 9:12–13). And it is just this consistency and faithfulness to his word that prompts Daniel's prayer in the first place and on which he relies, as he contemplates the promises made through Jeremiah (Dan. 9:2–3).[46]

Several responses are possible as we regard this presence of both mercy and justice in the biblical material. We could, of course, simply deem the two as inconsistent and privilege one strand or the other. There are traces of such an attitude in those who deny Amos 9:11–15 is authentic. For them the discrepancy between those verses and the bulk of the rest of the book is too great – they are incommensurable and we should, the argument runs, accept that Amos's 'real' message is the message of destructive justice on sinful people, whether Israelite or Gentile. This approach reveals a trajectory or tendency, the tendency to put one's message, one's gospel, in terms of either justice or mercy. Arguably, some presentations of the gospel today risk doing just that, that mercy is proffered in our gospel talks without due consideration of the justice of God (Bonhoeffer's criticism of 'cheap grace' still merits attention). Similarly, understandable passions for justice, especially social justice, sometimes sound as though there is no prospect of mercy for some, notably the rich; for wealth is, it seems, for some, the new unforgivable sin.

Yet in fact the presence side by side of mercy and justice is quite central to the Old Testament presentation of God. As well as the theophany of Exodus 34, key material in Deuteronomy, especially chapters 28–30, deals both with God's inevitable justice (e.g. Deut. 28:15–68) and his mercy (e.g. Deut. 30:3ff.). The emphasis of Amos, Isaiah and Jeremiah on both justice and mercy is therefore typical of this covenantal outlook.

Moreover, the reality of Israel's Old Testament experience shows all too painfully that human beings stand in need of both justice and mercy. A gospel without perfect justice entails us in a future that falls short of perfect justice. Berlin is quite right here that if one does really think values are incommensurable, then some or all of them will not be perfectly realized. Similarly, a gospel without perfect mercy is actually a gospel without hope for a human race that has universally, with the exception of Jesus, fallen into sin.

Yet in the cross God's just wrath against sinners is perfectly met. For judgment on sin is executed. In that sense, the cross is not a triumph of God's mercy in which justice is displaced and the need to administer it somehow ignored. Nor is the cross a triumph of justice which precludes mercy, for the cross is the supreme act of mercy, as well as an act of justice. There, undeservedly, the Son of God took my place, the place which morally I did deserve, and in his great love endured in the stead of sinners like me the wrath which would otherwise directly fall on us. This remains an act directed to me and my sin since by faith union I am united to Christ. One of the results of this faith union is that just as he is clothed in our sin, so we are clothed in his righteousness. But as he becomes sin for our sakes and in union with us, the just penalty for sin is observed. As he becomes sin for our sakes undeservedly and out of his gracious love for us, his mercy is manifest.

The penal substitutionary death of the Son, in pursuit of a single promised plan for redemption spanning human history (1 Peter 1:20), really is a testimony among other things to the simplicity of God, in whom all attributes are perfectly realized, without trade-off or competition or compromise. Considered in this light the penal substitutionary death of the cross is part and parcel of the sovereign and simple God. Indeed without it, there is no little difficulty in formulating an account of redemption which does not sacrifice either God's mercy or his justice. The penal substitutionary view of the cross underlines the moral coherence of the universe, not its incommensurable values.

In short, we may say the cross is plural – yet unified – and perhaps the greatest criticism we could launch against Berlin's incommensurable pluralism is that it is not cross-shaped.

It was said above that the cross was plural, in that it shows both justice and mercy perfectly realized. That takes us to the point that Christians do not necessarily deny plurality and diversity in the affairs of the cosmos, even though the Bible teaches the uniqueness of God and his sole monarchy. But just as Paul spoke about a better way, so perhaps we should speak of a better pluralism. By this I mean a pluralism which is ultimately coherent and commensurable, while Berlin's is incommensurable and ultimately breeds incoherence. Just as an incommensurable pluralism denies sovereignty and simplicity, so a Christ-based pluralism will affirm precisely sovereignty and simplicity.

However, we must note how it is that we are integrating, coordinating and rendering commensurable the diverse actions and values that human life contains: through Christ's lordship. In some respects, this principle is already recognized among us in our corporate life as Christ's church. We are rightly used to the idea of diversity of gifts and ministry within the church, but nevertheless we are instructed to have an orderly diversity, with an integrating principle, the edification of Christ's people under his lordship (see 1 Cor. 12 – 14). We should not, therefore, find principles of coordination or uniformity simply arbitrarily imposed by humans.

Yet are there not some obvious extensions to these arguments? Those same arguments about sovereignty and coherence under Christ apply with equal force more widely than the life of the church. If we are serious that the gospel involves God's kingdom realized through his Son, then the ambit of that kingdom should not be arbitrarily restricted by human decision. There is a real question to face, whether we have done something like this in our comparative slowness, within the context of English evangelicalism, to apply Christ's sovereignty to literature, or the visual or cinematic arts, or the sciences. What it is to write a Christian piece of literature, or do biology in a way that upholds Christ's lordship are certainly unfamiliar, indeed unfashionable, questions, given their association with that slightly unfashionable Dutchman Abraham Kuyper.[47] Yet defending the gospel against the claims of ideas such as Berlin's incommensurable pluralism seems to take us back to just this place.

After all, if we fail to do this we run the risk if instating a new kind of incommensurable pluralism, one where there is a realm where Christ is rightly lord: the world of the believer and the church. There, one set of rules and expectations apply. But there would also be other realms where different rules and expectations apply. This may well be how some Christians have at times behaved in the United Kingdom, comparatively reluctant to engage in the public forum, and with a tendency to leave matters of faith as essentially private. Yet it is hard to see how this differs in effect from incommensurable pluralism, and this, as we have seen, is an implicit denial of the kingdom of Christ.

In relation to humans . . .

We should move now to think of incommensurable pluralism in relation to humans. Perhaps the first thing to strike us here is the relationship with idolatry.

Idolatry

The reason why incommensurable pluralism takes us back to idolatry is that incommensurable pluralism seems inevitably to involve a very strong element of human sovereignty. In incommensurable pluralism we have values or virtues that govern our lives and the values are ones that we each select, arranged as we want, just as in idolatry we shape whichever gods we have chosen to our own specifications. More than this, we should note how we become invulnerable to criticism. The invulnerability comes from the way values, and hence value systems, are incommensurable. If they are incommensurable, then you cannot employ your values to criticize the values others have chosen, for your values *belong* in a different set from those other values. Your criticism will be met with the response that it does not apply, because it would be like comparing apples with oranges. In that respect the former Bishop of Edinburgh, Richard Holloway, affords a good example of this invulnerability to criticism as he utilizes Berlin's ideas of incommensurability to fire-proof from objections his defence of practising homosexuality.[48] We should remember, too, that this process renders evangelism impossible to defend, because one cannot categorize the values others hold as idolatry, from which they should turn to serve the true and living God (1 Thess. 1:9).

In this context it is relevant to recall the account that the redoubtable church father Tertullian provides of idolatry.[49] He points out that idolatry arises with perilous ease when real values are valued, but valued to the exclusion of others. For then indeed something of genuine value can stand in God's place, excluding God and obstructing proper sight of him.[50] That value can exclude the true biblical picture of God in whom all the genuine values are coherently found. Chesterton saw the tragedy of this with exceptional clarity in the passage I have already quoted. The point is not that the virtues to which Chesterton refers are not real virtues, established by God. The point is that shorn of their true integration in the one God, they function as idols. Indeed, the very fact that they do have an origin in God's ordained scale of values can give them a tremendous plausibility, as C. S. Lewis rightly saw in *The Great Divorce* as he discussed how divinely willed virtues could become all the more terrible as idols, because they were great virtues.

It is difficult, finally, to ignore some of the more pastoral issues idolatry tends to create. Idolatry (which is described in Hos. 1 and 2 as a 'whoredom') parodies

proper spiritual marriage, just as adultery parodies legitimate marriage. The
Bible notes our tendency to become like our idols (e.g. Ps. 115:8). We should
here recall that we analysed incommensurable pluralism earlier as polytheist,
with, in fact, a tendency to cosmic anarchy. What would that mean for people
who live and 'worship' (in the sense of ascribing great worth) within that world
view? If this analysis of polytheism is correct, it would not be entirely surprising
if it did not produce 'disintegrated' humans; that is to say, humans who miss
any final integration within themselves – humans who have no centre, to use
again the language of Yeats's poem. In the light of this, it is no cause for amaze-
ment that human urban life in the West is so marked by inconsistency and
lacunae: our culture has come to love its private-versus-public distinctions, with
different rules for each; we have come to thrive on differential application of
norms, permitting things for one group while denying them for another. No
one, for instance, will be holding their breath to wait for pro-homosexual
activists to be prosecuted under Britain's law and order legislation in the way
Harry Hammond was.

The appeal to self-righteousness – hypocrisy

This survey of our tendency to idolatry needs, perhaps, to be considered in
conjunction with another feature of the biblical description of humans. The
Bible tells us that humans are not simply given to wrongdoing while overtly
acknowledging their wrongness. We are not in the habit of raising our hands
and confessing, 'We quite see that we're doing wrong and intend to go on doing
what we know is morally indefensible.' Rather, we harbour a strong streak of
hypocrisy – a tendency to do wrong things while simultaneously asserting our
moral rectitude. Thus John 16:1ff. features Jesus' foretelling that the disciples
will be persecuted: this is not done because of a freely confessed hatred of God;
rather, it is done while – terribly – claiming to be loyal to God. The reality,
though, as Jesus makes clear in the surrounding material is one of hatred of
God and his anointed (John 15:23–24; 16:3). In a similar way, the final result
that Paul describes in the downward spiral of sin in Romans 1:18–32 comes in
verse 32, where Paul describes not a simple amoralism, where nothing is right
or wrong, but an inverted moralism, where what is wrong has been called right.

Incommensurable pluralism needs to be related to this streak for hypocrisy.
We have stressed above that incommensurable pluralism in effect allows us to
pick our supreme values, because it allows us to see values in splendid isolation
from each other, permitting them to be secure from criticism and competition.
If we do indeed have a tendency to hypocrisy, this is like leaving a gin bottle in
front of an alcoholic, because we will be inclined to choose our values in ways
that guarantee our rightness and also our immunity. As such, incommensurable

pluralism allows, dare one say it fosters, moral opportunism and hypocrisy: it allows the luxury of a self-indulgence that also rejoices in its moral self-righteousness. But perhaps that has become merely descriptive of much of contemporary Britain.

Conclusions

I therefore conclude, first, Berlin's incommensurable pluralism itself runs the risk of incoherence and can give rise to the very thing Berlin so fears, a ruthless and unaccountable tyranny and, despite its good intentions, the erosion of civic liberties.

As such, second, we must indeed go on looking for and proclaiming 'the' gospel. Looking for 'the' gospel implies singularity and coherence. This is quite compatible with recognizing plurality and diversity, but not compatible with a particular type of pluralism: incommensurable pluralism. This matters because the gospel is a question of obedience and God's will for our lives. An inconsistent series of gospels means God has inconsistent wills for us.

Third, we need to recognize that such incommensurable pluralism is polytheistic, and if we were to accept this kind of pluralism, whether tacitly or explicitly, we would by implication be denying God's monarchy and simplicity. In short we would have a different God. We would also be making ourselves even more vulnerable than we already are to some remarkable temptations: a temptation to idolatry and a temptation to hypocrisy.

This means that when we do encounter claims that a particular 'gospel proclamation' is drawing out another different strand of gospel teaching, we need to exercise considerable care as to whether this different kerygma or proclamation represents a diversity that is coherent or incoherent, commensurable or incommensurable. Where the diversity remains coherent, and the biblical foundation justified, we must joyfully admit the diversity, for it enriches our understanding of God's way with his world. Where the diversity becomes incoherent, then justifications arising from diversity and potential for enrichment cannot succeed.

Fourth, this survey of incommensurable pluralism takes us back to a sharp focus on the cross of Jesus Christ, and a renewed wonder at it, because it represents not the imperfection of values in God's plan of salvation or their incommensurability, but precisely their commensurability, as justice and mercy meet and are equally perfected, so that with God there is a just mercy and a merciful justice. Here, incommensurable pluralism signally fails to explain who God is, and what he has done for our salvation.

Notes

1. Originally published in C. Green (ed.), *God's Power to Save: One Gospel for a Complex World?* (Leicester: Apollos, 2006), pp. 17–54. Reproduced with permission of Inter-Varsity Press.

2. G. K. Chesterton, *Orthodoxy* (London: Bodley Head, 1909), p. 51.

3. Notably see F. Schaeffer, *The God Who Is There* (London: Hodder & Stoughton, 1968).

4. Similarly Reformed theology of John Owen's period (1616–83) distinguished archetypal from ectypal theological knowledge. Archetypal knowledge is the self-knowledge God has of himself and is complete and infallible. Ectypal knowledge, the kind humans have, is not complete but is nevertheless genuine in so far as it rests on God's self-knowledge and arises from his revelation.

5. See W. D. Mounce, *The Pastoral Epistles*, Word Biblical Commentary 46 (Nashville: Thomas Nelson, 2000), p. 392.

6. Note the use of *elenchein* in forensic and logical discourse with respect to a demonstrated argument; e.g. Aristotle in *Sophistical Refutations* is dealing with invalid *arguments*, and defines 'refutation' in terms of argument thus: 'For to refute is to contradict one and the same attribute – not merely the name, but the reality – and a name that is not merely synonymous but the same name – and to confute it from the propositions granted, necessarily, without including in the reckoning the original point to be proved, in the same respect and relation and manner and time in which it was asserted.' *Sophistical Refutations* 1.5.

7. Cf. Acts 17:30, where Paul envisages a general moral duty on pagans to repent.

8. S. E. Porter, *Idioms of the Greek New Testament*, 2nd edn (Sheffield: Sheffield Academic Press, 1994), p. 167, stresses the idea of replacement. D. B. Wallace, *Greek Grammar Beyond the Basics* (Grand Rapids: Zondervan, 1996), p. 378, notes the sense of opposition that *para* can carry.

9. Isaiah Berlin taught for many years at Oxford, notably in the fields of political theory, and was the first President of Wolfson College. He had earlier held the Chichele chair of social and political theory from 1957 to 1967.

10. See I. Berlin, 'The Pursuit of the Ideal', in H. Hardy and R. Hausheer (eds.), *The Proper Study of Mankind* (London: Pimlico, 1998), pp. 1–16.

11. Machiavelli, a Florentine public servant and man of letters, is best known, of course, for his short work on maintaining autocratic power, *The Prince*. His own preferred form of government, republicanism, is developed in *The Discourses*. His analysis has strong common features between the two works, although differently applied.

12. Vico was professor of Rhetoric at the University of Naples. He is best known for *The New Science*, which Berlin considered illuminated the way human creation is located and limited in particular historical environments.

13. Herder contributed notably to reflection on the relation between thought and language, and was a significant part of German reaction to the Enlightenment.

14. Berlin, 'Pursuit', pp. 6–9.

15. Berlin also calls this idea 'objective pluralism': here the description 'incommensurable pluralism' is preferred, because incommensurability is an idea Berlin frequently employs, and 'objective' is dangerously ambiguous in this context.

16. Berlin's work on the history of ideas and his contributions to the analysis and influence of German Romanticism are of enduring value.

17. I. Berlin, 'Two Concepts of Liberty', in H. Hardy and R. Hausheer (eds.), *The Proper Study of Mankind: An Anthology of Essays* (London: Chatto & Windus, 1997), pp. 191–242.

18. Chesterton, *Orthodoxy*, p. 51.

19. Stated within short compass, and with Berlin's usual elegance, in Berlin, 'Pursuit', pp. 11–12. As regards the incoherence point, see also I. Berlin, 'Vico and the Ideal of the Enlightenment', in H. Hardy and R. Hausheer (eds.), *Against the Current: Essays in the History of Ideas* (London: Pimlico, 1997), pp. 25–78. Berlin, 'Two Concepts', p. 241, derives much of its power from the argument about danger.

20. Thus Berlin, 'Pursuit', p. 7, merely speaks of 'Not all' the supreme values being consistent.

21. Berlin, 'Pursuit', p. 11.

22. See e.g. Berlin, 'Pursuit', pp. 7–8. Cf. Berlin, 'Vico', pp. 123–124.

23. A not unusual basis for justice, comparable to the Aristotelian idea of rendering to each what he deserves.

24. Berlin, 'Pursuit', p. 10.

25. Berlin, 'Pursuit', p. 10.

26. Berlin, 'Pursuit', p. 13.

27. Berlin, 'Pursuit', p. 9.

28. Berlin, 'Two Concepts', p. 242.

29. W. B. Yeats, *The Second Coming*.

30. Chesterton, *Orthodoxy*, p. 51.

31. I. Berlin, 'The Originality of Machiavelli', in Hardy and Hausheer, *Proper Study*, pp. 269–325.

32. Bernard Crick gives a lucid and brief account in his introduction to *The Discourses* (Harmondsworth: Penguin, 1970), especially pp. 61–67, on the question of politics and morality.

33. Berlin, 'Machiavelli', p. 301.

34. Berlin, 'Machiavelli', p. 301.

35. For the tendency during Stalin's Terror to produce 'moral' justification, see R. Conquest, *The Great Terror* (London: Macmillan, 1968).

36. An example cited by Bernard Williams, who sympathizes with Berlin's thesis. B. Williams, 'Conflicts of Values', in A. Ryan (ed.), *The Idea of Freedom: Essays in Honour of Isaiah Berlin* (Oxford: Oxford University Press, 1979), pp. 221–232.

37. A key idea in both Berlin, 'Two Concepts', and Berlin, 'Machiavelli'.

38. Especially Athanasius, *Contra Gentes* 6.

39. Texts cited in this connection include Jon. 4:2 and 1 Kgs 21:29.

40. W. Ames, *The Marrow of Theology*, trans. J. D. Eusden, 3rd Latin edn, 1968 (Grand Rapids: Baker, 1997), I.iv.23.

41. *Contra Gentes* 6.

42. *Third Oration on the Son* 1–2.

43. De Tocqueville (1805–59) was a French politician/writer best known for *Democracy in America*, trans. Henry Reeve, 2 vols. (repr., New York: Langley, 1841).

44. Berlin, 'Pursuit', p. 13.

45. See e.g. Williams, 'Conflicts'. Berlin and his followers are frequently more concerned, though, with a different value conflict: that between freedom and equality.

46. Cf. Neh. 9:31 for a similar point regarding God's pre-exilic actions.

47. Kuyper's case for the universal lordship of Christ applying to all the spheres of human conduct, not just the life of the church, is set out concisely in his *Lectures on Calvinism* (Grand Rapids: Eerdmans, 1931).

48. Lecture at Middlesex University, 1998.

49. Flourished AD 200. Tertullian wrote in Latin and lived in Carthage, in modern-day Tunisia.

50. *Pro deo adversus deum.*

24. APPROPRIATING AULÉN? EMPLOYING *CHRISTUS VICTOR* MODELS OF THE ATONEMENT[1]

Introduction

Gustaf Aulén is a name with which to conjure. A. G. Hebert's preface to his own translation of Aulén's best-known work in English, *Christus Victor*, struck a representatively laudatory note, while J. Macquarrie thought Aulén's case offered 'the most promising basis for a contemporary statement of the work of Christ . . .'.[2] It perhaps comes as a surprise to find that elsewhere Aulén has been castigated as in some respects superficial,[3] abounding in 'bold assertions without adequate proof',[4] and as having a doctrine of the incarnation which departs from the orthodox doctrine laid out at Chalcedon and later Councils.[5]

This broad spectrum of views, the gravity of some of the charges levelled at Aulén and the significance some attach to Aulén's work suggest we must dig deeper than a simple 'I accept Aulén' or 'I reject Aulén' or a broad 'I'm relying on Aulén.' The aim here is to establish quite what Aulén was arguing, how that might be evaluated and finally whether and how we might properly adopt Aulén's argument today. In doing this, this paper will try to show that Aulén's argument falls into two distinct parts,[6] a positive case and a negative case, and that the positive case, relating to the conquest of evil, in fact requires a notion that lies at the heart of penal substitution: justice.

However, we do well to recall why Aulén is so relevant to present evangelical deliberations on penal substitution. A rightly persistent question is, 'What is the objective work of the cross, the work extrinsic to human beings?' It remains relatively common ground among those identifying themselves as evangelicals that the cross does have an objective work. It is also common ground among us, I think, that the cross has a subjective work: it elicits a response in us and provides a model for our conduct. Yet many evangelicals are concerned to go beyond an exclusively subjective account, and defenders of penal substitution have asked those rejecting that doctrine, 'What is your account of the objective work of Christ, if you reject penal substitution?' Aulén's argument answers just that question: it suggests an objective work without penal substitution. Certainly, Aulén's argument has been used in this way in debates in the UK after the publication of *The Lost Message of Jesus.*[7]

Yet in fact Aulén's argument has a wider scope: he suggests not merely that there are other pictures of the cross than penal substitution, but rather that penal substitution is not a legitimate picture of the cross. Therefore, Aulén's argument is significant in our current debates because it offers opponents of penal substitution not only an alternative objective work of Christ in the atonement but also reasons to deny that penal substitution is a legitimate picture of the cross.

Aulén's work

Aulén's context

Before outlining Aulén's argument, he must be put in context. Born in 1879, he became professor at the University of Lund from 1913 where, with Anders Nygren, he was associated with so-called Lundensian theology. Prompted by the meeting of conservative Swedish Lutheran church life with the liberal theology emerging from some quarters of nineteenth-century Germany, the Lundensian approach tended to have some characteristic emphases. The following are relevant here.

First, theology is separate from metaphysics.[8] This partly perhaps explains Aulén's evident antipathy towards Anselm and certain scholastic approaches both pre-Reformation and afterwards:[9] the risk, he thinks, of seeking a rational understanding and justification of the affirmations of faith – *fides quaerens intellectum* in that sense – is precisely that it mixes faith and metaphysics. Second, theology is a descriptive discipline which has as its 'object of study the Christian faith'.[10] Third, the central task in this study is to 'remove all unnecessary accretions, and to bring out the very heart of the matter'.[11] This means Aulén, and indeed Nygren, are deeply concerned with separating out the underlying theme from the verbal formulae in which that theme may from time to time be expressed.[12] Particularly important is the axiom that the idea or theme can be separated from the form.[13] Such fundamental motifs provide the unity which underlies the varieties of verbal formulae.[14] Fourth, for Christianity, the key idea or theme, certainly for Aulén, is God's love.[15] Fifth, there is a commitment to the act of God in Christ, an affirmation to the importance of historic Christianity as against the allegedly moralizing liberal theology of A. Ritschl and others,[16] although there is also a willingness to use some of the biblical and historical criticism associated with that school.

For Aulén himself two other things require comment. First, he has a deep and persistent affection and respect for Luther.[17] Second, more importantly for current debates, Aulén is opposed to conventional theories of biblical inspiration, not least because historical criticism has, to his mind, made it impossible to think that the Bible has the uniformity a theory of inspiration suggests.[18] Moreover, he fears such theories of biblical inspiration mean the Bible carries its own authority as revelation, which would mean that the revelation of God in Christ ceases to be the supreme criterion for judging revelation.

Aulén keeps a special place for the New Testament, however. The New Testament writings are irreplaceable testimony to Christ.[19] The status of the unique testimony of the New Testament is certainly high in his estimation. Yet logically enough given his presuppositions, this falls short of the New Testament being the decisive benchmark of acceptable faith. Aulén goes on:

> But this [the unique testimony of the New Testament] does not mean that no other conceptions of faith are permitted except those produced within this most ancient testimony, nor that every one of the conceptions of faith found within the New Testament should without further consideration be accepted as legitimate parts of the Christian faith.[20]

Therefore, for Aulén, even the New Testament is not authoritative in itself to ground or exclude propositions of faith. This obviously differs from conventional evangelical understandings of the Bible such as that found in the Evangelical Alliance (UK) Basis of Faith.[21] Such a position on the Bible potentially affects evangelical attempts to appropriate Aulén's work. His theological method is not evangelical and does not claim to be.

Aulén's argument relating to Christus Victor

Aulén's subtitle for *Christus Victor* is *An Historical Study of the Three Main Types of the Idea of the Atonement*.[22] The types in question are what he terms the Latin view (penal substitution is, strictly speaking, simply one species of this type), which involves satisfaction of some kind; the subjective view, associated with Abelard;

and the dramatic or classic idea, which relates to the victory of God in Christ over what enslaves and tyrannizes humanity.[23]

Two observations are necessary. First, *Christus Victor* is ostensibly a 'historical study', without 'personal statements of belief', although it is fair to say that *Christus Victor* strongly implies the correctness of the dramatic or classic idea.[24] In fact, the argument of *Christus Victor* appears more prescriptively in Aulén's *The Faith of the Christian Church*.[25] We may fairly see *Christus Victor* as setting out Aulén's own position.[26]

Second, the types are treated as alternatives. Thus Aulén does not deal with how one could combine, say, the Latin idea with the classic idea, as different perspectives on the work of the cross. Rather, Aulén's argument is that there is essentially one perspective, the classic idea, with its related images. The reason Aulén does not think in terms of different perspectives is that he views both Latin and subjective ideas as resting on a view of divine and human action which is incompatible and inconsistent with the classic view, a point to be developed below.

His argument then breaks into two related parts. His positive case is that the classic idea has been unduly eclipsed and should be recognized for what it is: the authentic view of the early church and the New Testament. His negative case is that neither the Latin view nor the subjective view does justice to what God did in Christ. We must now flesh out these cases.

Aulén's positive case: the victory of Christ

Aulén on dualism and defiance of God's will

Aulén envisages a dualism in the world: 'To Christian faith history appears as an arena where the conflict between the will of God and that which is inimical to it takes place.'[27]

He hastens to add that this is not an absolute dualism, for God created this world. Rather, it is a dualism relating to conflict with God's will.[28] This conflict is universal in that it covers all human existence and God contests all that resists his will.[29] Defying God's will is central to Aulén's conception of sin:

> Sin is a perverse will, and therefore the opposite of that which it ought to be. Whether it appears as indifference or hostility to the loving will of God, sin is the opposite of this will. Where sin and egocentricity hold sway, there a power rules which is hostile to divine love . . .[30]

Sin for Aulén has a double aspect. Negatively, it is unbelief because it refuses the fundamental relationship between God and humans, which is God's loving

rule.[31] Positively, it is egocentricity, because something other than God rules –
there is another power in the individual's life: 'This other power which rules
man in sin is nothing else than his *own ego*.'[32]

Thus already Aulén has introduced notions of rule, so central to ideas of
victory. It is arguable, though, that the language of 'other power' in a human
being injects distance between the individual and her or his sin because the
terms tend to externalize the human will out from the human individual, even
moving, perhaps, towards the idea of a human being ruled by her or his will as
if it were somehow distinct from that human being. Clearly, though, Aulén's
argument envisages that sin has an individual component – unbelief and egocentricity at least include the individual level.

From here Aulén proceeds to note that 'Wherever this power rules, the fellowship with God is destroyed.'[33] This must follow since Aulén regularly defines the
divine–human relation in terms of God's will. However, Aulén does not have
an exclusively individual account of sin. He writes, 'Sinfulness does not belong
simply to separate individuals, it is characteristic of the whole human race.'[34]

He explains this more collective emphasis in terms of the network of relationships in which humans exist – we practise unbelief and egocentricity in
relations with each other:

> The solidary interrelationship of sin concretizes itself in inscrutable and obscure
> powers, a mysterious complex which cannot be accurately delimited and defined, and
> which slips away and becomes shadowy as soon as one tries to grasp and comprehend
> it. Nevertheless it shows its power in the most fearful manner and by the most cruel
> oppression of human life.[35]

However, this corporate aspect does not simply subsume the individual.
Aulén is emphatic that the individual aspect remains:

> No matter how much personal sin stands in an intimate connection with sin as a demonic
> power,[36] this personal sin is nevertheless something which adheres to and determines the
> personal will as such and is a result of this personal will and a reflection of its character.[37]

As a result, Aulén's account of sin has both corporate and individual elements,
both of which he argues must be retained.[38]

God's victory over the powers
Outline of the victory motif

Aulén's discussion of the classic view of the atonement takes place against this
understanding of the human predicament. He defines the *Christus Victor* idea

thus: 'Christ – Christus Victor – fights against and triumphs over the evil powers of the world, the "tyrants" under which mankind is in bondage and suffering, and in Him God reconciles the world to Himself.'[39]

Naturally, this prompts the question 'Who are the evil powers?' Aulén argues that the New Testament and patristic discussions of these ideas of victory bring several images to the fore: sin, death and the devil, along with 'law' (in Paul), and 'cosmos' (in the Johannine writings), while Luther, to Aulén's approval, includes God's wrath as another tyrant.[40]

Yet these evil powers are not identical. They fall into two different categories. The first category of powers have, for Aulén, a twofold aspect. Sin is not in this category. But death, law, wrath and the devil are 'on the one hand, tyrannical powers which enslave humanity, and on the other hand the instruments of divine judgment'.[41] As instruments of divine judgment, these powers serve the divine will. This means, according to Aulén, that the victory on the cross is, in a sense, God's dealing with himself, for in dealing with them he deals with powers serving his own will.[42] The significance of this will become clear later.

However, sin is an exception to this, and constitutes the second category of powers. It does not have this twofold aspect of being both tyrant and also instrument of judgment which serves the divine will. Aulén states, 'This hostile power cannot serve the divine will except in so far as the divine will overcomes it and turns it into good.'[43]

This must follow, because Aulén, as we have seen, has defined sin in terms of a will distinct from God that defies God. Sin therefore cannot be an instrument of that divine will in the same way that divine wrath is, for it arises from wills distinct from God. We should also note that sin, in a category of its own as power, is in fact logically prior, since death, wrath, devil and law arise as powers on account of sin. It may seem surprising that the devil is included in this list of logically subsequent powers, but the reasons why this is so in Aulén's scheme appear below.

Centrality of the victory motif

Aulén argues this view of victory over the tyrant powers is 'the dominant view' of both the New Testament and the early church.[44] A crucial part of his argument at this point depends on his first category of tyrannical powers: that they are both tyrants and also instruments of divine will. Using this twofold aspect, Aulén argues that victory over these powers is an act of reconciliation. God is reconciling the world to himself by his self-giving sacrifice in Christ and this is an act of victory.[45] Consequently, reconciliation and ransom language are not categories that are distinct from victory, let alone categories that support Latin views: they belong with victory. Hence Aulén's view that victory is the global motif.

In making this case, he lays particular stress on Irenaeus,[46] while for the New Testament he states that the classic idea 'has never found more pregnant expression' than in 2 Corinthians 5:18–19.[47] At first glance this is surprising since the passage does not contain explicit victory or defeat terminology, but, of course, Aulén has blended victory and reconciliation and hence sees the passage as an instance of the classic view. Further, Luther himself when properly understood was an exponent of the classic view rather than the Latin satisfaction view.[48]

Advantage of the victory motif

For Aulén the critical advantage of the classic idea is that it means atonement is a 'continuous' divine action, in which God is both reconciler and reconciled: all is of God. Atonement is 'from first to last a work of God Himself'.[49] God appears, it seems, as both subject and object of reconciliation, in particular, subject. In part, one suspects that Aulén stresses this so much out of a wish to preserve the principle that salvation must be by God alone since humanity is helpless in its sin. Given this framework that victory/reconciliation is a 'continuous' divine act, reasons Aulén, incarnation and atonement are properly and clearly related,[50] one of the great merits Hebert sees in the *Christus Victor* model.[51] This takes us to Aulén's negative case.

The negative case: the exclusion of Latin theories

Aulén's arguments for exclusion

Aulén's argument is not merely that *Christus Victor* is a model of the atonement that has been unduly neglected, so that with it we have a valuable extra perspective. It also asserts that the Latin model is defective, and hence one cannot, Aulén thinks, have Latin and victory views as complementary, different perspectives on the atonement. Aulén's reasons are, however, rather different from what might be expected. This should be stressed. The arguments debated among us over the last two decades against penal substitution are not those that were central for Aulén. Again, that means when hearing or making a claim to accept Aulén, we must clarify whether this acceptance includes the rationale that Aulén holds for his position.

Continuous action and the Latin view

The idea to which Aulén constantly returns is that the Latin view is not a 'continuous' act of God, an act of God, so to speak, from start to finish.[52] This is, he argues, 'the most marked difference' between the Latin view and the classic view.[53] The Latin view features an act from the human side. Aulén writes, 'It is at this point, in the payment of the required satisfaction, that the continuity of Divine operation is lost; for the satisfaction is offered by Christ as man, as the sinless Man on behalf of the sinners.'[54] Such payment made as a man undermines the message of grace and reinstates, it seems, merit and law.

This outlook is not just present in, but decisive for, Aulén's handling of the biblical evidence. Aulén, naturally, thinks that the Bible, or, rather more precisely, the New Testament, does not support the Latin view. However, his rationale for this conclusion repays attention. In discussing Romans 3:24, he suggests it lacks the idea of satisfaction being made by Christ on man's behalf, an offering 'made to God from man's side, from below', and for this reason contends that this does not support a Latin doctrine.[55] The offering 'from below', feels Aulén, is indispensable to the Latin view.[56] Similarly, when discussing Hebrews, Aulén suggests that Hebrews contains a double aspect – Christ's sacrifice is both an act of God and an act offered to him. Aulén writes, 'This double-sidedness is always alien to the Latin type, which develops the latter aspect and eliminates the former.'[57]

In other words, neither Hebrews nor Romans 3:24 supports the Latin view, because both texts lack this idea of offering from the human side. Aulén sees the discontinuity he describes as intrinsic and essential to the Latin view and, failing to find it, concludes these texts do not support the Latin view. Obviously the definition that stipulates discontinuity in the Latin view is a necessary presupposition for Aulén's case on the New Testament material. Aulén's own definition of the Latin view precludes defenders of penal substitution from relying on these traditionally cited texts.

Old Testament and church history

Aulén refers to the Old Testament material which supporters of the Latin view also cite. He observes, 'There is no doubt that there is plenty in the Old Testament that could serve as a basis for the Latin type of view . . .'[58]

However, there is a radical breach between 'Judaism and Christianity', and 'Judaism', as Aulén refers to the Old Testament revelation, has law as its dominating factor, so that in the New Testament we stand on the other side of a 'revolution'.[59] Accordingly, admitting the presence of elements supporting the Latin view in the Old Testament does not, Aulén thinks, affect his argument. Again, the method Aulén has for excluding material supporting Latin views repays attention: it depends on a displacement of Old Testament revelation.

Moving from the Bible to church history, Aulén suggests that the Latin view arises from Tertullian's and Cyprian's views of penance.[60] Aulén comments on such penitential thinking: 'Its root idea is that man must make an offering or payment to satisfy God's justice.'[61] He contends that this is essentially legalistic, and lays all its emphasis on what Christ has done as a man.[62] This, naturally, recalls his central criticism, that the Latin view involves a discontinuous act of God, and means that for Aulén the historical root of the Latin view carries assumptions of discontinuous act.[63] The criticism that there is no continuous act bulks large in his assessment of Anselm. He is well aware that Anselm himself does not assert penal substitution, knowing that Anselm saw satisfaction as an alternative to punishment, but he sees vital common ground in this feature of discontinuous act. He contrasts Anselm with the fathers: 'They show how God became incarnate that He might redeem; he teaches a work of human satisfaction, accomplished by Christ.'[64] Anselm, he says, treats atonement only as God's work 'in a sense', not 'in the full sense'.[65]

Aulén's governing perspective

So Aulén has theological, biblical and historical reasons for his negative case that penal substitution and other versions of the Latin view have no place in proper Christian faith. Yet the theological reason keeps reappearing even as Aulén discusses the biblical and historical matters. The Latin view is rejected on the basis of discontinuous act. One must conclude that the idea of continuous and discontinuous act was decisively important to him.

Evaluating Aulén's positive case

Recovering a diminished strand

One of the most attractive features of Aulén's work is that he draws attention again both to biblical texts and to historical, especially patristic, texts which stress Christ's victory. L. Hodgson describes this as 'a most valuable contribution'.[66] After all, theologically, the principle of the whole counsel of God requires that if a truth is taught in the Bible, we accept it. Pastorally, this restored focus on victory is very welcome, not least because it supports the assurance and security of salvation, and encourages Christians in present difficulties. Moreover, many would feel that Aulén's unashamed discussion of victory over the devil speaks of a full-blooded endorsement of spiritual realities, at odds with the anti-supernaturalism which has dogged post-Enlightenment Christianity in the West. Surely, then, Aulén's positive case can be accepted without further argument?

This is not, alas, so. The broad thrust of the criticisms we are about to examine is not that Aulén was wrong to point to the victory motif, but that he did not do full justice to that motif.

A demythologized devil? J. C. Diamond's criticism

I outlined earlier Aulén's dualistic view, that this world is the arena of conflict between God's will and that 'which is inimical to it'.[67] We saw the way this opposition to God, rooted in unbelief and egocentricity, is interconnected, comprising both individual and collective dimensions, culminating in a human network of sin that oppresses and tyrannizes.[68] Christ overcomes this multifaceted tyranny.

However, the surprising absentee here is a personal devil. Sin and evil have a fundamentally human origin. In this context J. C. Diamond draws attention to Aulén's distinction between forms of expression and the underlying motif or theme.[69] Diamond argues that 'devil' and 'demon' are for Aulén forms of expression, not underlying motifs, and that the underlying realities are sinful human wills, notably in their collectivity.[70] Close examination of *The Faith of the Christian Church* supports Diamond. Aulén describes the power of evil in solidary human interrelationships and says, 'In the New Testament we often meet more or less mythologically formulated expressions *for this complex of evil powers* (cf. Rom. 8:38; Gal. 1:4; Col. 2:15; Eph. 6:12).'[71]

Here the reference to the 'complex of evil powers' can be only to the powers generated by human collective sinfulness.[72] This interpretation receives further support from Aulén's later work. Thus he can note the doubts moderns have about the sick actually being demonically possessed (referring to the Synoptic accounts),[73] and go on to speak of humans being possessed by ideals: 'Even Peter could run errands for "Satan", "possessed" as he was by "the ideal of the Messiah" and its expectations.'[74]

He goes on to provide further instances of ideals as demonic:

> There are plenty of ideals which lead to disastrous results. This world would not be what it is today of [*sic*] money and status did not function as demonic powers. Hitler's Nazism spread like a demonic pestilence. Racial discrimination is a demonic power with enormously damaging results.[75]

Naturally many would firmly agree that such ideals are destructive, and aptly called evil, and that their conquest by God is vital, both as regards their obvious victims, for example Slavs, Jews, Christian dissidents and homosexuals in the case of Nazism, and as regards, to continue the example, those whom Nazism 'possessed' through their belief in it. What is more questionable is the inference that human ideological or social constructions exhaust the 'demonic' as a category.

On reflection, this reductionist turn is unsurprising since Aulén rejects any historical reference for the fall.[76] Thus human sinfulness cannot originate, as Genesis 3 outlines, with an external temptation. The demonic is not a pre-existing category or creature that comes from outside to tempt an originally pure humanity, since the demonic has a human origin. Despite the terminology, Aulén has a demythologized view of Christ's victory, arising in part from his rejection of Genesis 3 as referring to history.[77]

A number of misgivings now surface. First, it is highly questionable whether the New Testament's attitude to demons can be quite so easily dismissed. There is the obvious point that Jesus apparently treats demons as real personal entities in Synoptic exorcism passages.[78]

Second, is Aulén quite reproducing the thought of Irenaeus and Luther as he claims? Aulén acknowledges that both of them use 'grotesque' language to describe demonic opposition to Christ. What is far less clear is whether Irenaeus and Luther would consent to their thoughts about the demonic being rewritten as mere forms of expression which can be retranslated into Aulén's chosen underlying motifs.[79] Diamond notes that where the New Testament sees possession in terms of external evil forces, Aulén internalizes matters so that possession relates to the perverted inclination of our own wills.[80] Possession in that New Testament sense seems to be an empty set.

This means one might say that Aulén has abolished that characteristic Western way of describing the human predicament: that we are oppressed by the world, the flesh and the devil. In Aulén's scheme, this reduces to two: the world and the flesh. Far from being robustly supernaturalist at this point, Aulén seems if anything covertly anti-supernaturalist.

More than that, Aulén's claim to articulate the 'classic' view of the New Testament and the patristic period is much less straightforward. He retains some of the phraseology certainly, but distances himself from what New Testament and patristic writers thought the phraseology referred to. The claim to historical continuity is weakened.

Victory and justice

A further problem is the relation of victory to justice. Aulén quite rightly draws attention to the victory language associated with the atonement. What is less clear in Aulén's account is the intimate association of victory with justice. Thus John 16:11 speaks of the work of the Spirit in terms of conviction that the prince of this world now stands condemned – a justice concept. Earlier in John 12:31 Christ's victory is again associated with an act of judgment: 'Now is the time for judgment on this world; now the prince of this world will be driven out' (NIV). A rightly key reference for victory concepts is 1 John 3:8 and the statement that the Son came to destroy the devil's works. But this is in the context of a discussion about sin, in which we are told that sin is lawlessness

(1 John 3:4), that the Son came to take away our sin (v. 5), implying he came to take away our lawlessness, and that the Christian does what is righteous, just as God is righteous (v. 7: the terminology for 'righteous' coming from the *dikaios* word group, which includes justice ideas in its semantic range). Destruction of the devil's works is then related to the eradication of sin and this is loaded with justice concepts. Nor is this theme of victory with legal notions just Johannine, for Colossians 2:15 speaks of a victory (disarming the principalities and powers), but only after, or with, the cancellation of the 'bond' with its legal demands (v. 14). Victory and justice notions are joined.

Moreover, forgiveness of sin in 1 John has earlier been associated not simply with love but precisely with faithfulness and justice (1 John 1:9: 'he is faithful and just and will forgive us our sins and purify us from all unrighteousness', NIV). We rightly marvel at God's love in the sending of the Son, but strikingly here John grounds the confidence of our forgiveness in God's faithfulness and justice. Aulén, of course, dismissed the Old Testament evidence,[81] among other things because there even grace and mercy stood on a 'legalistic' basis; that is, was shaped by law concepts. But John bids us rely on just these concepts.

The significance of this is twofold. First the presence of justice concepts in this way raises the inevitable question 'How can a just God justly forgive the unjust?' This question prompts the reflections of Paul, of course, in Romans 3:24–26, where the sacrifice of atonement of the Son is a demonstration of justice, a point often made by defenders of penal substitution and an aspect of their argument with which Aulén does not directly deal. Put sharply, if victory in its New Testament fullness involves justice, victory necessarily raises the question of how a just God deals with those who deserve condemnation.

This takes us to our second point. If we exclude justice considerations from God's victory, what is the nature of that victory? It becomes difficult to see it as resting on anything other than power: it would not necessarily be immoral, of course, but it would at best be amoral. One problem this creates is that defiance of the Son's kingdom is met with judgment and condemnation (e.g. 2 Thess. 1:8–9). This implies that such defiance deserves punishment. But the justice of such punishment is far from obvious if the rule defied cannot itself establish its legitimacy because it is amoral. The risk here is that God's victory becomes naked power. Justice concepts tell us not merely that God is powerful, but that his reign is just. But, as we have seen, justice concepts pose the questions that penal substitution is designed to answer, and which victory (including its cognates in Aulén's scheme of reconciliation and ransom) on its own does not.

A further problem is that God's final eschatological victory is praised because of the way justice has been executed:

Hallelujah!
Salvation and glory and power belong to our God,
  for true and just are his judgments.
He has condemned the great prostitute
  who corrupted the earth by her adulteries.
He has avenged on her the blood of his servants.
(Rev. 19:1b–2)

Yet it is far from clear that this aspect of praise for God's victory is similarly stressed in Aulén's account.

Aulén faces a dilemma here. On the one hand, the Latin view insistently faces the question of God's justice – it is rightly said that Anselm's account in *Cur Deus Homo* springs from *iustitia*[82] – and Aulén is critical of the 'legalistic' relationships this implies. So his negative criticism of the Latin view requires some marginalization of justice notions. On the other hand, his source material for his positive view of Christ's victory requires recognition of justice notions. This is present in both New Testament and patristic sources.

Aulén's language may well reflect this dilemma. Speaking of his positive case he suggests that legal language associated with victory reminds us that God's dealings with evil have the 'characteristic of "fair play"'.[83] Yet when contrasting the classic idea with the Latin view, Aulén is keen to stress that on the classic view there is 'discontinuity in the order of justice', but not on the Latin view, in which there is 'continuity' of justice.[84] This means Aulén, overall, affirms that the classic view has both the 'characteristic of "fair play"', and yet also 'discontinuity in the order of justice'.[85] The manifest difficulty in holding both propositions is that a discontinuity in the order of justice seems necessarily to mean a lack of fair play.

In fact, to make much sense of Aulén's formulation, we need to know what the difference is between Latin views of 'continuous' justice and the 'fair play' that Aulén insists is present in God's dealings in the atonement. We also need to know why 'fair play' is not simply a different definition of God's justice from the ones stipulated by the Latin views. If it were simply a different definition, we could examine biblical material to see which definition of justice was best supported. Unfortunately the content of 'fair play' and its distinction from justice remains opaque in Aulén. It is regrettable that Aulén does not specify how there can be discontinuity in the order of justice that does not amount to injustice, nor how God can transcend the order of justice, while remaining righteous, as Aulén insists.[86]

Victory and sin

My next heading relates to a further way in which Aulén's account in fact gives an incomplete conquest of evil. The problem here centres on sin in Aulén's scheme. Earlier descriptions of Aulén's case pointed out that he has two categories of tyrannical powers: death, the devil, wrath, law and the cosmos on the one hand, and sin on the other. Members of the first category, it will be recalled, have a double aspect: they are tyrants and also instruments of judgment serving the divine will. Sin, though, 'cannot serve the divine will . . .'[87] The first category is also, in a sense, logically dependent on the second, in that it is sin that calls forth death and wrath, and so forth. Even the demonic is logically secondary in this sense, arising as it does out of solidary human defiance of God's will.

It will also be recalled that Aulén envisages the history of the world in dualistic terms in which God confronts and must conquer that which opposes him. He argues that in the cross there is victory and reconciliation when God as reconciler and reconciled, subject and object, deals with the powers that tyrannize humans in one continuous divine action.

However, Aulén's explanation of how this occurs in fact features the first category of powers only: he deals with death, the devil, law and wrath.[88] Because they have the double aspect mentioned above, their conquest is, as outlined earlier, in a sense God's dealing with himself.[89] Therefore the principle of continuous divine action, God's being both reconciler and reconciled, subject and object, is satisfied. Sin, on Aulén's own definitions, is not amenable to this kind of treatment. It is related instead to human wills, individual and collective, which defy God's will in unbelief and egocentricity. In conquering sin, the defiant human will, God does not deal with himself.

Aulén attempts briefly to gloss this difficulty by combining sin with death, commenting that they are regularly regarded as two 'expressions for the same thing'.[90] This, though, will not suffice, for Aulén's own definitions mean that sin and death cannot be reduced to the same thing. Sin is defined in terms of individual and collective defiance, with a notable insistence on the preservation of the individual dimension.[91] It is a question of our wills opposing God and, says Aulén, this does not serve the divine will.[92] Death is defined to include separation from God 'in accordance with God's will . . .'.[93] Sin, then, cannot be reduced to death and must remain a distinct category precisely because of the defiant human will, which is not in accord with God's will.

However, why should it matter that sin is a unique category that does not serve the divine will? In Aulén's dualistic conflict, God remains antagonistic to what opposes his will: 'Since the divine will is radically antagonistic to evil, and since God cannot, therefore, be reconciled to evil, this reconciliation entails the destruction of the power of evil and its dominion.'[94]

In the case of sin this should entail the destruction of the will that is locked in unbelief and egocentricity. The problem is, this is the human will, not just at a collective level, but, as Aulén himself insists, at an individual level. To be completely victorious in the cosmic battle, God must be victorious over these individual human wills, so that they are obedient, not rebellious.

At this stage it is clear that Aulén's scheme in fact demands God conquer individual human wills. This sits uncomfortably with his scheme in other respects. He has used a criterion of 'continuous' divine action in which God is both reconciler and reconciled, subject and object, to criticize and reject both Latin and also subjective views of the atonement. In the case of death, devil, wrath and law he preserves continuous action in which God is both reconciler and reconciled, subject and object, by his view that death, devil, law and wrath have a double aspect: they are outworkings of his will, so that God acts, in a sense on himself. Yet in the case of sin, which lacks this double aspect, God cannot be said to act on himself. For what Aulén's scheme requires is that God (subject) conquer the rebellious human will (object). But this is not a continuous divine action which is 'from first to last a work of God Himself'.[95]

Ironically, there is even a perverse resemblance to some presentations of the subjective view of the atonement, that God's action in the cross warms our hearts to submission and obedience instead of rebellion, so that Aulén emerges as a subjective Abelardian despite himself. Similarly Macquarrie envisages the classic view as actually incorporating a subjective aspect as humans contemplate and are inspired by Christ's own personal conquest of the demon of idolatry on the cross.[96]

This leaves the Aulén scheme with something of a problem. It cannot argue that the issue of sin can be ignored, because defiance of God's will is at the root of the dualistic view of the world and its history. Moreover, as has been said, human sin is the logically prior category compared to death, devil, law, wrath and cosmos. It could concede that God's final victory is not simply a continuous divine action in which he is both reconciler and reconciled, subject and object. To concede this, though, would be to surrender the most important criterion Aulén uses to delegitimate the Latin view. An uncomfortable dilemma, then, either to surrender the completeness of God's salvation or the argument which rules out the Latin views.

Summary

In short, while Aulén rightly stresses an important aspect of the atonement, victory, his positive case needs revision to capture the scale of Christ's victory and its nature. For his demythologized view of demons and his inadequate account of the dealing with sin, on his own definition, understate Christ's victory, while the biblical stress on the victory as a just and righteous act of merited judgment is not adequately represented in the idea God has observed the rules of 'fair play'. Moreover, the notion of just victory inevitably takes one to the questions of the justice of God.

The negative case

We turn now to Aulén's negative case, that the Latin view, including penal substitution, is not a legitimate picture of the cross.

The theological criticism: the Latin view involves 'discontinuous' divine action

Aulén's fundamental theological criticism of the Latin view is that it involves discontinuous divine action – the action is by a human being towards God. This criticism, though, is open to several objections, two of which relate to how Aulén applies his criticism, one to the content of the criticism itself.

Aulén's application of his criticism

The application of Aulén's criticism is open to objection on two grounds: that it is inconsistently applied, and that it is applied to a distorted account of the Latin view. First, then, we examine the idea that Aulén does not apply his principle of continuous action consistently. In the book *Christus Victor*, Aulén lays great stress on the work of Irenaeus, bringing out Irenaeus' doctrine of recapitulation.[97] He summarizes Irenaeus thus: 'He shows how the disobedience of the one man, which inaugurated the reign of sin, is answered by the obedience of the One Man who brought life. By His obedience Christ "recapitulated" and annulled the disobedience.'[98]

This is a good summary of Irenaeus on this point: Jesus is the new Adam, Adam as he should have been, so to speak. But Irenaeus' scheme of recapitulation requires that, as the first Adam's disobedience was as a human, so must the new Adam's obedience be as a human: hence the incarnation of the Son. But the obedience must be as a human. We need to look again at the dismissal of the Latin view by Aulén: 'It is at this point, in the payment of the required satisfaction, that the continuity of Divine operation is lost; for the satisfaction is offered by Christ as man, as the sinless Man on behalf of the sinners.'[99]

Continuity is lost, argues Aulén, because Christ offers as man. Yet Irenaeus' account of recapitulation stresses that Christ obeys as man. For instance, Irenaeus writes, 'So, "the Word became flesh" that *by means of the flesh* which sin had mastered and seized and dominated, by this, it might be abolished and no longer be in us.'[100]

But if the continuous-action principle means Christ cannot offer as man, then why should he be able to obey as man without violating the principle? Conversely, if Christ can act in obedience in his human nature and yet the act still be an act of which God is the subject, then the obvious question is why Christ, the Son of God, cannot act as a divine subject, but in his human nature, to make an offering as the Latin view suggests? Aulén's failure to deal with this point at any length leaves outstanding doubts as to whether he applies the principle of continuity of action consistently.

Second, there is the question whether Aulén applies his continuous-action principle to a distorted account of the Latin view. Aulén's use of the continuous-action principle necessarily suggests that the acts of Christ in his humanity in the Latin view are not acts of God. When attempting to state how God's involvement in the Latin view differs from the classic view, Aulén envisages the Latin view as being the work of God in that 'He is regarded as planning the Atonement . . .'.[101] This, though, inadequately describes the ideas of proponents of the Latin view, who envisage the atonement as an act of God. Thus Anselm, Aulén's *bête noire*, sees salvation as God's act, not merely his planning.[102] This is, moreover, integral to Anselm's argument. He insists God is our Saviour because if God does not save, then we should not be his servants, but rather the servants of the one who did save us.[103] The identity of our Saviour matters to Anselm and he would therefore strongly resist the description of his view as one in which man, not God, is the agent.[104]

However, the obvious response to this latter point is that, whatever Anselm's intentions, in fact his account of the atonement boils down to man (subject) acting on God (object), such that God is no longer reconciler and reconciled. This takes us to the content of Aulén's continuous-action criterion.

The content of the continuous-action criterion

Aulén himself has been criticized for using the continuous-action criterion from which to attack the Latin view.[105] The point here is that Aulén analyses actions by Jesus in his human nature as being other than actions of God. The attack circles around the notion that Aulén's account of the incarnation is defective. Fairweather's comments are representative. Fairweather notes that the Chalcedonian settlement of 451 involved the Son's being fully God and fully Man – one person in two natures is a convenient summary. As developed in subsequent anti-monophysite–monothelite debate, this Chalcedonian settlement was held to entail that the one person of the Son had, in respect of his two natures, two wills and two 'operations' (or modes of working). This line of thought was fully expressed in the Third Council of Constantinople (AD 681).

The Council concluded, 'We glorify two natural operations indivisibly, immutably, inconfusedly, inseparably in the same our Lord Jesus Christ our true God, that is to say a divine operation and a human operation . . .' The echo of Chalcedon in the 'indivisibly . . . [etc.]' terminology is unmistakeable. Certainly the logic is clear: *if the two natures retain their integrity after the incarnation, as Chalcedon insists, then that integrity will include the ways the natures work, their distinctive operations. Human nature will continue to work (operate) as human nature.*

The Council continued later:

> [W]e make briefly this whole confession, believing our Lord Jesus Christ to be one
> of the Trinity and after the Incarnation our true God, we say that his two natures
> shone forth in his one subsistence in which he performed the miracles and endured
> the sufferings through the whole of his economic conversation and that not in
> appearance only but in very deed, and this by reason of the difference of nature
> which must be recognised in the same Person, for although joined together yet each
> nature wills and does the things proper to it and that indivisibly and inconfusedly.
> Wherefore we confess two wills and two operations, concurring most fitly in him
> for the salvation of the human race.[106]

In other words, just as there are two natures, joined hypostatically, that is through the one person (the hypostasis) of the Son, so all that goes with those two natures, their natural wills and their natural operations, are alike performed by the one person. There is no objection, then, Fairweather reasons,[107] within Chalcedonian orthodoxy to the idea that the Son performs an operation in his human nature: it is God the Son's acting, he is the subject, but in a nature he has assumed. In answer to the question '*Who* is the subject of the actions of Jesus in his human nature?' Chalcedonian Christology and its successors answer, 'God the Son.' It is he who performs the miracles and he too who endures the sufferings.

However, if it is God the Son who is the subject of the actions, then Aulén cannot be correct to depict the Latin view as discontinuous action, in which God is not the subject. To establish his case, Aulén would have to show that the answer to the question 'Who is the subject of the human actions?' is a person other than God the Son. Yet that architect of the Latin view, Anselm, would strongly resist such an answer: he makes it quite clear in *On the Incarnation of the Word* that in the incarnation there is one divine person, not two persons, one divine and one human: 'For the Word made flesh assumed another nature, not another person.'[108]

The significance of this is clearer if we take a contemporary definition of penal substitution. J. I. Packer describes it as follows:

[T]hat Jesus Christ our Lord, moved by a love that was determined to do everything necessary to save us, endured and exhausted the destructive divine judgment for which we were otherwise inescapably destined, and so won us forgiveness, adoption and glory.[109]

Suppose one asks, '*Who* endured and exhausted the destructive divine judgment?' The answer within a Chalcedonian framework is, 'God the Son did.' Aulén's standpoint from which he launches his most persistent criticism of the Latin view is mistaken.

Aulén's account of incarnation and Trinity

Critics are right that there is something a little odd in Aulén's Christology. This arises, I think, from two crucial moves Aulén makes, although it is perhaps also questionable whether Aulén's translators have served him well here.[110]

The substance of God

The first move is Aulén's use of 'essence' or 'substance' terminology. This takes us into some perhaps abstruse but still highly important areas of trinitarian theology. Conventional Nicene trinitarian theology speaks of three divine persons who are of the same substance as each other. Typically 'person' is a term of relation (Father and Son are persons in relation), and because a relationship presupposes at least two, 'person' is a term that readily connotes plurality. 'Substance' or 'nature' is readily taken as referring to what each of the three persons is (each is just, wise, good, holy, but with the same justice, wisdom, goodness and holiness). It is associated with unity, for the persons are wise with the same wisdom, holiness, and so forth.[111] The usage of the terms 'substance' and 'person' remains well settled, and provides a resource to speak of the unity and plurality of the triune God.

Aulén compares the essence of God to the essence of a human being, concluding that it relates to 'disposition of . . . heart, will, personality and character . . .'[112] God's disposition is loving,[113] and Aulén therefore comments, 'God's essence is his loving will, not some obscure "substance" behind this will. It is meaningless to attempt to draw a distinction between God's will and his nature or his "substance".'[114] This ties in with the uncontroversial idea that God is not a material, physical substance; he is not made of 'stuff' in that sense. Moreover, Father and Son are of the same substance, he notes,[115] reproducing the terms of the Nicene Creed.

However, given that Father and Son are of the same, one, substance and that this substance is the one, single, divine loving will, it is natural to ask about the loving relations that exist between the trinitarian persons. For, on this view, the question is, 'What distinguishes the trinitarian persons in their relations between themselves?' When love is located at the level of *nature*, or *substance*, which all three trinitarian persons hold alike, there seems no way for the Father to love the Son in a way that is unique to him in his identity as Father.

This, though, stands at odds with Jesus' understanding of the Father's love for him. Notably, in John 5:19ff. Jesus says he relates to his Father as Son. He says the Father loves him (v. 20) and goes on to describe the Father's treatment of him, which includes the gift of 'life in himself' (v. 26), and the divine prerogative powers of life-giving and judgment. Yet this pattern of loving relation is not reversible: the Father gives these things to the Son, not vice versa.[116] What is revealed in the incarnation is a pattern of mutual love, but a pattern in which the Son loves *as Son*, and the Father loves *as Father*.

This matters because trinitarian theology stresses not merely that the triune God is eternally personal, but that the trinitarian persons are individuated: the Father begets the Son but is not begotten by the Son. They are not interchangeable with each other, but unique. Augustine pithily says that the Trinity is not a community of persons who are three friends.[117] His point is that in such descriptions as 'three friends' the relations are reversible and the persons in such a network are not distinguished and individuated by their relations. The biblical descriptions of the persons, Father, Son and Spirit, do convey not merely personal relations, but non-reversible personal relations in which the persons are individuated by their relations with each other.

This impression that Aulén's account of divine love undercuts the individuation of the trinitarian persons is heightened by the way he tends to discuss divine love only as divine love for sinful men and women.[118] The revelation of divine love in Christ is divine love towards human beings. We should agree with Aulén that it is gloriously true that God has shown his love for a sinful human world. What is more problematic is defining divine love by reference to this alone, as Aulén ultimately apparently does. Thus he states that divine love is characterized by spontaneity (it is uncaused) and self-giving.[119] This has important elements of truth for God's disposition towards us both in creation and redemption. It could not, though, be said in quite such easy terms for the love between the Father and the Son. Thus Jesus does not simply see the Father's love for him as uncaused: John 10:17 reads, 'For this reason the Father loves me, because I lay down my life that I may take it up again' (ESV).[120] This problem arises in part from too restrictive an account of what is revealed in Christ. Christ does not merely reveal divine love towards us, but also that there is a relation between Father and Son and that this is a loving relation between Father and Son. This revelation of the relation between Father and Son may not be exhaustive, but is nevertheless true.

This sense of difficulty about personal distinction within the Trinity is heightened by Aulén's later discussions: he speaks repeatedly of the threefold 'viewpoint' of Christian faith.[121] But such phrasing risks sounding as though the threefoldedness is only a viewpoint, and not an inner reality of the life of the Godhead. This impression is again reinforced by Aulén's use of the maxim *opera dei ad extra indivisa sunt* – the external works of God are undivided. Aulén rightly notes this maxim relates to the preservation of monotheism and adds, 'Every divine act is an act of the entire Trinity.'[122]

What he omits is the qualification that Augustine, a great advocate of inseparable operation in the Trinity, puts in, which is that although operation is inseparable, nevertheless particular actions have asymmetrical involvement: it is the Son who is incarnate, not the Father or Spirit, and so forth.[123] Augustine's phrasing tends to run that a particular person acts 'not without' the other persons, a formula that allows for both an inseparability of action (because the persons are inseparable) and also distinguishability and asymmetric participation in actions (for the persons are distinguishable and are in asymmetric relations). The characteristic objection to inseparable operation is that it can erode personal distinction. Aulén, though, lacks the qualifications Augustine puts in to avoid just this.

In these various ways, Aulén's accounts of divine substance and divine love tend to undermine the individuation of the trinitarian persons. This is significant because if the individuation of the trinitarian persons is not properly preserved, formulae in which the incarnate Son (subject) acts on the Father (object) can very readily be seen simply as a human (subject) acting on God (object), the phrasing which lies at the heart of Aulén's criterion of continuous action.

In fact, it is merely preserving the biblical data to envisage one person of the Trinity (subject) acting on another person of the Trinity (object): for example, God sends the Son (John 3:17). As a matter of simple grammatical observation, there are phrases and sentences where one person does something to another: 'the Father loves the Son' (John 5:20). One would add that the Father does not act on the Son despite the Son, against his will or in the Son's ignorance, for the two mutually indwell each other. The trinitarian persons are not 'pure' objects in that sense, but willing and consenting objects. To deny in principle that one person can so act on another is to exclude the idea that the Trinity is a community in which inseparable yet distinguishable persons genuinely love other persons, not just themselves. This denial uncomfortably resembles modalism.[124]

This point, naturally, is significant beyond the discussion of Aulén's continuous-action criterion, for some in the penal substitution debate argue that one person of the Trinity cannot be the subject of an action of which another trinitarian person is the object.[125] This, too, risks undercutting the real distinctions between the persons in a modalist direction.

These issues of relationality and individuation are enormously significant in the modern urban cultures of the West. In such cultures there are pressures for human persons to be seen atomistically rather than relationally and as uniform and indistinguishable rather than uniquely individualized. Against those pressures, classical trinitarian doctrine sets forth an account of personal identity which is relational and individualized, without being individualist. Yet modalist thinking, including Aulén's, impoverishes Christian apologetics and social engagement by obscuring this aspect of the gospel presentation of the triune God.

The incarnation – what was incarnate?

Aulén's second move relates to the incarnation itself. The issue here is what was incarnate in the human Jesus. Aulén answers, '[The] "substance" of the Father is "incarnate in Christ".'[126] We should note the term 'substance'. Aulén continues, 'It [terminology of incarnation] affirms that the "essence" of God, or in other words the divine loving will, "dwells" in Christ (John 1:14).'[127]

This second move is remarkable for two reasons. First, this statement about the incarnation of the substance takes place against a patristic tradition which insists that the Son (a term of trinitarian *personhood*) assumes a further *nature*. We have seen that Anselm uses just such formulations, and in doing so stands firmly within the Chalcedonian account of the incarnation.[128] But put sharply, Aulén has not preserved the person–nature distinction that Nicaea, Chalcedon and its successors have bequeathed to us, so that his account is of a divine nature or will being incarnate.

Now, of course, Aulén may be right to reject the Chalcedonian account of a divine person assuming a further nature, for Chalcedon attempts to synthesize the biblical data, but is not itself inspired. Yet it would perhaps have been useful to have signalled this rejection explicitly, particularly when he so emphatically castigates Anselm and others for forsaking patristic Christology.

The Chalcedonian tradition, in return, would regard Aulén's proposition of a divine nature becoming incarnate with little enthusiasm. There are several reasons. To begin with, Chalcedon and its successors stressed the integrity of both natures after the incarnation.[129] This could not quite be the case with Aulén's proposal: he does not think the divine nature is material, as we have seen, but for the *nature* to become incarnate it would have had to surrender at least this attribute of immateriality, so that the divine nature itself changed by virtue of the incarnation, a position distinctly redolent of the Eutychian heresy.[130]

The second reason why this account of an incarnate nature is remarkable relates to who Jesus is. The Chalcedonian answer to the question 'What was incarnate?' in fact is in terms of a 'who': the person we know as the Son, Jesus, was incarnate. However, this account of who Jesus is fits very poorly in Aulén's scheme, for he has insisted that it is the divine nature that is incarnate. Aulén writes, 'the "essence" of God, or in other words the divine loving will, "dwells" in Christ'.[131] In support he cites John 1:14. Yet in fact John 1:14 reads, 'And the Word became flesh and dwelt among us, full of grace and truth; we have beheld his glory, glory as of the only Son from the Father' (RSV).

Aulén's citation misses a number of things. John writes the Word dwelt 'among us' (*en hēmin*), not, as Aulén does, 'in Christ'. To 'dwell among' certainly implies presence, but not unity.[132] If so, to say John 1:14 deals with the Word (understood as essence or substance) dwelling in Christ, is to imply that there is not unity between Christ and the Word: it could even mean Christ is not to be identified with the Word. Moreover, the term 'the Word' cannot be taken as equivalent to God's essence or substance or will. Even by this stage of the Prologue in John there are hints that the Word exists in relation to God ('and the Word was with God . . .', John 1:1), and the indication that 'the Word' is to be seen in terms of the trinitarian persons is confirmed within verse 14 itself when the Word's glory is spoken of as the glory of the only Son.[133] It is, then, quite proper to see the Word becoming flesh as the incarnation of the person, the Son. For Aulén's argument to work at this point we would have to construe terms equating to Son as terms dealing with divine substance, not trinitarian persons. Clearly we are here back with the problem outlined earlier: that Aulén has an inadequate view of trinitarian persons.

Third, if the nature, not a person, is incarnate, the obvious question is, 'To what extent is this an incarnation of the Son?' Certainly some evangelical statements of belief (notably that of the Evangelical Alliance [UK]) retain more Chalcedonian-style phrasing than Aulén, speaking of the incarnation of the *Son*.[134] One might answer this by saying one cannot divorce the Son from his nature, and that if the nature is incarnate, then we should by extension be saying the Son is too. The problem with this response is that this reasoning is equally true of the Father and Spirit: they too cannot be divorced from the divine nature. This would therefore mean that the Father and Spirit are incarnate in the same manner as the Son: he is not uniquely incarnate. This sits poorly with conventional accounts. Thus Augustine summarizes Nicene trinitarian teaching on the incarnation thus: 'It was not however this same three (their teaching continues) that was born of the virgin Mary, crucified and buried under Pontius Pilate, rose again on the third day and ascended into heaven, but the Son alone.'[135]

Ironically, it was one of Anselm's opponents, Roscelin, who is associated with the proposition that all three persons of the Trinity were alike incarnate.[136] Yet Aulén's position seems to imply just the position posed by Roscelin.[137]

Indeed, if it is the divine nature that is incarnate in Christ, who is Jesus? Which person is he? The most obvious answer is that the 'who' of Jesus is a purely human 'who'. The trajectory of Aulén's argument is that the incarnation is not a trinitarian person, the Son, assuming a further, human, nature, but rather a human person being assumed by a divine will or essence. This might at least help explain why Aulén could think that Anselm denied that Jesus' work on the cross was a true work of God, but was rather a work by man, for the 'who', the personal identity who does it, is, on this view, only a man.[138]

In any case, the effect of this tendency to elide person and nature so that what is incarnate is a nature, a substance, is that Aulén lacks just the vocabulary to express, or indeed appreciate, what Anselm and others asserted: that the Son, a person, acts in a human nature, and, because the actor is a divine person, this is properly called an act of God. Naturally this tends to underline that Aulén's reduction of Anselm and others in terms of discontinuous action is a distortion.

Summary of Aulén's theological criticism
In short, Aulén's decisive objection to the Latin view is marred by his inconsistent application of his principle and anyway relates to a series of positions that are markedly and seriously at odds with patristic accounts of the incarnation and trinitarian theology – these positions relate in particular to the disappearance of the concept of person. This results in an account of the incarnation that overlooks the operation of two natures in their integrity, and envisages the incarnation as an incarnation of a nature, not a person, and in a trinitarian account markedly deficient in personal distinction.

Other considerations
After this, further consideration of the negative case seems almost superfluous. It should be added that biblically Aulén's case fails to reproduce the continuity between Old and New Testaments that the New Testament itself seems to envisage – the failure to deal at length with the citation in the New Testament of Isaiah 53 is especially striking, perhaps. Further, Aulén's rebuttal of the use of New Testament passages by defenders of penal substitution involved his presupposition of continuous as against discontinuous divine action, which, as we have seen, is open to grave suspicion.

In terms of the patristic evidence, some recent scholarship notes the similarities between Anselm and Athanasius at various key points. Especially important here is the idea of debt, which features in *De Incarnatione* 2–9 as Athanasius discusses why the Word had to assume flesh.[139] Debt, naturally, features in Anselm's account of why satisfaction was required. Indeed, in Athanasius *De Incarnatione* 9 we are told that the Son fulfilled the debt by his death as a substitute. This example tends to indicate the danger of asserting, as Aulén does, that substitutionary ideas are absent in the fathers. For they are present here at a decisive stage of Athanasius' argument. Space precludes dealing with early patristic candidates for teaching penal substitution as well as other accounts of the cross, such as the *Epistle to Diognetus* or the Homilies of Melito of Sardis.

Summary

This means that Aulén's negative case is open to objection theologically, biblically and historically.

Conclusions

First, it is not desirable to speak in any blanket way of 'adopting' or 'rejecting' Aulén's argument. We must distinguish between Aulén's positive and negative cases. Second, Aulén's positive case that victory is an important motif for understanding the cross remains undoubtedly valuable, but Aulén does not go far enough with the victory motif. It requires extension in two respects, and also a qualification. One extension is to remove the demythologizing elements in Aulén's account which restrict Christ's victory to human sin rather than including personal demons. This extension restores the victory motif to its original force.

The second extension is similar, and re-emphasizes Christ's victory as a just victory and not the mere application of force. This preserves the nature of God's actions as not being mere acts of power. However, this revision of Aulén's proposals brings back exactly the motifs of justice that penal substitution is designed to resolve. This means that Aulén's positive case when applied in this way does not preclude penal substitution but involves similar ethical values. The corollary of this is that an exclusion of justice values for the sake of excluding penal substitution will alter the character of Christ's victory, and change our worship from veneration of a just and loving God to adoration of amoral force. This would be apologetically fatal in our culture which is deeply suspicious of power as just that, amoral. This means that Aulén's original case risks reinforcing contemporary cynicism about religion as a mask for power.

The qualification relates to sin. We have seen how sin in Aulén's scheme does not in fact fit into his pattern of victory, by which God deals with himself in one continuous action. At this point Aulén has to surrender, it seems, the idea of victory and its cognates as an exhaustive account of the cross. There is more to Christ's work than Aulén originally allowed.

Third, Aulén's negative case by which he criticizes the Latin view revolves around a central criterion: the need for continuous divine action. This criterion is inconsistently applied, and applied to a distorted version of his opponents' cases. The criterion itself is related to a Christology which lies at odds with Chalcedonian orthodoxy and imperils the genuine distinction of persons within the Godhead, with consequent distortion of the incarnation of the Son. If penal substitution is to be rejected, it would have to be for other reasons than the major one Aulén himself cites.

How do I evaluate Aulén? I gratefully affirm aspects of his positive case with the extensions and qualification proposed, and deny his negative case. This means stating with care just what is meant by an endorsement of Aulén.

Notes

1. Michael J. Ovey, 'Appropriating Aulén? Employing *Christus Victor* Models of the Atonement', *Churchman* 124.4 (2010), pp. 297–330. Reproduced with permission.

2. J. Macquarrie, *Principles of Christian Theology*, rev. edn (London: SCM, 1977), p. 317.

3. T. Peters, 'The Atonement in Anselm and Luther, Second Thoughts About Gustaf Aulén's *Christus Victor*', *Lutheran Quarterly* 24 (1972), p. 314.

4. G. O. Evenson, 'A Critique of Aulén's *Christus Victor*', *Concordia Theological Monthly* 28 (1957), pp. 738–749 (740).

5. E.g. J. McIntyre, *St. Anselm and His Critics: A Reinterpretation of the Cur Deus Homo* (Edinburgh: Oliver and Boyd, 1954); E. R. Fairweather, 'Incarnation and Atonement: An Anselmian Response to Aulén's *Christus Victor*', *Canadian Journal of Theology* 7.3 (1961), pp. 167–175; and S. Rodger, 'Anselm: An Orthodox Perspective', *Greek Orthodox Theological Review* 34.1 (1989), p. 27.

6. L. Hodgson, *The Doctrine of the Atonement* (London: Nisbet & Co., 1951), p. 146, envisages a similar division.

7. See e.g. S. Chalke, 'Cross Purposes', *Christianity Magazine* (September 2004), pp. 44–48.

8. '[The] affirmations of faith are of a different nature than metaphysical theses, and that no combination of the theses of faith and metaphysics can be allowed.' G. Aulén, *The Faith of the Christian Church* (Swedish original, 4th edn, 1943; Eng. trans., Philadelphia: The Muhlenberg Press, 1948), p. 95.

9. Aulén's unease with what he envisages as a somewhat arid rationalism is a constant theme in *The Faith of the Christian Church*.

10. Aulén, *Faith*, p. 3.

11. Aulén, *Faith*, p. 5.

12. 'The essential element is not the forms as such, but that which underlies the whole, that which those forms seek to express.' Aulén, *Faith*, p. 77.

13. Aulén, *Faith*, p. 78.

14. Cf. Nels F. S. Ferré, 'Theologians of Our Time IX. The Theology of Gustaf Aulén', *Expository Times* 74 (1963), pp. 324–327.

15. Note especially Aulén, *Faith*, p. 130. Ferré speaks of the 'definitive centrality of agape as the fundamental motif of the Christian faith.' Ferré, 'Theologians', p. 325.

16. Aulén, *Faith*, pp. 79, 87ff.

17. Luther is, one might almost say, a touchstone in both *Christus Victor* and *The Faith of the Christian Church*.

18. Aulén, *Faith*, p. 82.

19. '[The New Testament writings] are the first and decisive testimony to that deed of Christ which is the fundamental fact of Christianity.' Aulén, *Faith*, p. 90.

20. Aulén, *Faith*, p. 90.

21. Article 3 of that Basis of Faith affirms 'The divine inspiration and supreme authority of the Old and New Testament Scriptures, which are the written Word of God – fully trustworthy for faith and conduct.' Its predecessor was Article 2 of the 1970 Basis of Faith, which was in very similar terms and affirmed 'The divine inspiration of the Holy Scripture and its consequent entire trustworthiness and supreme authority in all matters of faith and conduct.'

22. Gustaf Aulén, *Christus Victor: An Historical Study of the Three Main Types of the Idea of the Atonement* (Swedish original, 1930; Eng. trans., G. Hebert, London: SPCK, 1931; New York: Macmillan, 1969).

23. Aulén, *Christus Victor*, pp. 17–23.

24. A. G. Hebert's preface to Aulén, *Christus Victor*, p. v.

25. Aulén, *Faith*, pp. 223–241.

26. So too C. Gunton, 'Christus Victor Revisited: A Study in Metaphor and the Transformation of Meaning', *Journal of Theological Studies* 6.1 (1985), pp. 129–145.

27. Aulén, *Faith*, p. 167. Cf. Aulén, *Christus Victor*, p. 27; especially n. 1.

28. Aulén, *Christus Victor*, p. 27, n. 1.

29. Aulén, *Eucharist and Sacrifice* (Swedish original, 1956; English trans., Edinburgh: Oliver and Boyd, 1958), p. 141.

30. Aulén, *Faith*, p. 266.

31. Aulén, *Faith*, p. 262.

32. Aulén, *Faith*, p. 263; emphasis added.

33. Aulén, *Faith*, p. 264.

34. Aulén, *Faith*, p. 273.

35. Aulén, *Faith*, pp. 274–275.

36. The translators' term for sin's supra-individual power (*syndens överindividuella makt*).
    Aulén, *Faith*, pp. 270–271, n. 1.
37. Aulén, *Faith*, p. 276.
38. Aulén, *Faith*, p. 276.
39. Aulén, *Christus Victor*, p. 20.
40. Aulén, *Faith*, pp. 226–227. 'Cosmos' is in fact rarely mentioned as a tyrannical power
    by Aulén compared to the others.
41. Aulén, *Faith*, pp. 229–230.
42. Aulén sees this most clearly in the case of divine wrath, where the cross is an act
    of God's self-giving love by which his wrath is reconciled. See Aulén, *Faith*, p. 231.
43. Aulén, *Faith*, p. 229.
44. Aulén, *Christus Victor*, p. 22.
45. '[T]he victory over the destructive powers is at the same time a reconciliation.'
    Aulén, *Faith*, p. 230. Later, in respect of divine wrath: 'But this act of Atonement
    through which wrath is reconciled is at the same time a divine act, the act of divine
    love itself.' Aulén, *Faith*, p. 231.
46. Aulén, *Christus Victor*, pp. 33–51.
47. Aulén, *Christus Victor*, pp. 88–89.
48. Aulén, *Christus Victor*, p. 119.
49. Aulén, *Christus Victor*, p. 21; see also e.g. pp. 107 and 162–163.
50. Aulén, *Christus Victor*, p. 169.
51. Hebert, in Aulén, *Christus Victor*, p. v.
52. Gunton, 'Revisited', p. 130, also notes unenthusiastically Aulén's antipathy to
    'rational' theology as a consistent theme of criticism. More strongly Hodgson,
    Doctrine, p. 147, feels Aulén's anti-rational approach is itself disobedience to God.
    However, the use of reason is less central a criticism for Aulén than that of
    continuous action.
53. Aulén, *Christus Victor*, p. 21.
54. Aulén, *Christus Victor*, p. 163. See also pp. 21–22, 102, 107, 147.
55. Aulén, *Christus Victor*, p. 89.
56. Aulén, *Christus Victor*, p. 89.
57. Aulén, *Christus Victor*, p. 93.
58. Aulén, *Christus Victor*, p. 95.
59. Aulén, *Christus Victor*, p. 95.
60. Aulén, *Christus Victor*, p. 97.
61. Aulén, *Christus Victor*, p. 98.
62. Aulén, *Christus Victor*, p. 98.
63. Aulén, *Christus Victor*, p. 104.
64. Aulén, *Christus Victor*, p. 104.
65. Aulén, *Christus Victor*, p. 104.

66. Hodgson, *Doctrine*, p. 146.

67. Aulén, *Faith*, p. 167. Cf. Aulén, *Christus Victor*, p. 27; especially n. 1.

68. Aulén, *Faith*, pp. 274–275.

69. John C. Diamond, 'Aulen's Demythologized Interpretation of the Demonic', *Journal of The Interdenominational Theological Center* 1.1 (September 1973), pp. 21–35 (29). Hence the importance of locating Aulén in his Lundensian framework.

70. Diamond, 'Aulen's Demythologized Interpretation', p. 34.

71. Aulén, *Faith*, p. 275; emphasis added.

72. Macquarrie, *Principles*, p. 318, thinks Aulén has not adequately recognized the 'mythological background' of the principalities and powers, and proposes developing Aulén's classic view along demythologized lines, recognizing idolatry as that which enslaves humans. Diamond's point is that Aulén had already himself done something similar, and, for the reasons outlined in the text, his view is preferable to Macquarrie's.

73. Gustaf Aulén, *Jesus in Contemporary Historical Research* (London: SPCK, 1976), p. 145.

74. Aulén, *Jesus*, p. 146.

75. Aulén, *Jesus*, p. 146.

76. Aulén, *Jesus*, p. 279.

77. Following Diamond, 'Aulen's Demythologized Interpretation', and contra Macquarrie, *Principles*.

78. Aulén provides very little comment on Jesus' exorcisms, in either *Christus Victor* or *Faith*, despite the narrative significance of such exorcisms in the Synoptics.

79. This is an underlying question about Lundensian theological method, the apparent ease with which central ideas are discovered within a writer's forms of expressions that might well not be fully endorsed by the writer himself.

80. Diamond, 'Aulen's Demythologized Interpretation'.

81. Aulén, *Christus Victor*, p. 95.

82. E.g. K. McMahon, 'The Cross and the Pearl: Anselm's Patristic Doctrine of Atonement', in J. R. Fortin (ed.), *Saint Anselm – His Origins and Influence* (Lewiston, Queenston and Lampeter: Edwin Mellen, 2001), pp. 57–69 (57–58).

83. Aulén, *Christus Victor*, p. 70.

84. Aulén, *Christus Victor*, p. 107.

85. Aulén, *Christus Victor*, pp. 70, 107.

86. Aulén, *Christus Victor*, pp. 106–107.

87. Aulén, *Faith*, p. 229.

88. Aulén, *Faith*, pp. 229–231.

89. See especially Aulén, *Faith*, p. 231.

90. Aulén, *Faith*, p. 229.

91. Aulén, *Faith*, p. 276.

92. Aulén, *Faith*, p. 229.

93. Aulén, *Faith*, p. 229.

94. Aulén, *Faith*, p. 228.

95. Aulén, *Christus Victor*, p. 21; see also e.g. Aulén, *Faith*, pp. 107, 162–163.

96. Macquarrie, *Principles*, p. 320, does not necessarily endorse Aulén's criterion of continuous action.

97. Aulén, *Christus Victor*, pp. 37ff., 46ff. Recapitulation involves God's 'going over again', so to speak, the imperfect features of creation to make them perfect. This vindicates him as sovereign creator and entails a new Adam to recapitulate/'go over' by his obedience the errors of disobedience of the first Adam. W. P. Loewe, 'Irenaeus' Soteriology: *Christus Victor* Revisited', *Anglican Theological Review* 17 (1985), pp. 1–15, indicates that Irenaeus' soteriology in any case contains more elements than Aulén allows.

98. Aulén, *Christus Victor*, p. 46.

99. Aulén, *Christus Victor*, p. 163. See also pp. 21–22, 102, 107, 147.

100. *On the Apostolic Preaching*, St. Irenaeus of Lyons, trans. John Behr (New York: St Vladimir's Seminary Press, 1997), p. 31; emphasis added.

101. Aulén, *Christus Victor*, p. 163.

102. *Cur Deus Homo?* I.3. 'For God has shown the magnitude of His love and devotion towards us by the magnitude of his act in most wonderfully and unexpectedly saving us from the evils, so great and so deserved, by which we used to be beset.'

103. *Cur Deus Homo?* I.5. See also McIntyre, *Anselm*, p. 128, on why it is essential for Anselm that the divine person be the agent for our salvation.

104. This is not the first time that one encounters the point that Aulén rephrases other thinkers' arguments in ways they might well find unacceptable: cf. his demythologization of victory over Satan in Irenaeus, his reinterpretation of merit and satisfaction language in Luther into a victory framework, as well as the current instance with Anselm.

105. E.g. Fairweather, 'Incarnation'; W. J. Hankey, *God in Himself – Aquinas' Doctrine of God as Expounded in the Summa Theologiae* (Oxford: Oxford University Press, 1987); McIntyre, *Anselm*; Rodger, 'Anselm'.

106. Constantinople III, AD 681.

107. Fairweather, 'Incarnation', pp. 171ff.

108. *On the Incarnation of the Word* 11. See also 9 and 10. See McIntyre, *Anselm*, p. 127, for comments on Anselm's Chalcedonian approach.

109. J. I. Packer, *Celebrating the Saving Work of God* (Carlisle: Paternoster, 1998), p. 105.

110. That said, the regularity of the phrasing of the translators in Aulén, *Faith*, is striking, and the immediate concern of this chapter is the appropriation of Aulén in the English-speaking world; that is, through his works as translated.

111. Cf. the Athanasian Creed, for instance: 'the Father is almighty, the Son almighty, and the Holy Spirit almighty; and yet not three almighties but one almighty'.

112. Aulén, *Faith*, p. 213.

113. Note Aulén, *Faith*, p. 130.

114. Aulén, *Faith*, p. 213.

115. Aulén, *Faith*, pp. 211, 214.

116. Nor can these gifts simply be seen as gifts to the Son in his humanity, for John 5:26 speaks of 'life in himself', parallel to the eternal life that God the Father himself has. The human life the Son possesses is not 'life in himself' comparable to the Father's: apart from anything else, the Son's human life has a beginning.

117. *De Trinitate* VII.7 and VII.11.

118. Aulén, *Faith*, pp. 131–134. '[T]he divine love active in Christ is that love which seeks sinful man and enters into communion with him.' Aulén, *Faith*, p. 132.

119. Aulén, *Faith*, pp. 133–134.

120. It would be inadequate to reply that this is only of the Son in his humanity: the point would remain that the Father loves the person, the Son. In any case, even if this were simply referred to the humanity, the point remains that this is a caused love.

121. Aulén, *Faith*, pp. 254–258.

122. Aulén, *Faith*, p. 256.

123. Augustine, *De Trinitate* I.7.

124. For the persons are not being treated as 'other' from each other. Cf. Augustine on Sabellianism or modalism, *Answer to Maximinus* I.xiii.

125. E.g. J. D. Green and M. D. Baker, *Recovering the Scandal of the Cross: Atonement in New Testament and Contemporary Contexts* (Downers Grove: InterVarsity Press, 2000), p. 96.

126. Aulén, *Faith*, p. 211. This phraseology is not unique; see also p. 208: '[Christian faith] speaks of the Incarnation of the divine "essence", the divine love, in Christ'; p. 211: 'the "substance" of the Father is "incarnate" in Christ'; p. 216: 'it is the divine nature itself which is incarnate in Christ, not an intermediary being'. With such statements one should also note statements about the incarnation of the divine will, since Aulén identifies 'will' with 'substance': pp. 214, 221. Since 'love' is God's substance for Aulén, even Aulén's statements about the incarnation of divine love have to be read in the context of the incarnation of substance or nature: pp. 211, 212, 219.

127. Aulén, *Faith*, p. 211.

128. *On the Incarnation of the Word* 11. See also 9 and 10.

129. Thus the Council speaks of 'the distinction of the natures being by no means taken away by the union, but rather the property of each nature being preserved, and concurring in one person and one subsistence'.

130. In that the divine nature does not continue in its integrity after the incarnation.

131. Aulén, *Faith*, p. 211.

132. This would particularly be the case if the 'dwell among' of John 1:14 is an echo of God's presence among his people in the Tabernacle; see R. Brown, *The Gospel According to John Vol. I: I–XII* (London: Geoffrey Chapman, 1971), pp. 32–33.

133. A. J. Köstenberger, *John* (Grand Rapids: Baker, 2004), p. 40, comments, 'The major burden of 1:14–18 is to identify the Word explicitly with Jesus.'

134. E.g. The Evangelical Alliance (UK) Basis of Faith Article 5 confesses belief in 'The incarnation of God's eternal Son, the Lord Jesus Christ'. Its predecessor, in Article 4 of the 1970 Basis, speaks of 'the incarnate Son of God'.

135. Augustine, *De Trinitate* I.7.

136. Roscelin's work was the occasion of *On the Incarnation of the Word*.

137. Although possibly not for the same reasons.

138. This would not, of course, deal with the criticism that Aulén applies his continuous-action criterion inconsistently.

139. See McMahon, 'Cross'.

PART 4:

GLOBAL ANGLICAN FUTURES CONFERENCE (GAFCON) LECTURES

Global Anglicanism

GAFCON, the Global Anglican Futures Conference, has held two international conferences: in Jerusalem in 2008, and in Nairobi in 2013. Mike Ovey addressed both, and was intending to attend the third, planned to be held again in Jerusalem, in 2018.

25. THE GOSPEL 'HOW' OF THEOLOGICAL EDUCATION (JERUSALEM, 2008)[1]

Introduction

Yesterday our brother César Guzmán reminded us of the gospel matrix of theological education.[2] He brought us back to that easily stated but profound truth that theological education has a practical purpose: training people for gospel ministry in local churches. True, as we heard, theological education is not severed from the Academy. To that extent, theology takes its place as a true academic discipline, and a demanding one at that. But its focus is the local church, and the life of the people of God from place to place. All this, of course, is no innovation but deeply rooted in orthodox understandings of what theology itself is. Thomas Aquinas stressed that what he called 'sacred doctrine' was both practical, dealing with human action, and speculative, concerned with what God reveals.[3] Theological education is a training in this kind of theology.

Yet perhaps we should stay a moment with César's focus on the practical and the life of the local church. All of us are aware that in the life of the local church it is not simply the quality of a minister's teaching or preaching that testifies to the gospel, but the quality of life. Again, the apostle Paul provides a striking instance of this. In 1 Thessalonians 2:8 Paul describes the quality of his relationship with and life among the Thessalonian Christians. 'So deeply do we care for you that we are determined to share with you not only the gospel of God but also our own selves, because you have become very dear to us' (NRSV).

No doubt we could spend all of today on this verse, but let me make some brief comments. First, the proclamation of the gospel and the life of the gospel-proclaimer go together. Paul shares both. In this sense, the proclamation of the gospel is not the mere transfer of information, like a newsreader on a television station bringing one the news that there is a new head of state, a new lord. That there is transfer of information is true, and there must be that element, no doubt. But for Paul here, it is not just that.

Second, Paul's life is theologically significant in the context of 1 Thessalonians 1 and 2. Paul is reminding them in chapter 1 of the authenticity of their response: he summarizes in 1:9 and 10 how it is known that the Thessalonians have turned to the living God. In chapter 2 he reminds them of the authenticity of the message to which they have responded. He speaks clearly and unashamedly of the way he has proclaimed it, not from deceit or impure motives or trickery (2:3), not seeking to flatter (2:5), nor to receive praise (2:6), but with gentleness, love and care (2:7–8). The continuity of Paul's gospel life with Paul's gospel message is important, because he uses just that to reassure the Thessalonians about the authenticity of what they have heard and received.

Now what has that to do with theological education? Clearly this: in the practical setting of the Thessalonian church, it mattered that the one who proclaimed the gospel lived the gospel. And a theological educator who wishes to see ministers formed as Paul was must therefore be concerned not only with gospel knowledge, but also with gospel living. There is a character to be formed, as well as a mind to be trained. Both must reflect the gospel. Now the training of the mind, the content of theological education, we will return to.[4] What I aim to look at are some of the issues that relate to formation of character. Let me stress, I approach only some of the issues in this area, but we can at least scratch the surface.

The hidden curriculum

The perspective that we are exploring here is the way in which our educational methods themselves, the 'how' of theological education, actually serve to shape and mould those we train. Let me at this stage introduce the notion of the hidden curriculum. We may produce course documents that state what subjects are taught and examined, and that is our explicit curriculum. But alongside that there is a hidden curriculum. Perry Shaw defines the hidden curriculum this way. It is

> the potent sociological and psychological dimensions of education, which are usually caught rather than intentionally taught – the pervasive environmental features of

education that include such things as the nature of behaviours which are encouraged, the type of relationships modelled, and the values emphasised in the learning community.[5]

The hidden curriculum has both positive and negative elements. Thus, on the one hand, positively, there are things that are unintentionally taught, or, as Shaw says, 'caught'. On the other, the very process of selection which goes into any explicit curriculum ensures that some things do not appear or appear only marginally and those omissions also tell a story about what matters. In the UK context, I may, for example, as I teach the Doctrine of the Holy Spirit, not spend time on the way the Spirit was used in the theology of the nineteenth-century minister Edward Irving. My omission insensibly teaches something about how I view his current importance.

Now, this hidden curriculum may teach the right things both positively and negatively. What a student catches from his or her instructors may be just what the Bible asks. The things that are omitted or treated as marginal may be very rightly treated in this way. But Shaw poses the question for any instructor and institution as to what the hidden curriculum does in fact teach or model.

The hidden curriculum and gospel relationships

Let me at that point take us back to another of César's points. As he spoke about the gospel matrix he reminded us, 'The gospel is a reflection of the relational nature of God's being in his trintiarian reality; as such, the gospel itself is about relationships ... Through the gospel we enter the kingdom of God to enjoy the right order of relationships.'[6] These gospel relationships, of course, are personal relationships. To use the terms made famous by Martin Buber, they are I–Thou relations, interpersonal relations, subject-to-subject relations, as against I–It relations where an I relates to the other as an object, identified, knowable and masterable. Naturally, in the case of interpersonal relations with God, this is a very particular I–Thou relation, a relation in which we know God as Lord and Father. Yet relations with other human persons for the Christian are also to be I–Thou relations and not relations where one exploits another or treats them as a mere object in the world, a resource to use, as an It. This I–Thou, interpersonal, shape to the relationships the gospel brings is implicit, naturally, in the summary of the Law that Jesus provides: we are to love God and love our neighbour (Mark 12:29–31). However, these two commandments in which I am to love the other, whether that other be God or my neighbour, also has to be set in a wider interpersonal context. Jesus tells us further in John 15:9–12 that he has loved us (v. 9), and he tells us to abide in his love by keeping his command to love each other (v. 10).

Both these commandments, and the context in which they are framed, feature the interpersonal idea of love. The summary of the Law brings us to I–Thou relationships, not I–It relationships.

The question I want to pose at this point is whether our ways, the 'how' of our theological education, our hidden curricula, actually do promote these gospel relationships. Or do they subvert them?

Let me suggest two ways in which appropriate I–Thou relations can be subverted. We might, slightly loosely but conveniently, describe one of these ways as essentially modernist, the other as postmodernist.

Modernist subversion of I–Thou relationships

We begin with a modernist subversion of I–Thou relations. Consider the scene of theological education at least as it occurs so frequently in my own country. You have a room where someone stands at the front, or who sits chairing a circle of people, a whiteboard or blackboard or projection screen where, it may be, a passage of Scripture or a set of theological propositions is put, so to speak, under scrutiny.

Now there may be a certain inevitability to something like this taking place. Theological education certainly includes instruction, and there is transfer of information and expertise. If there is not some transfer of information and expertise, then one may ask in what sense theological education has taken place. But even so, we might want to voice some misgivings. They lie in two dimensions: my relation as an instructor with those I instruct, and my relation with what I am teaching.

Now, concerning my relation with those I instruct, Perry Shaw speaks of the set-up I have described as creating an emotional distance between instructor and learner.[7] This is not the same as having a relation of respect. Obviously there is an instructor–learner relationship between Jesus and his disciples, and it is a relation of respect, but not of emotional distance. The risk is that someone who has modelled to him or her an emotional distance between teacher and learner will take just that into their relationships in a local church as they teach there. It would scarcely correspond with Paul's attitude of sharing his very self with the Thessalonians in 1 Thessalonians 2:8.

But let me turn to the other dimension, the relation of teacher with what is taught. I take it that at some level all our instruction relates back to the word of God and ultimately, therefore, to the God who gave that word. Think again of the lecture or seminar room scene I have described. We may say we are taking Scripture seriously as we pore over every word and clause, but is there not a risk that as we do so we pass to a state of mind that sees even knowledge of the will of God as a commodity, as something we own, that we possess? It is a very telling turn of phrase to say, 'We have mastered the Letter to the Ephesians.'

Please do not misunderstand me at this point. I am not suggesting that the tools of rigorous scholarship that one associates with the modernist period are useless. At its best, modernist thinking, and the Enlightenment philosophies in which it was rooted, were highly concerned with truth and with intellectual integrity. But even that concern for truth can suffer distortion. Helmut Thielicke comments very perceptively on this:

> Truth seduces us very easily into a kind of joy of possession: I have comprehended this and that, learned that, understood it. Knowledge is power. I am therefore more than the other man who does not know this and that. I have greater possibilities and also greater temptations. Anyone who deals with the truth – as we theologians certainly do – succumbs all too easily to the psychology of the possessor. But love is the opposite of the will to possess. It is self-giving. It boasteth not itself, but humbleth itself.[8]

One of Thielicke's concerns is the way that this lust for possession can ruin relationships with other Christians who are not so trained.

> And in possession of this truth, he despises – of course, in the most sublime way – the people who as simple Christians pray to this Saviour of sinners . . . This disdain is a real *spiritual disease*. It lies in the conflict of truth and love. This conflict is precisely *the* disease of theologians.[9]

This aspect of the hidden curriculum would be a terrible thing, would it not? To have our explicit curricula teaching earnestly for the local church the truths of self-giving pastoral ministry and to have our graduates catching the disease of disdain from our hidden curricula. Quite simply, this will not help our graduates love their parishioners.

Yet this modernist approach to learning can also create the impression that what we study is an It, an object, a bounded thing to be mastered and treated as a commodity. But centrally, as César reminded us, what we study is the Word of God, and therefore who God discloses himself to be through his word. Now we do indeed have a personal relationship with God: in salvation we have been adopted by him as his children and are heirs of eternal life. He has loved us in the giving of the Lord Jesus, and we love him. He is, nevertheless, in this I–Thou relationship, Lord.

I would surmise that many, perhaps all, of us who are instructors have found ourselves with a pastoral problem along these lines. An able and competent student approaches one. They are diligent in study, interested, with no obvious unconfessed sin. Yet they speak of spiritual dryness and a sense of distance from God. The more they study the Synoptic problem, the less close to their Lord they feel. But if their Lord and his word have been rendered, so to speak, commodities, things to be owned, mastered, confined and bounded, then that would scarcely be surprising. For their Lord and his word have been insensibly treated as Its, and the tacit relationship operates as an I–It relationship, not as an I–Thou relationship. Buber himself comments very perceptively, 'But it is only the I–Thou relation in which we can meet God at all . . .'[10]

I stress once again that this subversion of the relationships the gospel seeks to establish is very far from the intention, but this would be one of the perils of involvement in modernist methods of instruction and approach to the object of knowledge: that with the concern for objective truth comes a lust for possession, what Augustine might see as *libido dominandi*.

Postmodern subversion of I–Thou relationships

This takes us to the question whether postmodern approaches and methods fare better. The postmodern Western mood is no doubt a highly complex phenomenon. But many strands within postmodernism would recognize the lust for possession of the object as indeed one of the problems of modernist methods of study. Within postmodernism, there is also an antipathy to the notion of external authority, and a suspicion of the notion of objective external truth, a suspicion characteristically associated with the idea that truth-claims are really power claims. Some, like Michel Foucault, see all human relations as power relations. And in terms of reading texts, the idea of author and authorial intention can readily be taken as imposing authority. And the suggestion can be that the reader is to be equally the author, finding and constructing meaning.

One may well feel that suspicion towards human authority under the sun is very frequently well taken. It is also certainly true that a postmodern stress that texts can be read in various ways can be fruitful and fits well with a basic humility before God and his word which accepts that God may bring forth fresh treasures and that we do not plumb the depths of the word of God so as to master it in any exhaustive sense.

Yet it is equally true that this style and approach can subvert the I–Thou relationships that the gospel establishes. While this postmodern mood may not accept the notion of an objective It, a bounded thing to be scrutinized, nevertheless, at its strongest the mood that says the reader is the author, whether one is reading the word of God or whether one is reading a letter from a parishioner, is something that does not treat the other as a Thou either.

One might say this mood goes beyond Buber's scheme. For, not only is there no I–Thou relationship, there is no I–It relationship either. There is only the postmodern I, the postmodern ego. If there is only an 'I' and what the 'I' thinks or chooses to think another might have said, then there is no genuine relationship, certainly not of an I–Thou form in which the other, the Thou to whom I relate, has a givenness and an independence of me and my opinions. Put bluntly, a postmodern solipsism, a 'there's-only-me-ism', where there is ultimately only the 'I', that kills relationship. It certainly kills an I–Thou relationship with God in which I say 'Lord' to God and obey him as such. And the parishioner whose pleading letter about marital desertion is rewritten with postmodern wit and playfulness by a reader as an ironic celebration of the single life is unlikely to feel there is authentic relationship either.

The critic George Steiner observed early on in the emergence of this kind of approach that it has the 'covert thrill of violence' in the way that it allows the reader to treat others.[11] We may return here to one of the most perceptive exponents of postmodernism, Foucault. Foucault, we recall, saw statements about truth as claims to power. But he also saw claims to power in a certain light. He asks rhetorically, 'Shouldn't one therefore conceive all problems of power in terms of relations of war?'[12] This is striking, to see relationship reduced to war. It is devastating to think of an interpretative approach and technique as presupposing relations of war, when the gospel speaks of relations of love and peace.

Common features of relations in modernism and postmodernism

What both of the approaches we have looked at readily share is a propensity for the 'I' to dominate. In the case of the modernist style, this domination comes from rendering the other an It, an objective object in the world to be mastered. In the case of the postmodernist style, domination comes from rendering the other not even an object with its own objectivity, but something that exists only in so far as it is construed and constructed by the 'I'. The common feature is domination, and it is right to see both methodologies as opening the door, no matter how unintentionally, to what Augustine calls the *libido dominandi*, the lust to rule and dominate.[13] For Augustine, this was what marked out and characterized the city of this world, not the city of God, and it is, after all, the city of God that we are training people to serve.

Intellectual vice and intellectual virtue

Inevitably I think we ask how significant this may be, and we may possibly even feel somewhat resigned, along the lines that these problems have a certain inevitability. We may even feel that, at least in the case of the modernist I–It approach, it does take the issue of truth seriously. At its best there is a genuine intellectual virtue there.

For my own part, I do not wish at all to downplay the significance of the intellectual virtue of truth. After all, we serve a God who does not lie and whose word is truth. I do, though, want to ask, first, whether our definition of intellectual virtue has not become a little narrow, and indeed, second, whether a narrow view of intellectual virtue, too exclusively in terms of truth, will not paradoxically leave the value of truth itself open to corruption.

Intellectual vice

Let me begin by thinking about intellectual vice. We have noted the way that our hidden curricula can promote not gospel relationships, but a lust for mastery, *libido dominandi*. It is possible that our hidden curricula promote a sense of the 'I', the self, in our students that is essentially individualistic, not merely individual. Characteristically, and understandably, students are tested and examined as individuals and often ranked with some precision, and with high intellectual ranking enjoying prestige and approval from us as teachers. Those with lower ranking may not attract our approval so significantly, or even our interest.

Now, individual assessment and handling may be necessary and desirable in some respects. Yet I do recall my own experiences as a law student where rivalry and individualism were taken as read in this kind of educational environment. And an individualist educational ethic can become intensely competitive. Competitiveness can create conditions ripe for arrogance, pride and pugnacity. And competitiveness is a marked aspect of the social profile from which many of the students I am privileged to teach are drawn (Ivy League university, 'alpha' personality, high achiever). One only has to watch them play touch rugby.

W. J. Wood comments very perceptively on the consequences of this: 'Arrogance, dishonesty, pride, pugnacity, laziness, and many other vices undermine our ability to think well and to pursue the truth. A vicious character can undermine good thinking just as effectively as some physical debility.'[14]

His point is that what one might think of as the prime intellectual virtue, truth, is undermined by these vices. Contentiousness and rivalry, for example, may lead one to deny the truth when another asserts it, precisely because it is another who has said it. Arrogance can lead one to repudiate a perfectly legitimate criticism, and the sense of one's significance can lead one on that quest to find something new, something original, no matter how eccentric, a thought that one can call one's own and possess, of which one is proprietor and master. Is that not, to be honest, a snare for the academic, the yearning to have a school of thought or line of argument named after one? For one's doctoral thesis to be all too definitive?

As I mention the temptations that can beset us in the Academy, I should make a further observation. To be a successful academic does not require us to be a whole human being. No doubt many of us have met individuals from time to time who are enormously gifted in one discipline or another, but whose skills in that cannot be employed in, or seem irrelevant to, the rest of life. Their virtues are not integrated into a whole life. And one of the problems that we face with a narrow definition of intellectual virtue too exclusively in terms of truth is that it may lead to a life where the virtues themselves are not integrated. Where truthfulness does not walk with consideration, graciousness, humility and mercy. G. K. Chesterton commented long ago on the disastrous tendency in the modern era for the virtues to become dissociated:

> The modern world is full of the old Christian virtues gone mad. The virtues have gone mad because they have been isolated from each other and are wandering alone. Thus some scientists care for truth; and their truth is pitiless. Thus some humanitarians care only for pity and their pity (I am sorry to say) is often untruthful.[15]

Again, we must remind ourselves that those we teach are being prepared for a practical task, serving in local churches. And as we have seen from the example of Paul, this requires lives that are consistent with the gospel. Now I take it that the gospel is consistent, coherent and the life it brings is integrated. In that case, clearly we look to be forming characters whose virtues are integrated, not people who have so developed one virtue that it serves actually to choke others. A coherent gospel implies, so to speak, integrated gospel workers.

Intellectual virtue

Naturally at this point, I am arguing for the inseparability of the virtues. Again, this is nothing new in orthodox Christian thought, for Aquinas argues that moral virtues cannot ultimately operate without at least the intellectual virtues of understanding and prudence.[16] This is something we must investigate more closely (in the next chapter) as we consider the question of the content of theological education, the 'what' of the explicit theological curriculum. But vitally, for our present discussion, he also argues that intellectual virtues require moral virtues.[17]

Our question here is how best we nurture moral virtues, especially through our hidden curricula that may support our intellectual and academic programmes. Let me make some observations under two broad headings, coherence and humility.

Coherence

We have been observing the way that lack of coherence between explicit and hidden curricula, and lack of coherence between the pursuit of truth and other virtues can subvert our aims to equip and form gospel-hearted ministers. We may well, then, want to pursue factors that make for coherence in the experience of our students.

First, we as their teachers must strive to model the integration of Christian virtues, not their incoherence, or the optional nature of, say, charity, when discussing theologians with whom one disagrees. Our personal holiness and love of Christ are not irrelevant if we want to see a holy learning in our students. This is obviously one reason why one would be extremely slow to contract out teaching of, say, John's Gospel to an unbelieving lecturer at a local secular university, no matter how eminent. For that would speak precisely of the separation of intellectual virtue from the others.

Second, as between ourselves on a particular faculty, a quest for an essential coherence as between our subjects and as between ourselves is also desirable. Clearly we will not attain unanimity on all issues – that would not be so in the Academy or the typical local church. But there does come a point where a faculty looks less like a team involved in ministry and more like a loose confederacy of people temporarily in league while they pursue their own agendas.

Third, we will want to ensure that learning is properly related to worship. It is not even enough to say that a particular community of students and teachers worships together as well as learns together. What we learn and how we worship must surely be consistent with each other. To use a slightly caricatured example, there is no point reciting the Nicene Creed with conviction in a chapel together if the Creed is not then taught with conviction.

Humility

Our second heading is humility. A moment's reflection tells us how importantly the New Testament regards this. Luke repeatedly enjoins humility, not least because the humble will be exalted and the proud cast down. Humility, naturally, works in two relational directions: horizontally and vertically.

Horizontally, in terms of relations between humans, a theological education, or a theological educator who models humility, will not behave with contentiousness and arrogance. Humility opens the door to a generous listening to others, and a refusal to try to overwhelm them with intellectual aggression. It encourages a proper interaction with questions and objections.

Vertically, in terms of relation with God, humility discourages the attitude that seeks to possess and master God's Word, or to tell others what God should have said on particular topics. Humility opens the door to a trust that God does speak and speaks truthfully, but does not insist that one has grasped him and his word exhaustively. In that sense learning humbly really does reflect the relationships the gospel establishes, and there would be something odd about expecting a minister who has been taught in ways that make him proud, to be able to live the gospel life of humility. But humility is the model, and not just from Paul. For Philippians 2:3 warns us strenuously to be humble and drives this home with the example of the Lord Jesus in the incarnation. Naturally, we would want Christ's ministers not simply to speak of him, but to live him.

Discussion

- How can we best encourage both humility and good learning in those in our charge?
- Are there particular educational techniques that hinder or help gospel-shaped theological education?

Notes

1. See <https://www.gafcon.org/resources/the-gospel-how-of-theological-education>. Reproduced with permission of Global Anglican Futures Conference. Editor's note: this chapter has been lightly edited for reading purposes, but I have tried to retain its context. Over the three-day conference, César Guzmán spoke on 24 June, Mike Ovey on 25 (this chapter) and 26 (next chapter).
2. César Guzmán, 'A Gospel Matrix for Theological Education', <https://www.gafcon.org/sites/gafcon.org/files/resources/files/A-Gospel-Matrix-for-Theological-Education.pdf>.
3. *Summa Theologiae* 1a.1.4. 'Hence, although among the philosophical sciences one is speculative and another is practical, nevertheless Sacred Doctrine includes both . . .' (*Unde licet in scientiis philosophicis alia sit speculativa et alia practica, sacra tamen doctrina comprehendit sub se utramque*).
4. Editor's note: see next chapter.
5. P. W. H. Shaw, 'The Hidden and Null Curricula', *Theological Educator* 1.2 (2006), p. 3.
6. Guzmán, 'Matrix', p. 5.
7. Shaw, 'Hidden and Null', p. 4.
8. H. Thielicke, *A Little Exercise for Young Theologians* (Carlisle: Paternoster, 1996), pp. 16–17.
9. Thielicke, *Little Exercise*, p. 17; emphases original.

10. M. Buber, *The Eclipse of God: Studies in the Relation Between Religion and Philosophy* (Atlantic Highlands, NJ: Humanities Press International, 1988), p. 128.

11. Editor's note: a phrase from George Steiner's 1980 preface to an edition of *Tolstoy or Dostoevsky: An Essay in Contrast* (London: Faber and Faber, 1980; first published, 1959), p. iii.

12. M. Foucault, 'Truth and Power', in C. Gordon (ed.), *Power/Knowledge* (New York: Pantheon, 1980), pp. 109–133 (122–123).

13. Augustine, *City of God* I.

14. W. J. Wood, 'The Crisis in Contemporary Epistemology', <http://wheaton.edu/FandL/pdf/wood.pdf>, accessed 1 August 2017, p. 21. He adds elsewhere, 'Intellectual vices include traits such as gullibility, superstitiousness, willful naïveté, closedmindedness, and being prone to self-serving beliefs,' p. 25.

15. G. K. Chesterton, *Orthodoxy* (London: Bodley Head, 1909), p. 51.

16. *Summa Theologiae* 1a2ae.58.4.

17. *Summa Theologiae* 1a2ae.58.5.

26. THE GOSPEL 'WHAT' OF THEOLOGICAL EDUCATION (JERUSALEM, 2008)[1]

Introduction

Let us spend a few minutes reviewing the material that we've covered over the last few days. César Guzmán reminded us to begin with of the gospel matrix of theological education.[2] Since then, we have considered the implications of the gospel and the relationships it establishes for the 'how' of theological education, and the way that instructional methods themselves must reflect the I–Thou relationships which the gospel establishes. We thought about the impact of the gospel on the 'who' of theological training and how it is the faculty may be established, how theological educators may be encouraged, who will train so as to produce gospel ministers for the local church. After all, as César reminded us, training takes place with the local church in mind: it is highly practical in that sense. And today we move to discussing the question of what should go into a programme of theological education.

The gospel as the principle of knowledge

Let us stay, though, for a moment with the thought that it is the gospel that establishes relationships, relationships in the first instance with the God who saves and adopts us, and in the second instance with our fellow-believers who are, like us, in union through faith with the Lord Jesus Christ. The gospel is the principle of relationship, it is the principle of salvation, but is also a principle of knowledge. The gospel is an epistemological principle.

Permit me to expand on that. As we come to faith in the Lord Jesus Christ, we come to recognize him for who he truly is. He is one person in two natures, he is both the son of David, born in David's house, and the fulfilment of promises about the Messiah. He is also the eternal Son of the Father. This identity is who he really is, and in faith, we know him for who he really is. And as we know the Son in faith we know that he is the Son of someone, eternally the Son of someone, and that someone is his Father. And since the Son is eternally Son, his Father is eternally Father. We may well find our minds taken to John 17:6 and Jesus' high priestly prayer. Jesus comments: 'I have made your name known to those whom you gave me from the world. They were yours, and you gave them to me, and they have kept your word' (NRSV).

This repays some detailed attention. By name, we readily understand something essential to the identity of the person. So Jesus' comment that he has made God's name known is a claim to have given a profound revelation, a revelation which does not deal simply with the acts of God in space and time but with who God is. And yet there is a puzzle over this question of name, isn't there? For God also gave his name to Moses (Exod. 6:3–4). John's Gospel, however, consistently ranks the revelation that Jesus gives higher than that of Moses. We think, for instance, of the contrast in favour of the revelation that Jesus brings in John 1:17, and the implicit criticism of the idea that Moses has had a complete theophany in John 1:18.

The question therefore arises, 'In what way is the revelation that Jesus brings superior?' The name given to Moses is characteristically taken as reminding us that God is uncreated, that he is a self-existent being. That is undoubtedly the truth. For it is a consistent part of the Old Testament polemic against idols, that God is uncreated while the idol is created (see Jer. 10:1–16, for instance). But Jesus brings a name that Moses cannot bring. For what Jesus reveals, as has often been noted, is his own identity, his identity as Son, eternal Son of the Father. This identity dominates the disagreement between Jesus and the corporate character termed 'The Jews' in John's Gospel, and comes to a head in chapter 19:7, where the Jews tell Pilate that Jesus must die for claiming to be the Son of God. But in claiming to be Son, Jesus is also saying something about God: he is saying God is his Father and the Jews well appreciate this as their reaction back in 5:18 makes clear. In short, in revealing himself as the Son, Jesus reveals God as Father. That is the name he brings, the name he alone can bring because he alone is Son.

All this is simply the basic but glorious truth summarized in the Nicene Creed. Yet we need to note something further about John 17:6: this name is given and revealed to those whom the Father has given to Jesus. On reflection, there is something surprising about that. The surprise is that the identity of the Father is not something that is simply appropriated as a piece of information. That is to say a piece of information available to all human beings without distinction, whether or not they believe in Christ. We might say that in principle we can reveal to people that the earth is round, whether or not they believe in Christ. But the revelation that the name of God is Father is not something universally accessible in that kind of way. Jesus is quite specific. It is given to those whom the Father gave the Son from the world. The phrasing takes us back to John chapter 6, of course, and Jesus' discourse on the bread of life. There Jesus states that the Father gives to Jesus those who will come to him (6:37). The thought is that if the Father gives, then the person he has given will come to Jesus. And coming to Jesus is one of the ways in which the Jesus of John's Gospel describes belief in him (6:35).

We need, though, to apply that thought about the people whom the Father gives, to John 17:6. Jesus is saying that he has revealed the Father's identity to those who have faith in him, faith that is by virtue of the Father's giving. This line of thought is reinforced by the reference in John 17 to those whom the Father gave as being 'from the world'. 'From the world' carries the implication that this may be where they came from and where they once belonged, but it is where they are no longer. For the world is the realm of human disbelief and rebellion in John's Gospel. By the Father's generosity, people are drawn from the world of unbelief and given to the Son and they come to the Son, that is believe in him, and trust that he is the Son, and therefore that the Father is Father.

In this way, the great trinitarian truths of the unity yet eternally inter-relating Father, Son and Spirit are truths known only in faith, known only through the gospel which proclaims the Lord Jesus as Son. The principle of knowing God as he truly is, as he is in eternity, is therefore the gospel. We may well follow Aquinas in saying that the subject matter of theology, what we know in theology, is God himself and creatures in their relation to him.[3] If therefore we treat the subject matter of theology from the point of view of knowledge, we can do so only as believers; we can do so only through the gospel. We cannot study God from any other perspective, whether that perspective is of human experience, or human speculative philosophy, or the consensus of the majority, or the ecstatic mystic experience of the privileged few. For, quite simply, it is not from those perspectives, or by those means, that we know God.

Making the gospel the principle of knowledge

Naturally, the question then is, 'How do we implement this idea that the gospel is the principle of theological knowledge?' We have seen that the gospel brings us to the knowledge of God through believing the truth about Jesus' identity, that he is the Son. In that case we must clearly look for where we are brought to that knowledge of Jesus' identity, and that can be only in the Bible. Jesus himself regards our Old Testament as testifying about him (John 5:39), and as setting out what he must do and endure (Luke 24:26). Similarly the New Testament is manifestly Christocentric. So to realize and to implement the gospel as the principle of theological knowledge the Bible must necessarily be the priority of our study.

This is, after all, nothing more than the mainstream of orthodox Christian thought down the centuries. Thus Hilary of Poitiers insists on the priority of biblical testimony about God over against human speculation about God on the grounds that God is his own best witness.[4] And this again simply recognizes the nature of our relationship with God that the gospel establishes. It is an interpersonal I–Thou relationship. In an I–Thou relationship one accepts that the other must disclose himself or herself; the other is not simply an object that I investigate, but one to whom I listen as he or she speaks of who he or she is. This is especially the case where the I–Thou relationship is one where one party is Lord and has a perfect self-knowledge. Put that way, Hilary's notion that we must let God witness to himself is simply common sense.

Moreover this primacy of the Bible is authentic Anglicanism. Article 6 of the Thirty-Nine Articles reminds us that the Bible is sufficient to instruct us about salvation.[5] The First Homily (the Homilies, we should remember, are described by Article 35 as containing 'godly and wholesome Doctrine') states the place of the Bible not just as sufficient but as necessary: 'Unto a Christian man, there can be nothing either more necessary or profitable, than the knowledge of Holy Scripture; forasmuch as in it is contained God's true word, setting forth his glory, and also man's duty.'[6]

This historic position for the primacy of the Bible in theology is not an assertion that there are no other kinds of human knowledge. It is, though, to assert that theology and the education which follows it have a special character among the various kinds of human knowledge. This has long been recognized and Thomas Aquinas provides a helpful framework for discussing this. In 1a.1.5 of the *Summa Theologiae* Aquinas faces the question of whether Christian theology, 'sacred doctrine' in his terms, is an inferior discipline or mode of knowing to others. We should note in passing how contemporary this question is in modern universities in the West, with that seemingly endless and often ill-tempered discussion as to whether a university should permit there to be a department of Christian theology at all.

Aquinas's answer is that Christian theology is not an inferior discipline, but a superior one. He has several reasons for this judgment. He notes that it deals with nobler subject matter, God himself, and has a higher end, 'eternal bliss'. Yet what catches our attention in our present discussion is that Christian theology is superior because it has not lesser certainty but greater certainty than purely human sciences, be they physics or history. It is based on revelation from God. The significance of revelation is that this is knowledge not based on human reason, but on God's knowledge, whether of himself or his creatures.[7] In other words, revelation is valuable because of who God is, the uncreated creator of all. As uncreated, he has perfect self-knowledge; as creator of all he has perfect knowledge of his creatures. A word of knowledge that comes from him, then, is knowledge indeed.

From this perspective, Aquinas is in a position to note the relations of Christian theology to other sciences. Are they useful? Definitely, but as handmaids,[8] whose propositions are weighed in the light of the revelation the Bible gives.[9] This follows as the night the day. Once we have a view of God as the uncreated creator of all who knows perfectly, it must be his statements that correct and evaluate human knowledge; not the other way round. Nor is this a peculiarity of the medieval theological synthesis. This is the tone of the high Reformed theology of Frances Turretin,[10] and it is the logical implication of Article 20 of the Thirty-Nine Articles, which indicates that the Bible cannot be contradicted, even by the traditions of the church: 'it is not lawful for the Church to ordain any thing that is contrary to God's Word written . . .'

You may feel I am labouring this point. Perhaps this is because I see theological curricula in my own country that do not see disciplines such as sociology or history or philosophy as handmaids which assist but are subordinate to a theology based on revelation in God's Word written. Rather, such disciplines are in practice given positions that correct what a theology based on revelation would hold. We are told that, for example, the clear teaching of Paul must now be seen in the light of, which in effect means corrected by, current social, psychological or other claims. We should be quite clear, I think, that this approach in principle assumes that valid theological positions arise independently of canonical revelation and can not only contradict that revelation but actually be preferred to it. This would be possible, would it not, only if knowledge of God were possible outside the gospel. And if such knowledge were possible outside the gospel, then, to paraphrase the apostle Paul in Galatians 2:21, Christ came and died to no purpose. How could we expect someone educated on a basis that sees gospel knowledge as redundant or erroneous then to go out and be a minister of that gospel? The idea seems incoherent.

Actualizing the gospel as the principle of knowledge

It follows from what I have been saying about the gospel as the principle of knowledge and the understanding that the gospel takes us to the Bible that a theological education must be an education in the Bible. What would that look like?

Breadth of coverage
It would mean that curriculum choices must respect the need for students simply to be taken through as much of the biblical text as possible. We may feel that it is not possible to explore each book in as much depth as we would like over, say, the space of three years. But the extent of our biblical coverage is a key point. It empowers students, by making them less vulnerable to a distorted selection of biblical material, whether from us or others. It is an antidote to error. The Homily on Scripture comments forcefully, 'Ignorance of God's Word is the cause of al [*sic*] error . . .'[11] It models to them the point Paul makes in Acts 20:27 that a Christian minister is concerned with all that God says. It also equips them better to treat God's Word as a unity.

The unity of the Bible
We do well to stay with the notion of unity. For the idea of unity is what will shape not only our biblical studies teaching, but also our biblical and systematic theologies. The North American theologian John Frame provides a concise account of the relation between the different disciplines of exegetical, biblical and systematic theologies:

> While exegetical theology focuses on specific passages and biblical theology focuses on the historical features of Scripture, systematic theology seeks to bring all the aspects of Scripture together, to synthesize them. Systematics ask, What does it all add up to?[12]

It is, of course, a basic principle of interpreting particular biblical texts that they must be construed in context. With any text, not just biblical ones, reading individual sentences so that they contradict each other may be an amusing party game, but it scarcely is calculated to help us know the mind of the author. Even so, with purely human texts we are sometimes justified in finding contradictions. This scarcely surprises us, since consistent, coherent thought is difficult. Yet with a text originating with God, we rightly expect and seek consistency and coherence, not just between, say, 1 John chapter 1 and chapter 4, but between, say, Paul and James on justification.

The rationale for this is not a bibliolatry, but a conception of who the God is who has originated the biblical texts. As Paul comments in Acts 20:27, when we speak of the plan or purpose or counsel of God, we speak of it in the singular, and as a whole. Given the sovereignty, wisdom, knowledge and truth-fulness of God, this must follow. For to suggest that God has inconsistent plans, or plans that come to be implemented as one or another fails, would be to suggest he is not sovereign in salvation. To suggest that there are mutually incompatible values within his purpose would be to impugn his wisdom and knowledge, and so on.

In other words, the God who meets us in the gospel, eternal, uncreated Father, creator of all, necessitates a commitment at the level of our exegesis to the unity of individual texts, and leads us to seek for resolution and synthesis in the face of apparent contradiction. This again is part and parcel of the authentic Anglican approach to Scripture. Article 20 reminds us that the church does not have liberty to follow any exegetical conclusion. We read of the authority of the church, 'neither may it so expound one place of Scripture, that it be repugnant to another'.

At the level of biblical studies this means in concrete terms that there will not be, say, a Marcionite approach to the Old Testament, that reads it as incon-sistent with or independent from or free-standing from the New Testament. Within New Testament studies it would not be appropriate to suggest that, say, Paul and John have inconsistent pictures of the cross. Please do not misunder-stand me at this point. The issue is not that different books, different corpora, different genres and different texts have different perspectives. They clearly do. The issue is rather that when those different perspectives are elevated into contradiction and incompatibility, to repugnancy, to use the terms of Article 20, then the unity of the Bible that derives from who the God of the gospel is starts to evaporate. We will return a little later to why that matters so much.

Let us pass, though, from exegetical theology to biblical theology. We may see biblical theology, following Frame, as drawing out the developing themes of the Bible and tracing through their narrative structure and sequence. An example would be following through the theme of death from Genesis 2:17 to the fearful second death of Revelation 20:14, with the associations that are generated en route of exclusion, wrath, physical death, spiritual death in sin, and so on.

Naturally the kind of exegetical theology we have just outlined inclines one to this kind of biblical theology. In fact, one might even ask whether we have equipped our students to do exegetical theology as richly as we should have if we have not also taught them this biblical theology. There is a certain delicacy required in this task. There is the presupposition of the unity of the Bible that permits and requires something like this. But equally the best biblical theology does not flatten out the particularities of the themes as they appear in the text. The strictures of James Barr about totality transfer from one occurrence to another remain chastening and warning for putative biblical theologies.[13]

Systematic theology likewise on Frame's account is a working through of the consistency and unity of the Bible. Frame also says, 'Systematic theology seeks to apply Scripture *as a whole*.'[14] In this way, systematic theology is not merely a biblical discipline, in the sense that it works with the data of Scripture, but one with a very particular presupposition: that Scripture genuinely is a whole.

At times, doubtless, systematic theology has failed to be truly biblical in respecting the data on which it rests, and doubtless too it has not always preserved the unity of the Bible as it should have. Yet when faithful to its calling, it is trying precisely to preserve the fullness of revelation. This is clearer still in Helmut Thielicke's comment '[Systematics] attempts to include the whole of the study of revelation and to assign its details to their proper place in this whole.'[15]

The purpose of dealing with the whole of revelation in this way is, as Frame says, so that it may be *applied*. Frame's comment is perceptive. Among other things the Bible is a book that tells us, as the Homily on Scripture puts it, our duty. It continues, 'For in Holy Scripture is fully contained what we ought to do, and what to eschew, what to believe, what to love, and what to look for at God's hands at length.'[16]

As soon as one recalls that one of the functions of the Bible is to tell us God's will for human life, then the task of systematics as a way of synthesizing the data of the Bible becomes a way of maximizing God's address to human life. It is an enormously practical discipline and in a sense Christian ethics is impossible without it. Karl Barth, though, stresses another aspect of the task of systematics: 'Dogmatics [systematic theology] is the testing of Church doctrine and proclamation . . . The concrete significance of this is that dogmatics [systematic theology] measures the Church's proclamation by the standard of the Holy Scriptures . . .'[17]

We need to draw together the role of systematics as maximizing the ethical application of the Bible and the role of testing the proclamation of the church. Both reflect the attempt to make the lordship of God real in the life of the church and of the believer. It is, though, a relationship of lordship that charac- terizes the personal I–Thou relationship that the gospel establishes. For instance, the cry of one whose heart has been regenerated and enlightened by the Holy

Spirit is precisely 'Jesus is Lord' (1 Cor. 12:1–3), while Paul in Colossians can describe the process of conversion as one where we have been transferred from the realm of darkness to the kingdom of God's Son (Col. 1:13; cf. also Acts 26:18).

In this way the picture Frame gives us is of a systematic theology that is not antibiblical, or abstract and irrelevant, but precisely one that respects and implements the idea of the unity of the Bible and also is of critical practical importance for grounding our day-to-day obedience and the faithfulness of our witness. It is something a local church ministry cannot safely do without. My guess is that many of us face two questions: first, whether the systematics we teach does respect the unity of the Bible in this way, and second, whether we teach systematics at all, or have dismissed it as an arid irrelevance in favour of other disciplines.

The particularity of the Bible

It has long been recognized that the texts of the Bible are given to us from within a location in time and space and human history. Thus considerations of Israelite social customs can help us understand, say, the book of Ruth. Likewise, though, we would need to say with James Barr that the Bible is given to us not just in a particular historical and social location, but also in a linguistic location. Barr writes, 'Language is not a tool but is essentially an entity in which the biblical material is built and within which it exists.'[18] From this, Barr makes the point that right interpretation of the Bible needs training in the biblical languages.

This, naturally, touches us on a raw spot. Language training is not easy at the best of times and is in any case time-consuming. We may also point to preachers of our acquaintance who do not know the biblical languages but who preach faithfully enough. Yet in a sense we would want to challenge this. If the Bible really is as precious as we say, as the Anglican formularies indicate, indeed, as it itself teaches, more precious than fine gold (Ps. 19:10), then we would want the Bible taught in local churches not merely passably or adequately but as best we may. My own country has a saying, 'Do not let the good be the enemy of the best.' And equipping a minister with a command of the biblical languages enhances their ministry remarkably: it extends the range of scholarly material they may use, and so on, but most importantly it maximizes their own direct contact with the text. There is less mediation through the work of translators and other scholars, and less dependence in that way, and more direct encounter with God through his word. There is a maximizing of directness in the I–Thou relationship that a preacher or teacher has. I imagine we all want that for our students.

The perspective of the Bible

The Homily on Scripture says this: 'In these books we may learn to know our-selves.'[19] One of the peculiarities of our personal relationship with God is that although he must reveal himself if we are to know him, and we must therefore listen, he already knows us. His disclosure to us is not just a revelation of who he is, but a revelation of who we are. We see this almost painfully in the teaching of Jesus. Thus in Luke 11:42 he charges the Pharisees with being those who neglect justice and the love of God. This was scarcely, it seems, their own self-image. But by Jesus' words, a Pharisee could come to know himself, and turn to God in repentance and faith. Clearly, some did.

This bears on theological education in at least two respects. First, this gives a perspective for human history and for church history especially. The progress and failures of the people of God since the ascension are to be seen in the light of Jesus' lordship and his command to take the gospel of repentance, faith and forgiveness of sins to the ends of the earth. As such it furnishes examples to learn from, and be warned and encouraged by, but all within the perspective of the reality and purpose of God that it sets out.

Second, the Bible provides perspective on the non-revealed academic disciplines. The Bible both celebrates human understanding of God's creation (e.g. Job 28:1–11) and notes its limitations because of our finitude (e.g. Job 28:12–28) and sin (Rom. 1:21–22). From that point of view, naturally, a study of some secular disciplines will be useful and fruitful, enlightening us about an individual culture's self-understanding and goals. At its best this helps signifi-cantly in contextualizing the gospel for the culture in which a group of ministers have to work. Thus to understand contemporary England, knowing something of Friedrich Nietzsche's outlook illuminates some of the obstacles the gospel faces and also some of the more astute insights some English people have on life in this sinful world. Knowing something of Jean-Jacques Rousseau helps one grasp some of the mechanisms behind the current tensions in English family life, and so on. To that extent, teaching in the areas of current world views, or sociology or psychology, can have its place. But these human schools of thought are set within an overall perspective, the perspective the Bible itself gives on us, for 'In these Books we may learn to know ourselves.'[20]

And without the Bible?

Let me close this brief survey with one final reflection. What does theological education look like without this priority for a biblical understanding? It seems to me we can discern two dangers. First, the danger of incoherence. We may have space in our curricula for psychology, history, counselling, New Testament, and so on. But each of these disciplines, shorn of the biblical perspective, tends to become a free-standing discipline which does not fully integrate with others, but tends to generate its own values. It is one thing to prepare our students for the complexities and subtleties of life. It is another thing entirely to send them out with a series of fundamentally dissonant understandings of life, so that their New Testament training says to solve the problem of a parishioner's adultery one way, while the counselling training says that answer is wrong.

Second, the risk is that if we do not listen to God's self-revelation as the basis and norm for our training, we will establish something else. We may speak of God, but that word will have become a label for a content of our devising, and not of God's revealing. To use the word 'God' for something we have devised attracts a striking biblical description and analysis. It is idolatry, for it is a view of God formed by human imagination and art (Acts 17:29). And of this the Bible calls us to repent.

Discussion

- How can we best contextualize theological education without theological compromise?
- What elements in theological education are necessary across all cultural contexts?

Notes

1. See <https://www.gafcon.org/sites/gafcon.org/files/resources/files/The-Gospel-How-of-Theological-Education.pdf>. Reproduced with permission of Global Anglican Futures Conference. Editor's note: this chapter has been lightly edited for reading purposes, but I have tried to retain its context. Over the three-day conference, César Guzmán spoke on 24 June, Mike Ovey on 25 (the previous chapter) and 26 (this chapter).
2. César Guzmán, 'A Gospel Matrix for Theological Education', <https://www.gafcon.org/sites/gafcon.org/files/resources/files/A-Gospel-Matrix-for-Theological-Education.pdf>.
3. *Summa Theologiae* 1a.1.3.
4. E.g. *De Trinitate* I.18.
5. Article 6 begins, 'Holy Scripture containeth all things necessary to salvation . . .'
6. Homily 1, 'A Fruitful Exhortation to the Reading and Knowledge of Holy Scripture', in *The Homilies* (Lewes: Focus Christian Ministries Trust, 1986), p. 1.
7. See especially *Summa Theologiae* 1a.1.6, 1a.1.7, 1a.1.8.

8. *Summa Theologiae* 1a.1.5.

9. *Summa Theologiae* 1a.1.6.

10. *Institutes of Elenctic Theology*, Topic 1, questions 8–10.

11. Homilies 1.1, 'Fruitful Exhortation', p. 4.

12. J. Frame, *The Doctrine of the Knowledge of God* (Phillipsburg, NJ: P&R, 1987), p. 212.

13. J. Barr, *Semantics of Biblical Language* (Oxford: Oxford University Press, 1962).

14. Frame, *Knowledge*, p. 212; emphasis original.

15. H. Thielicke, *A Little Exercise for Young Theologians* (Carlisle: Paternoster, 1996), p. 28.

16. Homilies 1.1, 'Fruitful Exhortation', p. 1.

17. K. Barth, *Dogmatics in Outline* (London: SCM, 1966), pp. 12–13.

18. J. Barr, *The Concept of Biblical Theology* (London: SCM, 1999), pp. 78–79.

19. Homilies 1.1, 'Fruitful Exhortation', p. 2.

20. Homilies 1.1, 'Fruitful Exhortation', p. 2.

27. THE GRACE OF GOD *OR* THE WORLD OF THE WEST? (NAIROBI, 2013)[1]

May the words of my lips and the meditations of all our hearts be now and always acceptable in thy sight, O Lord, our Rock and our Redeemer.

Introduction

My first really significant encounter with worldwide Anglicanism came at theological college. It was 1990 and an East African priest was on secondment with us. He preached in the college chapel. He posed a question. 'Which gospel?' he asked. 'Which gospel do you Westerners want us to believe? The one you came with or the one you preach now? Which gospel?' I was horrified, not because what he said was not true. I was horrified because it was true.

My East African brother's question has nagged away at me ever since. But how has it come about that we have a different gospel now from the one we first preached? What is this difference between what we Westerners say now and what we said then?

I think the difference is nothing less than the grace of God and what we mean by it. The difference comes from the way that Western culture and the Western church deny or distort God's grace. The modern West, in both culture and church, is, overall, graceless, and has become so because of its worldliness.

That is why I have called this plenary talk the grace of God *or* the world of the West. Ultimately you cannot have both. It is either/or. My prayer is that as global Anglicans we choose grace, not the world of the West. For those of us who have tried to have grace and the world, I pray for our repentance. My fear is as global Anglicans we will try to have grace AND the world, and that God justly hands us over to the consequences of our sin in rejecting his grace as it truly is and builds his kingdom through others.

But I must now explain why grace is at stake, why the culture of the West denies grace and how the Western church distorts grace.

Why is grace at stake?

Let me begin with grace.

On first hearing, you may well be thinking that I am simply crazy. People in the Western church still talk about grace. They talk about it a lot. If anything, the charge is that traditional believers like me lack grace. So what am I getting at? It's this. It's not enough just to say the word 'grace' a lot. The issue is what we mean by it, and whether we mean what the Bible means or whether we have made up our own meaning for ourselves.

Cheap grace?

Now the kind of grace that I think the Western church talks about, and come to that Western culture when it thinks about grace at all, is this: cheap grace. Cheap grace. I am borrowing from the German theologian Dietrich Bonhoeffer. He says this:

> Cheap grace is the grace we bestow on ourselves. Cheap grace is the preaching
> of forgiveness without requiring repentance, baptism without church discipline,
> Communion without confession. . . . Cheap grace is grace without discipleship,
> grace without the cross, grace without Jesus Christ, living and incarnate.[2]

We especially need to note three points. This grace is *worldly*. Bonhoeffer means that it conforms to the patterns of the world, is no different from the world and listens to the world.[3] Crucial. Bonhoeffer was warning us about mixing Christian grace with the world's idea of grace, and at worst substituting the world's view of grace for the Christian view. For Bonhoeffer, who was writing in the 1930s, that influence from the world came from the tragic infatuation of some German Christians with Nazism. The precise kind of worldliness may be different now from Nazism then. I'm not saying that modern Western culture and the modern Western church is pro-Nazi. I am saying it is pro-world, just as, in their different way, Nazi Christians tried to be.

This worldliness is at the heart of Bonhoeffer's criticism. He is echoing the Barmen Declaration of 1934, when German Confessing Christians rejected the idea that Christ's people should listen to any other voice claiming to stand on a par with his. The Barmen Declaration comes back to that time and again: the imperative that Christ's people listen to him, the good Shepherd, and not to any competing voice. It is Christ alone, not Christ and something else – whether the something else is Nazism or liberal democracy or an understandable pride in establishing oneself as an independent country.

But what does this cheap grace that conforms to the world look like? Bonhoeffer points especially to two things that mark out cheap grace from real grace:

- This grace is *repentanceless*.
- This is a grace we *bestow on ourselves*; in other words, it is a grace we give each other when we see fit, rather than according to the pattern of God.

We need to look at both aspects: the lack of repentance and bestowing grace on ourselves.

Cheap grace and the lack of repentance

To begin with, why does it matter if we have a cheap grace that lacks repentance? First, it matters because it distorts the gospel of Christ. So Mark 1:14 describes Jesus preaching the gospel. Those are the words in Greek, proclaiming the gospel, and the content of Jesus' gospel is, 'Repent and believe.'

At Jerusalem, we global Anglicans rightly and emphatically pointed to the great commission given to us by the Lord Jesus in Matthew 28. You have that repeated fourfold theme of 'all', don't you? All authority is given to Jesus, proclaiming all he has taught. To all nations. Being with us for all time. And that commission gives us both the right and the duty to proclaim what Jesus has taught. The right because all authority is his. The duty because he, the one with all the authority, has told us to do so.

But people can cite even this great commission in Matthew 28 superficially. The key issue is, precisely *what* has Jesus taught? What is the *content* of his teaching that he tells us to proclaim to all? Here we must compare Scripture with Scripture, as good Anglicans do, and read Matthew 28 with Luke 24. Again these are words of the risen Christ. Let me read to you from Luke 24:45–47:

> Then he opened their minds to understand the scriptures, and he said to them, 'Thus it is written, that the Messiah is to suffer and to rise from the dead on the third day,

and that repentance and forgiveness of sins is to be proclaimed in his name to all nations, beginning from Jerusalem.' (NRSV)

We heard in this morning's sermon from Ephesians that Christ is central to us, and this is how he is central, the one through whose name there is forgiveness of sins.

So what is the content of what we proclaim to all nations? Luke makes it clear, doesn't he? The content of the great commission is the proclamation of repentance and forgiveness of sins in the name of Jesus. Peter picks up just that in the climax to his first speech in Acts 2. There he is, he has explained that Christ is risen from the dead and that this Jesus has been crucified by the people he is talking to. They ask him what they should do. And his response (Acts 2:38) is to tell them to repent and be baptized in the name of Jesus for the forgiveness of sins. Repentance and the forgiveness of sins. It's there again, isn't it? And so it goes on throughout the Acts of the Apostles. A high point, of course, is Acts 17:30, where Paul says that God now commands all people everywhere to repent, because there is coming judgment.

And you can see why repentance really matters. Classically I repent when I recognize my sin and I rely on the mercy of Jesus for my forgiveness. There is horror at my sin, but more than horror: there is a despair of myself and hope solely in Christ. Of course, we can then see why repentance is integral to becoming a Christian. I am turning from the flesh, the world and the devil towards God. That's why our baptismal services have repentance. Now if there's no repentance, then where am I with regard to the world? Well, I haven't turned away from it. I'm trying to love God and the world at the same time. But no human being can face two ways at once, and you can see why cheap grace with its lack of repentance means that you remain facing towards the world and not facing towards God.

And we can't say that the Anglican tradition is just different. Think of the Book of Common Prayer services for Morning and Evening Prayer. They begin with extensive prayers of repentance. Think of the 1662 version of the Lord's Supper. The Exhortations underline we must not approach the Lord's Table lightly but repentantly. Baptism likewise involves repentance. This means that for centuries repentance has played a vital part both in Anglican worship, in our sacramental services and our ordinary services of Morning and Evening Prayer. And this is explained very clearly in the Homily about repentance – we should remember by the way that the Jerusalem Declaration[4] refers us to the Thirty-Nine Articles, which in their turn point us to the two Books of Homilies. GAFCON has recognized the Homilies as a spiritual resource for our guidance. So what does the Homily on Repentance say?

no doctrine is so necessary in the church of God, as the doctrine of repentance and amendment of life. And verily the true preachers of the gospel – of the kingdom of heaven, and of the glad and joyful tidings of salvation – have always, in their godly sermons and preaching unto the people joined these two together; I mean repentance and forgiveness of sins even as our Saviour Jesus Christ did appoint himself.[5]

And then there's a reference to Luke 24.

So, godly preachers in the Anglican tradition, when they preach the gospel, join repentance and forgiveness of sins together, following Christ.

The Anglican Reformers weren't out on their own here. In the continental Reformed tradition, John Calvin states that 'with good reason the sum of the gospel is held to consist in repentance and the forgiveness of sins'.[6] The Lutheran Philip Melanchthon in his Apology for the Augsburg Confession makes exactly the same point.[7]

Now, you have heard church leaders from my country and from North America. How much honestly have you heard or seen this Luke 24 gospel of repentance and forgiveness of sins? Too little, I think. I think you have heard about Millennium Goals, and you have heard a lot about inclusion, an awful lot about inclusion, but an inclusion without repentance. And therein lies the tragedy, because if you offer inclusion without repentance, then you are offering inclusion without the forgiveness of sins. And that is desperate, isn't it? First of all there is the question of blessing. In Acts 3:25–26 Peter refers to the blessing of the Gentiles under the Abrahamic covenant. He explains what this blessing is – the forgiveness of sins. There again Paul in Romans 4:7 quotes the psalmist David, 'Blessed are those whose iniquities are forgiven' (NRSV). But in cheap grace, because there is no repentance there will be no forgiveness, because it's thought to be unnecessary. And the distinctive blessing of sins forgiven? Well, that's lost.

That profoundly alters our relationship with God. He is no longer the God of the huge and generous mercy that he freely gives as he justifies us by his grace alone through faith in the Lord Jesus alone. Remember the parable that Jesus tells in Luke chapter 7. The two debtors, one of whom owes a little while the other owes a fortune. Jesus teaches that the one who was forgiven much loves much, and the one who was forgiven little loves little.

Do you sense in the Western churches this great love of sinners who have been forgiven much by their heavenly Father? I see admirable concerns for social justice in my own church, as well as genuine good intentions and kindness towards others, and a certain affection for God. But remember that the parable of Luke 7 is told in the context of the woman who washes Jesus' feet and dries them with her hair. There is an exuberance, a passion, a sense of her being overwhelmed by the goodness of the Lord Jesus to her that I think is alien in a church whose services no longer reflect the priority of repentance and the humble seeking of God's face as we turn away from the world.

The next aspect is something I say with trembling. When we read Luke 15, we read three parables that tell us in fact about God's joy at the repentant. It is joy in which we are expected to share. If I'm honest, I think the way that the Western churches have, not always explicitly denied but, minimized various sins and their eternal consequences means that God would find little to rejoice over in terms of our repentance. We don't really do it.

Now I want to be careful as I say that, because Western churches do repent of some sins: the legacy of racism, the history of colonialism, sins of social injustice within their cultures. But what fascinates me is that these are sins that the world recognizes as sins in Western culture. It's very safe in Western culture to say that racism is a sin. Very safe to repent of it. It even wins a certain admiration from the world.

It's always difficult to be sure about people's motives, but when Western churches repent of the history of colonialism and the murder of indigenous peoples, are we doing it because it is offensive to God or because it is – rightly – offensive to the world? I think the acid test of whether our repentance is really towards God is when God and the world disagree. If the benchmark of what counts as sin and requires repentance is really God's will, then we will repent ourselves and call for repentance when God has said something is sinful, and will do so even when the world says otherwise. I very much fear that we fail this acid test, because I'm afraid that where we do repent, we repent of the things that the world finds offensive. As we all know too painfully, things that the Western world doesn't find offensive, like sexual sins, the Western churches are increasingly disinclined to condemn. Repentance like that: Is it really turning to *God*, or acknowledging the *world*?

This question of repentance is huge. Biblically and historically and pastorally. In the parable of the lost son, the father speaks of a son who was lost and is now found, who was dead and is now alive. This is fantastic. The great commission, properly understood in those Reformation terms of repentance and forgiveness of sins based on Luke 24, is the most wonderful news there could be. Yes? We can take news to people which means that they can wait confidently like the Thessalonian Christians for the return of the Lord Jesus who delivers from the wrath to come.

The second thing I want to pick up is this self-bestowed grace. Self-bestowed grace just assumes that grace will come and that it is inconceivable that God could do other than we want. Traditionally, this self-bestowing attitude is called 'presumption'. Or we can just call it 'taking God for granted'.

The Bible teaches us that presumption is deadly. So, in the Old Testament, the kingdom of Judah took it for granted that God would not finally judge them and they could take him for granted because they had the temple. In Luke 3 we find people coming before John the Baptist with presumption, and John rebukes them for it, telling them not to presume on the fact that they are physical descendants of Abraham. Again the problem is taking God for granted. And when Satan tempts our Lord Jesus Christ, he uses presumption again and Christ has to reject it – he will not take God for granted.

The theological tradition of which Anglicanism is a part, and in which the African Augustine played such a huge role, has thought long and hard about presumption. Thomas Aquinas puts it like this:

> presumption is an inordinate trust in the Divine mercy or power, consisting in the hope of obtaining glory without merits, or pardon without repentance. Such like presumption seems to arise directly from pride, as though man thought so much of himself as to esteem that God would not punish him or exclude him from glory, however much he might be a sinner.[8]

Aquinas relates presumption to pride and comments that such presumption despises God's justice.[9] We think so highly of ourselves we cannot imagine God being just towards us and punishing *us*; others, perhaps, but not us. Note too that Aquinas states presumption lacks repentance. But why bother to repent when we presume on God? So cheap grace with these two characteristics, lack of repentance, and presumption or self-bestowed grace, relates intimately to pride. To humanity that is curved in on itself, absorbed by itself and not looking outwards to God and neighbour. Lack of repentance and presumption are two sides of the same coin.

As you look at the conduct of the Western church, and what it tolerates and thinks needs no apology and no repentance, do you not sense presumption, taking of God for granted? To our shame I think I do.

Now obviously a Westerner listening in may think this shows the usual obsession with sexual ethics, and same-sex relations in particular. Here we must remember that the kind of behaviour we're talking about, which the Western churches either openly approve or tacitly tolerate, is a symptom of something deeper. Rosaria Champagne Butterfield catches this brilliantly in her spiritual autobiography.[10] She describes how the Lord Jesus brought her out of a same-sex lifestyle. And she reflects on the way that same-sex behaviour is a manifestation, as are other forms of sexual sin, as are our malice, gossip and violence, of our underlying pride and our claim to be owners and disposers of ourselves and our bodies without regard to our creator. For her, pride took this form of same-sex behaviour. For others of us it will be heterosexual adultery. For others of us, greed. For others, power. And so on. But the fundamental disorder is a disordered love of ourselves which leads us to imagine that God cannot possibly judge us – presumption. So that is cheap grace. Not biblical, not Anglican and desperately short-changing a world that needs to hear the gospel of repentance and forgiveness of sins.

Why is the West a cheap-grace culture?

Where has it come from? Let me look first at Western culture and why it is a cheap-grace culture. Why has Western culture become so graceless?

Now we can all see that Western culture seems to have little room for God and less time for him. The culture may call itself secular, which could suggest neutrality. But actually it is hostile to speaking of God. That's why more and more human rights cases in the UK relate to Christians and their freedom of belief. This should amaze us. Western culture is a product in large part of Christian cultural contributions. That is so whether you are talking about the world view that enables the scientific revolution. That is so whether you are talking about the world view that enables a strong account of the need to respect the human individual. Why then so little room for God?

Kant and maturity

Intriguingly I don't think Western culture started down this path simply by saying, 'We don't think God matters.' It didn't start with God at all. It started in large part with what we thought about human beings. The starting point is anthropology, not theology. This is strikingly clear in Immanuel Kant's 1784 essay 'What Is Enlightenment?' He says:

> Enlightenment is man's emergence from his self-incurred immaturity. Immaturity is the inability to use one's own understanding without the guidance of another. This immaturity is self-incurred if its cause is not lack of understanding, but lack of resolution and courage to use it without the guidance of another. The motto of enlightenment is therefore . . . Have courage to use your own understanding![11]

Let me try to set out what Kant is saying. His key idea is maturity. Humans have arrived at maturity. Because they are mature, two things follow. First a mature person is a competent person. Mature people make rational and correct decisions. Mature people need no external guidance. Second, there is a question of rights. An ethical question. Mature people are entitled to exercise their own judgment without external interference. So Kant uses maturity for two things. Maturity underpins both the claim to competence that human beings make and also the ethical claim to independence that human beings make. It means I do not need you to tell me what to do and it means you have no warrant in telling me what to do. In everyday terms, you should mind your own business.

Well, on Kant's view, why on earth would you need God to reveal things to you? You do not need him to tell you his law. You can work it out yourself, and of course bound up with this maturity is the idea that I can do righteousness. Mature people have self-control and since we are self-controlled we can will the good. Therefore not only do I not need revelation but I do not need justification and imputed righteousness from the Lord Jesus because logically I can do it myself, as a mature person.

Think how offensive classic Anglican theology is to Kant's view. Take Homily 1, which is on Scripture:

> Therefore as many as be desirous to enter into the right and perfect way unto God, must apply their minds to know Holy Scripture; without the which, they can neither sufficiently know God and his will, neither their office and duty.[12]

Of course, it's not surprising when you think about it that in order to know what God desires you should listen to what he says. But that's the thing about Homily 1 – it's concerned for relationship between persons, which involves listening. Yet it's not only our need for revelation that Anglican theology asserts, but our inability to be righteous in and of ourselves in any complete sense. Take this statement from Homily 2: 'For of ourselves we be crab trees, that can bring forth no apples. We be of ourselves of such earth, as can bring forth but weeds, nettles, brambles, briers, cockle, and darnel.'[13]

Think about it; the fruit we bear is not apples – we cannot bring forth apples because of what we are after the fall: people whose hearts are inclined to evil (Gen. 6:5; 8:21). Kant's maturity is utterly different, isn't it?

Maturity and entitlement

After Kant, this maturity is assumed and treated as an entitlement. It's not something that you have to earn.

This takes us to something vital in current Western culture: our sense of entitlement. I think we can see this in two areas. The first is our emphasis on rights. The second is the growth, socially speaking, of narcissism, a destructive form of self-regard that I'll explain more later.

So, first the growth of rights.

Europe and North America are very much rights cultures. For us in Europe it's the European Convention on Human Rights, especially the rights that flow out of equality. Please note several features about this.

Individualism

First, individualism. We all wonder why Western Europe is so individualist. But of course it's individualist: it has a doctrine of rights that the individual holds, and in many ways that's as basic as it gets. The basic building block of society is the individual, not the family, because the individual is the right holder. What's more, those rights are just there. You don't have to earn them; they are just there. You don't have to qualify for them. You just have them; you're born to them.

Incoherent – rights without foundation or duties

Second, when you come down to it, this is incoherent. There is strangely little discussion of *why* you have those rights and where they come from. The history of these ideas in Europe is that people are thought of as having rights because those rights are God's gift to his human creatures. So the Americans put it in terms of men and women being endowed by their creator with certain inalienable rights. But in modern Europe you can't assert God or creation in the public arena. So there's a problem. Roman Catholic thinker Marcello Pera points out that this means that the modern West is busy trying to forget where it came from.[14] It's an amnesiac culture. It's intriguing, isn't it? How can you have a strong sense of identity as a culture when you won't acknowledge your history? The modern West wants all the benefits of a society with individual rights, but doesn't want the basis on which they were actually formed. It's like climbing a tree, sitting on a branch and then chopping off the branch you're sitting on. It's the same kind of problem that atheist German philosopher Friedrich Nietzsche spotted in the mid-nineteenth century. He posed the question of whether Europe could keep its morality without its God. He mocked the English especially for thinking this was possible. As someone brought up in England, I reckon he was spot on, as is Marcello Pera. Because if, as the modern West says, you can't talk about God's giving us these rights, where do they come from? People don't want to say the rights are only given by society, because society could then take them away. So what are you left with? Well, the individual. And the individual becomes king or queen. Lots of individuals, which means lots of kings and queens, or people who think they are.

Now don't underestimate the problems this creates. You've got this robust doctrine of rights. But can you really build a society just on rights, the rights of the individual? What happens when those rights conflict, one individual with another? I think that's what some of you in the Global South observe about us, that our individualism breeds various conflicts, and in particular an individualism where the individual prefers himself or herself to the good of others. As it happens, these problems were seen long ago in the nineteenth century by another Catholic thinker, Giuseppe Mazzini. Mazzini argued it is not enough to speak of rights. We must speak of duties too. In fact, he said, when we look at Christ we must look for duty first because that is where Jesus leads us. Think of his summary of the Law. And Mazzini says, 'The origin of your duties is in God. The definition of your duties is found in his law. The progressive discovering of the application of his law is the task of humanity.'[15]

But you can see the problem for the West, can't you? It's all very well to talk of individual rights, but where do *duties* come from? Why do we Westerners have all these declarations of rights, and not declarations of duty? What do you all sense about this in the West? Do you sense we have as robust a sense of our duties as of our rights?

Attractive

And this is enormously attractive. Whether we like it or not, we have managed to evolve a system in which there are fundamental individual rights and we talk about those a lot, but we have very little to say at a fundamental level about human duties. Now we may feel that it's incoherent to talk about rights without duties. But my goodness, it's attractive. And that is what the modern West is holding out to us culturally speaking. Tempting, isn't it?

Plausible

But this is not only attractive; this is plausible. It's plausible not least because of the technological achievements of the West. When I look at my computer or use my phone, I am deeply impressed by what human minds have done. Remember that Kant used the word 'maturity' to imply our competence and our ability. Doesn't it tempt you to think that Kant is right? Surely we are as competent, we are as able, as he said. If I may say so frankly to you in the Global South, I am not sure that you have fully taken this on board: Kant's value system is going to look very plausible in your cultures, as well as very attractive.

Powerful

Not only is this attractive and plausible; this culture is now enormously powerful. The assumption of maturity and the sense of entitlement that goes with it create values that are being pumped around the world through this technological achievement. You cannot keep it out by border posts or immigration control. People will read this stuff and they *will be* impressed by it; and because we in the West just say it all as part of our presuppositions, it will become for you the air that you breathe too. Sometimes, of course, the West is much more overt in imposing values. As a UK citizen I am still deeply ashamed of the way a few years back our Prime Minister David Cameron tied foreign aid to pro-same-sex policies in a speech. Western culture says a lot, it shouts a lot, and it spends a lot. Do not underestimate its power to reshape your cultures in its own image. And remember, it will *want* to do so. Because it thinks it is righteous. I'm sure you sense that too, don't you, the Western sense of self-righteousness about its doctrines of individual rights?

So that's the first thing to say about our sense of entitlement: the way it creates and is also supported by this doctrine of individualist rights without duties.

Entitlement and narcissism

Let me take you now to the social phenomenon of narcissism. I'm using this especially because of recent work by American social psychologists Jean M. Twenge and Keith Campbell. They have a simple starting point. They conducted a prolonged survey of surveys done on American students entering study. The surveys are standard and among other things they test for narcissism. Twenge and Campbell put it like this:

> the central feature of narcissism is a very positive and inflated view of the self. People with high levels of narcissism – whom we refer to as 'narcissists' – think they are better than others in social status, good looks, intelligence, and creativity. . . . [N]arcissists see themselves as fundamentally superior – they are special, entitled, and unique. Narcissists also lack emotionally warm, caring, and loving relationships with other people. . . . [T]he result is a fundamentally imbalanced self – a grandiose, inflated self-image and a lack of deep connection to others.[16]

Now Twenge and Campbell aren't saying that this profile fits everyone. They are saying, though, that it fits more and more people and that the attitudes that underlie this are more and more socially acceptable. For Twenge this is painfully evidenced as the quest for self-respect morphs into a quest for self-esteem; not quite the same thing. She sees it encapsulated in the chorus of a Whitney Houston song which says, 'Learning to love yourself is the greatest love of all.' It almost stops you in your tracks, doesn't it? The greatest love of all is loving yourself. And some schools adopt the strategy of increasing self-esteem with young children by teaching them precisely that and playing that song. My colleague who is director of Youth and Children's ministry read an earlier draft of this address – her comment was, 'This is basically what our education system is now about!'

The key word here is 'entitlement'.

Narcissism – theologically

We need to make clear two things that flow from this. First, theologically, this is not a doctrine of works righteousness. It is not saying you earn your way to eternal life. This is not Pelagianism but the different beast of entitlement. Entitlement is not about what we do or earn so much as thinking so highly of ourselves, just by virtue of who we are and our natures, that we think good things automatically belong to us and it is intolerable that we should be frustrated.

Narcissism, disappointment and rage

Second, Twenge and Campbell point to the disappointments this entitlement attitude causes. Of course it disappoints. Not everyone can become a pop star. Not every essay gets an A. And the person with the entitlement attitude is ill-equipped to cope. Twenge and Campbell discuss how prone disappointed narcissists are to anger and rage. Of course, disappointment can make any of us angry, but Twenge and Campbell note how extreme it is. For me it is very interesting to read what Twenge and Campbell say about entitlement and the rage that follows frustration, after what happened in my own country in November 2012 when the majority arguing in favour of a particular kind of pro-women bishops legislation could not get its way. The only word that describes it is 'rage'.

The dangers of dissent

This explains why certain kinds of dissent are deeply problematic now in Western culture. If you challenge entitlement, the perception is that you have attacked rights, and are attacking people's self-esteem, and these are perceived as great moral errors. And that is why the modern West in its culture will hear only a word of cheap grace, because cheap grace does not demand repentance and it can be bestowed by ourselves. But the real grace, linked with repentance and forgiveness of sins, now challenges Western culture at a very deep level, and it's no surprise when you read in Western media how frequently the comments about religious conservatives are comments of rage. The summary phrase is, 'How dare you say that!'

The Western church and cheap grace

But where is the Western church in all this? Why has the Western church become prone to promoting cheap grace?

Bafflement at the failure of modernization

First of all, let's remember how puzzling the situation is for Western churches. Think of it: so much of the leadership of major Western denominations, including the Church of England, has made a virtue of trying to modernize itself. That's the language used, and the project is to bring the church into line with the world around it. Now the theory behind that was that if the church did this, people in the secular West would come back to church in their droves. That hasn't happened. People within the Church of England don't much like the term 'managing decline'; but make no mistake, that is frequently but not invariably the mindset. But if you have committed yourself to a programme of 'modernization', then it is baffling to find that the modern world still doesn't want you. But it will be enormously costly at an emotional level to try to think through why. It seems almost impossible for past and present Church of England leaders to ask whether their modernization programme is part of the problem.

You will be asked in the Global South to go in for 'modernization'. Please don't fall for it. It's a recipe for disaster – look at us.

Spiritualized narcissism?

Second, you may be thinking that I'm being too hard. So let me describe a recent service of evening prayer at a conference of relatively senior leaders within dioceses in the Church of England. Those leading the service had a presentation which spoke of three calls. The first call was to love God. The second call was to love your neighbour. The third was to be yourself.

Does anything strike you about that? What strikes me is that self is right up there with love of God and love of neighbour. And this was not given to us by the Lord Jesus but is something we have made up and put on a level with the other two. These three calls were then explained. Most time was on the call to be yourself, which involved identifying your desires and following them. It looks remarkably like the sense of entitlement and self first that Twenge and Campbell discern in the entitlement culture, doesn't it? It's a spiritualization of narcissism, I'm afraid.

Roots for putting self at the centre

Third, let us try to see something of the roots. Remember I said that Kant's Enlightenment thinking didn't start by talking about God. It started by talking about humanity, about ourselves. That is what has happened in the Church of England, I think. Let me take you back over 100 years to the publication of the hugely influential *Lux Mundi* essays in 1889.[17] Several essayists shared the key point that when John 1:9 speaks of the true light enlightening all, it means that even before the incarnation of the Lord Jesus we already had divine light and reason within us. We have the divine light of reason within and so can tell from within what is right and wrong. But this means, of course, that we are back to talking about us. Again, our anthropology may be shaping, is shaping, our theology.

Crucially, John definitely does not mean this. If we had that divine light of reason within us, already illuminating us so that we could tell right from wrong, as the essayists thought, then the world would not have rejected the true light when he did come into the world. That is exactly the point that John makes in verses 10 and 11: that the world was made through him, that he had his own people, and Christ was still rejected. John's references to light are best taken as a reference to the light of life, the creative activity of the eternal Word, which John has in view in 1:4–5.

Fourth, if the divine light is already at work illuminating the reason, giving this knowledge of right and wrong, and this applies to the whole human race, then the logic is we should listen to the world, isn't it? It implies we should indeed let the world set the agenda, because the world already has this eternal light within it. I fear that this is what much of the current Church of England sounds like to me – let the world set the agenda.

This is important for listening and weighing what a Western church says. The issue is not so much 'Is there an explicit reference to Christ's agenda?' but rather, of course, 'Is the agenda that of Christ as attested by the Scriptures, or that of my inner Christ who has always illuminated me?'[18] A second question is, 'Is the world setting the agenda with equal authority to Christ's?'

But as you go through John's Gospel, you can see, can't you, that John doesn't mean that. In John 7:7, Jesus himself tells us that the world hates him. It hates him because he testifies against it that its deeds are evil. Now that's impossibly wrong on the *Lux Mundi* view, isn't it? If you're following those essayists, then Jesus would be quite wrong to see the sharp distinction that he does, in fact the sharp opposition that he does, from the world towards him.

Now, I've shown briefly that this exegesis of John 1:9 is desperately wrong. But please understand that this theology has been running round, and indeed running, the Church of England for decades. And it opens the door to cheap grace, because it says 'yes' not just to Jesus but also to the world. It's not an explicit 'no' to Jesus, but it is a Jesus *and* the world approach. As you look at us in the Church of England, I'm afraid you're looking at a church which has an increasingly worldly view of grace, a cheap grace in which repentance is redundant, and which we can safely bestow on ourselves because we already have divine light within us and we know when God will give grace to us. Frighteningly, on this view God will never disagree with us, because his voice comes from within us. As I look at what is happening to the church in which I was ordained, I'm very struck by the way that what Twenge and Campbell say about narcissism and entitlement applies. They analyse the almost religious feel of Western narcissism like this: 'The quest for self is in some ways the misguided quest for the divine spark within.'[19] It could come straight from *Lux Mundi*.

Conclusion

Now we have teased out why cheap grace with its worldliness is inevitably going to be there in Western culture and in one of the dominant forms within the Western church. Joining Jesus with the world so that we say Jesus *and* the world is always going to be popular at least as a way of appeasing the world. And the Western world right now does issue challenges to the church to modernize. By which it means, catch up with worldly opinion.

But while the world may want cheap grace, it is not what the world needs. To cheap grace Bonhoeffer opposed costly grace, a costly grace which costs us everything in that it is grace that we receive repentantly and with humility, not presumption. That is the grace associated with the forgiveness of sins and peace with God. The world's needs are many, we all know that, but this is its greatest need: that its sins be forgiven. And that is why it is absolutely imperative that we at GAFCON preach not cheap grace, but costly grace to the world, not because we hate the world but because we love it, as our Saviour did.

Notes

1. See <https://www.gafcon.org/sites/gafcon.org/files/resources/files/The_Grace_of_God_or_the_world_of_the_West.pdf>. Reproduced with permission of Global Anglican Futures Conference.
2. D. Bonhoeffer, *The Cost of Discipleship* (London: SCM, 1963), p. 47.
3. Bonhoeffer, *Cost*, pp. 46–47.
4. See <https://www.gafcon.org/resources/the-jerusalem-declaration>.
5. Homily 32, 'An Homily of Repentance, and of True Reconciliation unto God', *The Homilies* (Lewes: Focus Christian Ministries Trust, 1986), p. 366.
6. *Institutes* III.3.1.
7. Commenting on Article XII of the Augsburg Confession. T. Tappert (ed.), *The Book of Concord* (Philadelphia: Fortress, 1959), p. 186.
8. *Summa Theologiae* 2.2.21.4.
9. *Summa Theologiae* 2.2.21.1.

10. Rosaria Champagne Butterfield, *The Secret Thoughts of an Unlikely Convert* (Pittsburgh: Crown and Covenant, 2012).

11. Kant uses the pithy Latin motto 'Sapere aude!' E. Kant, 'An Answer to the Question: What Is Enlightenment?, in H. S. Reiss (ed.), trans. H. B. Nisbet, *Political Writings* (Cambridge: Cambridge University Press, 1991), p. 1.

12. Homily 1, 'A Fruitful Exhortation to the Reading and Knowledge of Holy Scripture', *Homilies*, p. 1.

13. Homily 2, 'A Sermon of the Misery of All Mankind, and of His Condemnation to Death Everlasting by His Own Sin', *Homilies*, p. 10.

14. M. Pera, *Why We Should Call Ourselves Christians: The Religious Roots of Free Societies* (2008), trans. L. B. Lappin (New York and London: Encounter, 2011).

15. G. Mazzini, *The Duties of Man* (London: Everyman [Dent], 1907), p. 21.

16. J. M. Twenge and K. Campbell, *The Narcissism Epidemic: Living in the Age of Entitlement* (New York: Free, 2009), p. 19.

17. C. Gore (ed.), *Lux Mundi: A Series of Studies in the Religion of the Incarnation* (London: John Murray, 1889).

18. 'Christ as attested by the Scriptures' was the formula adopted by the Barmen Declaration of 1934, para. 21.

19. Twenge and Campbell, *Narcissism*, p. 65.

SERMON AT THE THANKSGIVING SERVICE FOR MIKE OVEY

All Souls, Langham Place, London, 13 March 2017

Revd Dr Peter F. Jensen, retired Archbishop of Sydney

> For to me, to live is Christ and to die is gain.
>
> (Phil. 1:21, NIV)

Here is the world's stark truth: you are either alive or you are nothing. For us, in our world, you live only once; make the most of it; better forget death until he calls for you. Don't talk about it; don't think about it. Death is the end of our being, our consciousness, our life and our loves – it is the great Oblivion, the great Nothing. We return to the dust and are no more.

The contemporary world seems so assured. We know what life and death are. That is why we party. Why hope for more? Why fear the end? When we die, the memory of our existence is like an echo fading into silence. People will judge us; perhaps an obituary, perhaps a eulogy; it matters not; they usually say nice things.

But this is a charade, a desperate and melancholy charade. It cloaks pain, anxiety, loneliness. We are like children, hands in front of faces at what frightens. And yet, what if God is the judge, and *he* delivers your final funeral speech? To this we have no answer that satisfies the heart and stills our anxious fears.

In such a world, the stark truth of Paul sounds like the beating of a mighty but alien drum: *For to me, to live is Christ and to die is gain.*

To live is Christ . . . Into the chaos of Paul's life had come Jesus Christ. Paul was given a new identity and a single focus. He was a new man in Christ Jesus, he had been translated from the kingdom of darkness into the kingdom of God's own dear Son. In the midst of that great redemption, brought about by the power of the Holy Spirit of God, Paul found the most precious of all gifts: the forgiveness of his sins.

Once he was dead in his trespasses; now he was alive, forgiven. His debts which were many, were cancelled, their deadly legal demands nailed to the cross. The Saviour whom he had once thought of as cursed by God, he now knew was pierced for our transgressions. The apostle cast aside his moral accomplishments, his privileges of birth, of education, of status, his professional advancements. Rubbish, he called them, and garbage they were. For him, the greatest privilege was 'the surpassing worth of knowing Christ Jesus my Lord'.

Because he lived *by* Christ, he lived *for* Christ, striving in all things to please him. He prayed that Christ would be honoured in his body, whether in life or in death. For that reason, he engaged daily, like all Christians, in the great struggle to put to death the deeds of the body by the power of the Spirit; to deny the grip of sin and the world and the devil in his life, and to live instead by faith in his Lord and the word of his Lord. He lived for Christ.

His losses were nothing. His life was dominated by his Lord. This one thing I do, he said, 'forgetting what lies behind and straining forward to what lies ahead, I press on towards the goal for the prize of the upward call of God in Christ Jesus' (Phil. 3:13–14, ESV). 'For to me, to live is Christ and to die is gain.'

What gain is this? Not the oblivion which is the best hope of the modern world, whose end is destruction, whose god is their belly and who glory in their shame, whose mind is set on earthly things; but the glory which is the work of the living God: '[O]ur citizenship is in heaven, and from it we await a Saviour, the Lord Jesus Christ, who will transform our lowly body to be like his glorious body' (Phil. 3:20–21, ESV).

We Christians grieve, but we do not grieve as those without hope; our hope is a person, and such a person: 'For ever with the Lord!' Our hope is to be *with* our resurrected Lord, and living *for* our resurrected Lord, and being *like* our resurrected Lord, for ever. However happy, healthy and fulfilled we are in this life, it is nothing compared with the eternal weight of glory beyond all comparison that is our future. Paul calls this great gain 'going home'.

'For to me, to live is Christ, and to die is to go home.'

But was Paul a mystic, dreaming of the heavenly future and unconcerned for this world and the people thereof? On the contrary: this chapter shows that it is his focus on Christ which fills him with a fervent love of neighbour. He is in prison, he suffers, he wishes to go home, he says, 'My desire is to depart and be with Christ, for that is far better.' But then he says, '[T]o remain in the flesh is more necessary on your account' (Phil. 1:23–24, ESV). His love for the Philippians is passionate and clear; his business, to serve the Lord by serving them.

He speaks from no luxury penthouse. He is in a prisoner's chains for Christ; his future, dubious; his enemies, legion. There is also the painful truth that among his enemies are those who claim the name of Christ – perhaps former converts or colleagues – who now preach the gospel out of envy and rivalry, out of selfish ambition, thinking to afflict him further in his imprisonment. Here is no wild ascetic; no paper saint; no clownish entertainer; no dressed-up popinjay; no sleek ecclesiastic. Here is one who carried the cross, who bore the shame and who is able to say even of his betrayers, 'What then? Only that in every way, whether in pretence or in truth, Christ is proclaimed, and in that I rejoice'; 'For to me' – and surely for you? – 'to live is Christ and to die is gain.'

It is clear that Mike Ovey made the same confession of faith: for me, to live is Christ. All of us who knew him, knew that this was true of him. He would say that his true identity, the meaning of his life, the focus of his ambitions, arose from his redemption through Christ, and he lived for Jesus.

Of course, he was far from perfect – but that's exactly the point, isn't it? He was a sinner, who had no claim on God, no right to be right with God, no reputation or achievement or goodness which merited God's favour, however much it may have impressed the world.

But that is the point – you live by and for Christ, not from the garbage which is human achievement or goodness, but by grace which covers our sins and brings forgiveness.

We are rightly met here today to thank God for Mike, to laugh perhaps, to weep, to remember and smile, to recollect with deep gratitude. All correct. But he himself would say to us, his life does say to us, that the first act of gratitude to the Lord today is that he took so sinful a man as Mike Ovey and redeemed him, saved him, forgave him, transformed him, empowered him, gifted him, enriched him with the love of his wife and family, set him in the church and enabled him to preach the Saviour who was pierced for our transgressions. Here is the first point and the main point, at which we say together, 'Praise the Lord!'

Of course, there is so much more. All of us here are grateful for what the Lord gave us through Mike. We will have our stories, funny or serious, about events, classroom incidents, blindingly brilliant teaching, wisdom, care and love; about Mike as a child, Mike as a husband and a father, and about so much more. He was indeed one of the best of friends; he was intellectually acute; he was learned; he was courageous; he was filled with spiritual insight; he lent his courage to us timid souls so that we were emboldened to live for Christ. He was a fearless friend of the truth because he walked by faith.

What are you thanking God for?

Personally, I think of him in his time in Sydney as one who became an honorary Aussie without ever losing his Englishness. He and Heather came into a foreign country and a foreign community; it is not always an easy transition. And yet they endeared themselves to everyone; and I mean everyone – it was not just faculty and students; it was the cleaners and the kitchen staff and the office workers who loved them.

I think of his support in times of need. My way of putting this is to say that it was like being shoulder to shoulder on the same rugby team. You could throw the ball without looking and know that he would catch it and take it forward. Not for Mike an academic aloofness; his love for neighbour and his love of the gospel and God's church meant that he could always be relied on to give himself to the cause of gospel fellowship. As Paul says, in this very passage, giving me the very words I long to use because it is the Mike I knew: 'I thank my God in all my remembrance of you . . . because of your partnership in the gospel from the first day until now . . . with one mind striving side by side for the faith of the gospel' (Phil. 1:3, 5, 27, ESV). That was Mike and it meant so much to us all; and that is why, humanly speaking, the loss is so acute for us all.

I think of his theological prowess, whether one to one, in writing, in the leadership of the College, in the classroom, in the pulpit. We have lost no ordinary minister of the new covenant; the Lord has taken one of the choicest of his witnesses from us. I can never forget his talk in GAFCON, Nairobi, where he gave one of the best addresses I have ever heard, holding riveted as though by a divine gift, an audience from so many different cultures and languages.

I think too, however, of sitting with him through his suffering as he struggled with the strain of being a Christian leader in the midst of conflict. His courage and his cheerfulness hid from many that he was vulnerable. He bore deep and permanent scars, inflicted as he gave service through leadership. Indeed, you may be sure that all who lead for Christ make mistakes, but also that they bear in their body and heart the marks of the crucified Christ. This was Michael and we thank God for him.

I think, also, of sitting with Mike and Heather at their table with their dear children, being embraced and loved, and rejoicing in the intimate fellowship of their home. For one of the most wonderful titles any of us can be granted by God's mercy is 'husband' or 'wife', 'mother' and 'father', and it is no accident that the Scriptures see a connection between our homes and our ministries. And for those of us who had the immense privilege of receiving their hospitality, and knowing their children, we know that as the loss is so keen, so the thanksgiving can be so true for a father and a husband who pointed to Christ and lived so human a life.

And yet, let me go further. There is a special contribution we must not forget, because it is both so essential and so rare: it is Mike's vision for the churches and for theological education. What was this vision? Mike was utterly persuaded about the need of healthy and growing churches for the future of the gospel in this land. And he rightly connected this with theological education. He regarded his own experience of theological education with distaste. For him, it did little to prepare him for the ministry of word and sacrament. Mike was deeply disturbed and even alienated; he determined that if there was something better, he would do what he could to find it and promote it.

He understood this as few of his contemporaries did. He knew the vital importance of healthy churches, churches in which the people live for Christ in an alien world, taught the gospel and valuing it above all else. He knew that a church can rarely rise above its pastor; if the pastor is poorly trained, the church will be weak and vacillating. He knew that theological education is the key issue. A denomination can hardly rise above its seminaries.

He knew that this is more urgent than ever in a world which thinks that death is mere oblivion. Some, of course, have natural skills to make up for poor education. But they are the exceptions. He saw that a deep acquaintance with Scripture requires years of study as well as adequate training to preach it. If the ministers of the gospel are not properly prepared for ministry, the churches will wilt and the mission of Christ will be compromised.

And he determined to train the pastor-teachers who are Christ's gift to his church so that through their ministry the body of Christ would not be victim to every wind of doctrine, but might build itself up in love. He wanted to see graduates who know the Lord and can make him known. How did he do this?

First, he put the knowledge of God through sacred Scripture at the heart of the Oak Hill experience. God's revelation was a trust, of which we are the stewards. The Bible was not treated as a book to be deconstructed, but as the living and abiding word of God to be understood, trusted and obeyed. It is clear in its testimony to Christ; it is authoritative; it is sufficient; it is unified. We are, he would say, stewards of knowledge, not masters of knowledge. There are many subjects in the curriculum, but one task, to know God and be equipped to make him known, and one authority, Christ Jesus who rules through his enscripturated word. You were taught to teach the Bible in such a way as to affirm truth and to deny error, both key aspects of a godly ministry.

Second, he made community essential to that by which we learn and grow. He saw that a good seminary is the product of its faculty: godly and able ministers of the new covenant, the humble stewards of the knowledge of God, who admit into their fellowship others who are learning Christ so that they may all be shaped by his word and made better fitted for his service. He aimed to create a community of faith, hope and love, a community in which all learn Christ. Of course, its academic standards are the highest, for when we are set the task of learning Christ, our minds and hearts and souls are energized and motivated as by nothing else. But we learn not in rivalry but in fellowship.

In this vision, the good seminary is the product of its faculty; but the test of a good seminary is its graduates and the churches which will flourish and grow as the word of God is preached. And the overwhelming evidence is that if you want good churches, you need a good seminary. Thus his vision was not for Oak Hill, but for England and beyond. To see the inestimable benefit of hundreds of faithful churches, faithfully taught, faithfully listening, faithfully sharing the glad tidings that Christ is Lord. Oak Hill and all good seminaries need to attract hundreds of men and women who enter training not for a job but for a mission to the world.

Mike saw the seminary as a pastoral community in which we encourage and rebuke, hear the glad tidings and are summoned to repentance. Then, it can be the seedbed of the preaching ministry for the churches. In our world, you cannot bypass such a seminary or substitute for it some quicker, cheaper option. Not if you want a ministry equipped for the challenges of today.

There is of course much else. But if our thanksgiving for him today does not include the resolve that excellent theological training will be available in this country, not least through Oak Hill, we will have met in vain. Here is his legacy: What will you do to sustain it?

For me, to live is Christ and to die is to be with Christ.

The news of Mike's death came to us in the brilliant sunshine of a Sydney summer as the people gathered at our annual CMS summer school. Those of us who knew him were shaken to the core; the Lord had suddenly removed one of the chief captains among the people of God, at a time, in our judgment, when we needed him most. Ana was with us, and so the grief was for, and with, family as well. And for the family, the grief can hardly abate, even with the passage of time, for loss is loss.

And yet, God is God. We trust his wisdom and we know his power; we believe that he works out all things according to the counsel of his perfect will. With God, sometimes life is very hard; without him, it would be inexplicable and horrible. There is always a reason for the cross, and the cross leads home to the crown.

This we do know and it explains why the grief of the Christian is of a different quality: that to die is gain. The God of all comfort assures us that there is a future where there is no more death, no more tears and that our dear brother has passed into the very presence of the Lord he loved so well. And he has already heard the words which you and I long to hear: 'Well done, good and faithful servant; enter into the joy of your Lord.' For him, the trumpets have sounded on the other side.

For us, there is a time of waiting; Mike's death has created an absence which for some is almost unbearable. But God is still our Father, whether we are here or at Home; Mike's absence from us is so painful – but it will not last for ever. The day will come when we too will be with Christ.

For Mike – for me – I trust for you – this is what we say to the world: life is no charade and death is no oblivion. Rather, we know as of a surety that as Mike lived for Christ, so at the right time for him he went Home. And so, through our tears, in our sorrow, we hear, for our comfort, the strong and certain note of the gospel of Christ, the risen Saviour. And we thank God for the witness of this great servant; we follow his witness by thanking him above all for the Lord Jesus Christ, by whom and for whom we live until we ourselves see him face to face.

AFTERWORD: MIKE OVEY – THE BEST POSSIBLE GIFT

Daniel Strange, Acting Principal, Oak Hill College

Introduction: the one about the monster and the whirlpool

As a lover of all things classical, the late Principal of Oak Hill College would be grinning at my somewhat dramatic illustration taken from Homer's *Odyssey*, as a *homage* to his infamous oblique introductions to lectures (and much human conversation, for that matter).

Like Ulysses, our hero Mike Ovey captained the good ship Oak Hill in a way that swashbucklingly but expertly had to steer between twin perils: Charybdis the whirlpool, and Scylla the monster. I had the great privilege of being his first mate on the adventure.

Our whirlpool was the decidedly 'mixed' formal theological education we had both received and that we wouldn't wish on anyone else. Through bitter experience we recognized that cut from the moorings of biblical authority and the apostolic Jesus revealed therein, academic theological studies is a vortex of vain human imaginings; not healthy but gangrenous; not integrated within itself but angrily dissonant; not for the church but for itself; too much Athens and not enough Jerusalem. We recognized that the emperor has no clothes and needed to be called out.

Our monster was an ecclesiastical anti-intellectualism and amateurism towards theological training. Although in part a reaction to the perils of the whirlpool, it was knee-jerk, pragmatic and worryingly short-termist. The results could be shallow and simplistic, an unwillingness to engage with the world and its complexities, cut off and so cut out of conversation – a ghettoized Jerusalem with little interest in anything Athenian, resulting in a poverty of seeing the implications and applications of biblical truth. Lots of machete, but little scalpel. We recognized that we didn't want to take part in the race to the bottom, where pragmatic considerations have often resulted in an attitude which asked how little theological education one could get away with before getting into 'real' ministry.

Of course, constantly defining yourself against what you are *not* is never the most edifying pursuit. Fortunately the course which the college under Mike's leadership was charting was founded on a distinctive and exciting biblical vision *for* theological education. Mike was determined not to get bitter but to get better. Moreover, he was determined to train students to be better than himself.

It's a mystery of sovereign providence that the Lord would call Mike home with the journey only just gathering momentum. But we are so thankful to the Lord that the narrative we had been working on in the months before his death was completed and had gained enthusiastic acceptance within the college community at Oak Hill and beyond. We call it *The Best Possible Gift*, and it consists of two big pictures.

The best possible gift

Mike's vision for theological education centred around the pattern for gospel ministry set out in Ephesians 4:11–13:

> So Christ himself gave the apostles, the prophets, the evangelists, the pastors
> and teachers, to equip his people for works of service, so that the body of Christ
> may be built up until we all reach unity in the faith and in the knowledge of the
> Son of God and become mature, attaining to the whole measure of the fullness
> of Christ. (NIV)

Ephesians is a big-picture letter. Paul paints for us a huge God, a God who brings all kinds of blessings in Jesus, but those many blessings are part of one plan. God's overall plan is that Christ is the head of all, head as ruler, head as King, head over the whole cosmos, natural and supernatural. This truth is both wonderful but also challenging: wonderful because of who God has appointed to be head – no one less than the Lord Jesus who died for us; but challenging – disturbing even – because we realize we are not the centre of everything. There are all kinds of blessings for us as God's adopted children, but we're not the most important thing there is. The universe doesn't revolve around us, but it's so tempting to pretend it does.

Moreover, unlike so many of our plans, this plan packs a punch because it's put together and run by a God who raises the dead. Paul hammers this. God's power is so far-reaching that he brings life to the dead, life both in raising Jesus from the dead after crucifixion, and bringing us to life when we were dead in our sins and our wrongdoings. This is power on a scale outside our comprehension.

As he has brought us to new life as we believe in Christ, he realigns our relationships so we are brothers and sisters, living stones in the same building, a new humanity, and by being that, we are a living vindication of the wisdom of God. It is a huge privilege to know that as God's new humanity, we are the way by which he vindicates, demonstrates, his wisdom.

Of course, we want to ask how we in our local churches, or in our organizations, can live lives that vindicate God's wisdom, and in particular what kind of minister is needed to help a local church be that.

This takes us to Ephesians 4, and what the Holy Spirit says here about the life of God's people. First, there's the idea of unity in verses 1 to 6, and then from verses 7 to 16 there is the theme of Christ's gift to his people, and how that works out.

Paul speaks of the characteristics we should have as a people together. He wants us to be local churches, individual Christians, marked by these qualities. These qualities are outward looking. So I live humility out in the way that I treat others. It's the same with gentleness, and generosity. I'm not kind, sitting alone on a desert island – I'm kind on a Sunday morning when I help someone. And, of course, I'm not loving on my own. I love someone else.

That all rests on, it's explained by, this language of oneness. I'm to be like that because my brothers and sisters are part of one body, because the one Spirit is at work in us all. As we read the statements about oneness, we are aware that there is a particular kind of oneness at stake here. It's a oneness that hinges sooner or later on what the one God has done, and on how we will together have one faith. It's not about being part of one organization, like everybody working in the Royal Bank of Scotland or a supermarket chain. It's about the way that you and I are brought together as we all believe in the one set of promises God makes to human beings, about salvation through his one and only Son.

This is critical. I can be part of a denomination where we have the same pension plan, the same employment policies, the same-shaped buildings, and all that can look like being united. And sometimes that's helpful practically. But it's not the unity the Holy Spirit is talking about here. Above all the Spirit is talking about unity of faith here, because there is one God, one Lord Jesus Christ who has done all that he has in carrying out one plan of salvation. We must not substitute anything for that, let alone deny anything that goes into that. But how do we get there? Yes, clearly Paul wants this kind of unity. So how do we get it? How do we keep it? How do we grow it?

This is just what Paul goes on to explain in the following verses as he talks about the gifts of Christ. With any gift, one of the big things is who gives it. Some people are brilliant present givers because they've got generous hearts as well as credit cards to match. They are willing and able to give. So who is doing the giving here? Crucially, we are told that it's Christ – the one who's been appointed head of the cosmos, and who is the ascended one. He ascends like a conquering king.

In Paul's time a conquering king came back laden with treasure, gold, artworks, jewels – you name it. Dripping in wealth. That's the image of the ascended, conquering king. And Jesus is ascended and conquering, because he's conquered both death and Satan.

But Paul doesn't stop there. This magnificent towering figure of Jesus, the ascended victorious Jesus, is the very same Jesus who descended.

Jesus is the descended one: he came in humility, to his own people, to the world that he created – and his human creations murdered him. And he did that willingly, carrying out his Father's plan. This means that our Lord Jesus Christ is the right kind of giver. He is the one who descended, willing to be lowly, willing to endure death and humiliation for our sakes, and to bear our sins on himself in our place. And he is also the one who has ascended in victory, rising from the dead.

As he is the most willing and able giver, can you possibly imagine what kinds of gifts he will give?

That takes us to this critical verse, verse 11: 'So Christ himself gave the apostles, the prophets, the evangelists, the pastors and teachers' (NIV). Notice the way Paul puts it. He gives people, people who are ministers. *He gives ministers, not ministries.* This verse does not say that Christ has given you something, namely a ministry. He says that Christ has given *us*, namely ministers. We ourselves, as ministers, are the gifts.

That means, for all those aspiring to be pastors, teachers and gospel leaders of various descriptions, the issue is: How can we be the best possible gift of Christ? It is not primarily what we will personally enjoy, or will make us look good. When we ask how we can be Christ's best possible gift, we are acknowledging all over again that it is not about us, not about how everything centres around us, our ease, our prestige, or whatever. There is a real challenge for us here: we are not to make our training choices for selfish reasons. We are not even to make our choices basically to please someone we admire. We are to make them on the basis of what will make us the best possible gift.

Why must we be so clear on this? Because when we have said that we as ministers are gifts, we have to ask who is given those gifts. In Ephesians 4, the gifts are given to the people of God, not us. Remember that we are in view here as gifts, not as receivers of gifts. We may be receivers in a subordinate sense, but what the text has in view is not that a talent or a ministry is given to me, but that I as a minister am given to somebody else, given to the people of God. It's not about me.

Overall, what Ephesians 4 is talking about is gifts that Christ gives. Those gifts consist of Word ministers (because all those gifts of ministers are ministers of the Word), and those gifts of ministers are given to his people. More, these gifts have a purpose: so that God's people can be safe. Secure. Protected. Why? Because stuff happens inside and outside a local church that blows it around, and crucially blows it away from what God has said. Verse 14 stresses how false teaching endangers God's people. How does Christ keep his people safe? Among other things, by giving them Word ministers.

Not just safe though, but also serving (v. 12). How do God's people know how they should be serving, reaching out to each other and out to the world around them? We have our lives shaped and formed by God's Word being ministered to us. I learn how to behave in the office, how to relate in the gym, how to conduct myself at a party, as Word ministers teach me about diligence, honesty, wholesome conversation, and so on.

This is all so that we can be united under the headship of this one Christ, joined together in a common faith, a common bond, a common allegiance to him and with him – and there we are right back to these themes of unity that open this chapter. How can we walk the walk as Christians together who vindicate God's wisdom in our common faith? On the premise that Christ has given the gifts of ministers to his people who will keep them safe, serving and united under his headship.

Training for worlds yet to be

Let's look forward in the light of Ephesians 4. Again this is a big picture, but this time looking ahead to worlds yet to be. Why worlds yet to be? Because the church needs ministers in those yet-to-be worlds. Who will we minister to in those yet-to-be worlds, remembering that as ministers we are gifts for them?

First, the world yet to be will be fallen and fractured

Not just fallen, but fractured: different outlooks, different standards of living, different customs, different subcultures. Our big cities can already be very like that. Our fallen, fractured worlds resemble a whole plane of ice floes, floating close to each other with big cracks between. And this world is changing. Now, this is stating the obvious, because human life has always been changing. New kings, new queens, good harvests, bad harvests, that has been true since whenever. Our world is changing – but more than that, today it is fast changing. Very fast changing. So fast changing that you can easily feel out of it, excluded, dizzied, disoriented. Isn't that just how some of us feel at the pace of techno-logical change? Changing, but fast changing.

Second, this creates a world that is both confused and confusing

Our world is fractured and fast changing, it's fallen and changing, but primarily it doesn't have the Word of God; it's starving for the Word of God, and so of course it's confused. Don't we feel this when we click on any news feed? Swathes of description, but so little actual understanding of what is happening. And it's not just that our world, fallen, fractured, changing and fast changing, is confused; it is confus*ing*. We are set within it. We often are bewildered by what we see going on, by the mixed messages we get. We're living in a culture that simul-taneously thinks it's hugely free because of its lax sexual ethics and at the same time has a maze of rules to wade through if we want to put up a conservatory. It's crazy. And Christians are not immune to being confused.

Third, that makes for a perfect storm

Ministers will constantly have to cross the fractures as we minister to a fallen world; those fractures are going to be changing and very fast changing, and our footing's none too sure because this world is confused and confusing. And just when we think we've sorted out one species of confusion, our fast-changing world will have moved the goalposts. And so the task as Christ's gifts is to minister in these yet-to-be worlds. We have to ask what those worlds would actually need from any Word minister of the Lord Jesus Christ. Not what *we* would *like*, but what *they* will *need*; not even quite what those worlds will like necessarily, but what they will *need*.

First, because we're living in this fractured world, in a world of floating ice floes, those worlds will need us to have *breadth* of knowledge and understanding. Second, that understanding must have *depth*. Unless we understand things deeply we won't see the changes in our world in their proper biblical light. We won't quite see how things connect, how one ice floe may drift towards or away from another. Those worlds will need from us an understanding that is not just broad and deep, but one that fits together, that fits together as far as possible all the different disciplines and bits of knowledge we may have.

Third, because this world is changing and fast changing and the ice floes keep drifting in different directions, ministers need to be *adaptable*: to be able to see when a previously successful pattern of ministry just no longer quite clicks; to be able to spot what's wrong, and then reinvent what we do and how we say things. We mustn't change the content of what we say, because the gospel doesn't change, but we must be able to adapt how we say it. And then when we've done it in 2030, we will have to do it all over again in 2040, and 2050. That's a huge demand – a joyful demand because it is wonderful to see someone first turn to the Lord Jesus Christ, and it is wonderful to see Christians growing in their understanding. But it is demanding.

Loving Jesus so deeply that we can present him simply

If that is what those yet-to-be worlds need from us, how do we become Christ's best possible gift? To begin with, theological education – Christian theological education – must aim for a student to become more like Christ.

In particular, Christian theological education wants students to come out with a bigger view of our infinite God than on day one of their study. We can think, and sadly sometimes in our country it's been true, that theological study leaves people with a smaller view of God. That's not Christian theological education. There's a really lovely part in *Prince Caspian*, one of C. S. Lewis's Narnia stories. Lucy returns to Narnia and sees the Christ figure, Aslan the lion, once again.

> 'Aslan,' said Lucy, 'you're bigger.'
> 'That is because you are older, little one,' answered he.
> 'Not because you are?'
> 'I am not. But every year you grow, you will find me bigger.'[1]

If we are really growing as Christians, then God, his Son, his Spirit will get bigger and bigger for us as we see them more and more for who they are, as we understand them more deeply.

And as we grow more like Christ, as we have a bigger view of an infinite God, the aim is for us always to keep growing. Any theological education must equip the student to keep growing, keep learning, refining our understandings, reading God's Word better and better. As we are equipped and enthused to grow ourselves, that equips us genuinely to minister to others, equipping them and enthusing them in their turn to grow in the knowledge of the Lord Jesus Christ.

Isn't this the minister the Bible is pointing us to, one who knows and loves the Lord Jesus himself or herself, wants to know him more, and can help and inspire others to the same? Think what the churches of our land would look like if they had ministers like that. Think what it would mean for bringing good news to the lost. For binding up the broken-hearted, and comforting a world facing death with no hope of resurrection or forgiveness.

Conclusion: the best possible training

Wouldn't it be wonderful for this to be the pattern for ministers in all those yet-to-be worlds? It's what they need: ministers who love Jesus so deeply that we can present him simply. Those are the ministers Mike Ovey wanted to train, and for the last twenty years of his life his centre of operations was at Oak Hill College in London. However, it's a vision that could apply to any theological college.

The pattern is a virtuous circle of servanthood between college, its students and our churches.

The college's task is to serve students by enabling them to become the best possible gifts of Christ to his church. Training must be highly adaptable to meet the challenges of rapidly changing times. The curriculum must be integrated, with the Bible at the centre, and the different theological disciplines not isolated or compartmentalized but interacting with each other, and inexorably moving towards ministerial application. Faculty must be recruited who can model servant leadership not only in what they teach, but also in the way they teach.

Mike was convinced that the best way to be trained was to be immersed in a learning and worshipping community for a dedicated and rigorous time of study and formation. Such a context offers students essential time to listen, debate, reflect, pray and grow in love for Christ in the fellowship of others. This is not a time out of ministry. Rather, it is a redirection of ministry for a time and for long-term gain. Lifelong skills, lifelong habits, lifelong relationships, lifelong learning.

In this kind of community, students are taught to see themselves as servants of, rather than masters over, the church and the Word of God. They are stewards of the mysteries of God. They do not possess knowledge of God: it possesses them. The aim is not merely for students to receive the information they need for ministry, but for the transformation which comes from reflecting with others on being Christ's gift to God's people. Students learn to love Jesus more deeply so they can explain him more simply.

Given the challenges the church faces in our culture, Mike was convinced that training should be interdenominational and pan-evangelical. We train together recognizing our distinctive polities, thus displaying a gospel unity while also encouraging firm convictions on secondary matters.

Mike wanted to encourage churches to be ambitious for the gospel. He wanted to see more people coming to believe the gospel, and more believers living the gospel more deeply. This growth can happen when, in the goodness of God, congregations are taught and mobilized for mission by more leaders who are better trained. The college must look to the churches to support and expand the work of the gospel in genuine partnership to produce more and more, and better and better, gifts to the church.

This was Mike's vision, and an inspiring one for those who worked with him. Certainly it is an aspirational vision, and one that has never been more urgent. Men and women are still dying in their sins. The world is as fractured and fragmented as ever it was, and even more so. We have an incredible message of hope for a hopeless world. For that we need more training, not less.

Oak Hill College has to navigate without Mike at the helm; but resolved and galvanized, we know where we are going. As we plough forwards on the course Mike set, I leave us with the challenge he would give to prospective Oak Hill students:

> I suspect many of us feel that the kind of theological training we're going to outline here is very costly. Very costly financially, very costly relationally as you leave other ministries and perhaps geographically distant from friends.
>
> Fair comment. Absolutely. It is costly. But I must tell you it is too costly not to. Not having Word ministers who are Christ's best possible gift means what? It means God's people are more unsafe from false teaching, un-serving of each other and the world and un-united under Christ's headship but under some substitute. My fear is that what I have seen in the UK over my Christian life are churches which are more and more unsafe, un-serving and un-united.
>
> Please do not short-change the people you will minister to by not training properly to be Christ's best gift.
>
> Costly? Too costly not to.

Note

1. C. S. Lewis, *Prince Caspian: The Return to Narnia* (London: HarperCollins, 1951; repr., 1994), p. 141.